The Black Prince
and King Jean II
of France

The Black Prince and King Jean II of France

Generalship in the Hundred Years War

Peter Hoskins

Pen & Sword
MILITARY

AN IMPRINT OF PEN & SWORD BOOKS LTD
YORKSHIRE – PHILADELPHIA

First published in Great Britain in 2020 by
PEN & SWORD MILITARY
An imprint of Pen & Sword Books Ltd
Yorkshire – Philadelphia

ISBN 978-1-52674-987-1

Typeset by Concept, Huddersfield, West Yorkshire, HD4 5JL
Printed and bound in England by TJ Books Limited, Padstow, Cornwall

Pen & Sword Books Ltd incorporates the Imprints of Aviation, Atlas, Family
History, Fiction, Maritime, Military, Discovery, Politics, History, Archaeology,
Select, Wharncliffe Local History, Wharncliffe True Crime, Military Classics,
Wharncliffe Transport, Leo Cooper, The Praetorian Press, Remember When,
White Owl, Seaforth Publishing and Frontline Publishing.

For a complete list of Pen & Sword titles please contact
PEN & SWORD BOOKS LTD
47 Church Street, Barnsley, South Yorkshire, S70 2AS, England
E-mail: enquiries@pen-and-sword.co.uk
Website: www.pen-and-sword.co.uk
or
PEN & SWORD BOOKS
1950 Lawrence Rd, Havertown, PA 19083, USA
E-mail: uspen-and-sword@casematepublishers.com
Website: www.penandswordbooks.com

For Grace and Sebastian

Contents

Preface ix

Acknowledgements xi

List of Illustrations xiii

List of Plates xv

PART ONE: THE PROTAGONISTS

1. Edward of Woodstock, 'The Black Prince'   5

2. King Jean II, 'The Good' 25

PART TWO: THE PRINCIPLES OF WAR, COMMAND AND
LEADERSHIP IN THE HUNDRED YEARS WAR

3. The Principles of War 55

4. Command and Leadership in the Hundred Years War 59

PART THREE: THE PRINCIPAL CAMPAIGNS OF KING JEAN II
AND THE BLACK PRINCE

5. The Siege of Aiguillon, 1346 69

6. The Black Prince's *Chevauchée* in the Languedoc, 1355 79

7. Normandy and the Siege of Breteuil, 1356 105

8. The Poitiers Campaign, 1356 109

9. The Battle of Nájera, 1367 151

Conclusions 167

Appendix: The Location of the Poitiers Battlefield 173

Notes 179

Bibliography 183

Index 185

Preface

The idea for this comparative study came from an interview that I gave for a podcast on Jean II. My interviewer drew my attention to the lack of literature on Jean II in English. My first thought was a biography, but then I started to consider his career and life in the context of the Black Prince. Their careers ran in parallel for much of the first period of the Hundred Years War. However, while the Black Prince had a glittering military career, Jean left a less than glorious record in arms. Why should this English prince succeed when the king of the most powerful country in the medieval world failed so disastrously?

Jean is known best for his defeat by the Black Prince at Poitiers in 1356, but I began to appreciate that there was much more to this man than first meets the eye. He was quick of temper, headstrong and often arbitrary in his judgements, but he was a reformer and in many ways a man of principle, whatever his failures as a commander in the field. He was a man with considerable personal courage, hence the epithet '*le Bon*' attached to his name, which in the Middle Ages was a reflection of his acknowledged bravery rather than of any goodness in either his character or behaviour. In contrast, Edward of Woodstock, the Black Prince, seems to have been a man of cool judgement who fought and won two great battles, at a time when pitched battles were rare. These men had much in common: descent from King Philippe III of France, the French language, culture in the broad sense and the chivalric code. However, as I have already suggested above, there were many contrasts. Most notably, Edward was a future king from his birth but predeceased his father and never acceded to the throne, while when Jean was born none would have foreseen that he would become King of France.

In judging these men and their achievements we must also acknowledge that we are not comparing like with like. Edward, other than to a limited extent during his period as Prince of Aquitaine, did not have the broad responsibilities of a head of state. In modern parlance he was either a divisional or army commander in the field. Jean as Duke of Normandy before coming to the throne had similar limited responsibilities in the field, but as king he took on the broader responsibilities as head of state, commander-in-chief and chief of defence staff, all anachronisms of course, as well as a field commander. Thus, he had the challenges which Edward never faced of raising armies on a national scale, financing campaigns and bringing about reforms to redress deficiencies in French mobilisation and fighting tactics. In studying these men it must be remembered how young they were by modern standards for the responsibilities they held. Edward was only 16 at the Battle of Crécy and 26 when he won his great victory at Poitiers. He died just short of his 46th birthday. Jean, eleven years older than Edward, died just before his 45th birthday. He had also had considerable responsibility at a young age, being just 27 when he commanded the forces besieging Aiguillon. He became king at 31.

Acknowledgements

Thanks once again to Rupert Harding for his support for the idea which led to this book. My thanks are also due to Andrew Vallance and Linda Taylor for their review of the draft and for their helpful comments and suggestions.

List of Illustrations

FIGURES

The Valois Succession to the French Throne   26

MAPS

The Aiguillon Campaign, 1346   70
The Siege of Aiguillon, 1 April to 20 August 1346   72
The Black Prince's *Chevauchée* in the Languedoc, 1355   83
Crossing the Garonne and the Ariège, 28 October 1355   89
Crossing the Garonne at Carbonne, 18 November 1355   99
Normandy and Breteuil, 1356 106
The Poitiers *Chevauchée*, August to October 1356 110
The passage of Brantôme, 8–10 August 1356 112
Crossing the Vienne, 14 August 1356 114
Romorantin to Poitiers 119
Battle of Poitiers – Initial deployments and opening moves 135
Battle of Poitiers – Attack of the vanguard 138
Battle of Poitiers – Attacks of the Dauphin's and the Duke of
    Orléans' divisions 140
Battle of Poitiers – The final phase 141
The Nájera Campaign 154
The Battle of Nájera 160
The Poitiers Battlefield 174

List of Plates

Edward the Black Prince as a Knight of the Garter.

The tomb of the Black Prince in Canterbury Cathedral.

Fourteenth-century portrait of Jean II by an unknown artist.

King Jean.

Franc à cheval of Jean le Bon, 1360.

Vestiges of the ramparts of Aiguillon, dating back to Roman times.

Vestiges of Breteuil castle. It was built in the twelfth century by Henry II of England and demolished in 1378 after being retaken for the French by Bertrand du Guesclin.

The Battle of Poitiers: This photograph was taken after the driest summer for fifty years. The Miosson was little more than a minor stream but in wet weather it can be a much more significant river. The bridge replaced an earlier structure washed away by the river in flood in 1982. The land in the foreground would be susceptible to flooding in such conditions. Beyond the road on the right, where grass has not been planted, marsh plants are evident even in dry weather.

The Battle of Poitiers: Baker's 'broad deep valley', with the river Miosson in the middle-ground and the road running up the hill towards the prince's position near the Croix de la Garde.

The Battle of Poitiers: This hedge has been allowed to grow to more than 3 metres, or 10 feet, in width. Such hedges would be formidable obstacles.

The Battle of Poitiers, as depicted in Froissart.

A reconstruction of a belfry, or siege tower, as favoured by Jean II, at Tiffauges castle.

The arms of war of the Black Prince. The white label of cadency, a horizontal bar with three downward points, differentiates the prince's arms from those of his father and shows that he is the eldest son.

The church of St Vigor in Quettehou where the Black Prince is believed to have been knighted at the start of the Crécy campaign in July 1346.

The formidable defences of the *cité* of Carcassonne, which were sufficient to deter an attack by the Black Prince in 1355.

The Battle of Nájera: The bridge across the Najerilla looking towards the town and the high ground behind which trapped the fleeing Spanish army.

The Battle of Nájera: The flat ground on which the battle was fought.

The Battle of Nájera: The high ground on the approach to the battlefield looking north from the road between Navarette and Nájera.

The funeral procession of King Jean.

The thirteenth-century north door, known as the Valois door, of the basilica of St Denis in Paris – the final resting place of a number of French monarchs, including King Jean II.

PART ONE

THE PROTAGONISTS

Edward of Woodstock, the Black Prince, and Jean de Valois had much in common. Both were descended from King Philippe III of France, and both grew up speaking French as their first language. They shared a common culture and the same code of chivalry. They were both unwaveringly loyal to their fathers. They both had a strong sense of honour and were men with strong religious convictions. They also both exhibited great physical courage. Both could be ruthless when occasion demanded, although such ruthlessness could often be in tension with chivalry and honour. What made the difference between extraordinary success on the one hand and ignominious defeat and capture on the other? In trying to answer this question we shall first explore the lives of these two warriors in the round, with the objective of subsequently putting their military careers in perspective.

Chapter 1

Edward of Woodstock,
'The Black Prince'

Edward the Black Prince was born at Woodstock in Oxfordshire on 15 June 1330, the eldest child of Edward III's queen Philippa. He was born during the dying days of the regency council appointed to oversee the minority years of his father's reign. Edward III seized power from his mother and Roger Mortimer the Earl of March, who had dominated the regency, on 19 October 1330. In contrast to King Jean II of France, Edward, despite his nickname the Black Prince, was portrayed as the epitome of chivalry. The herald of Sir John Chandos in his chronicle heaped praise on the prince: 'This frank prince of whom I tell you, from the day that he was born thought only of loyalty, of free courage and of gentleness, and endowed was he with prowess. So much of this prince was of such lofty mind that he wished all the days of his life to give all his mind to upholding justice and integrity, and therein was he nurtured.' There is much more in the same vein, including his goodness and nobility, and praise for his support for the church and in particular the feast of the Holy Trinity. His strong religious views were at the heart of his criticism of Pedro the Cruel, claimant to the throne of Castile. Nevertheless, admittedly by no means uncommon in his time, he fathered at least one and perhaps two illegitimate sons. Why then, with the widely held view that he was the epitome of chivalry, and the respect and admiration of contemporaries, including the French, did he earn the epithet the Black Prince? The answer is that we simply do not know. It has been suggested that he had a preference for black armour, but there is no evidence to support this. There are no contemporary records of the use of the term, although it was in common use by the end of the sixteenth century. Shakespeare in *Henry V* refers to 'Edward, Black Prince of Wales'. However, there is little doubt that he had a fearsome reputation during his lifetime and a tapestry in Angers castle, commissioned in 1373, is said in one panel to show Edward III and his sons as the riders of the Apocalypse, and a second is reputed to show the prince as the lead rider. Perhaps his nickname owed something to the chronicler Jean Froissart's dark account of his conduct at the sack of Limoges in 1370, although as discussed below there is considerable doubt about the veracity of his account.

The Earldom of Cheshire had since the mid-thirteenth century been a traditional estate for the king's eldest son and from his birth Edward was seen as the future holder of the title. This was confirmed in 1333. In 1336, on the death of the king's brother John of Eltham, the opportunity came to confer the earldom and its revenues on the prince. The following year the title of Duchy of Cornwall was created and the title of Duke of Cornwall given to the young prince, the first time such a title had been used in England. His title of Prince of Wales had to wait, but he was appointed to this office a little before his 13th birthday.

King Jean II started life as an improbable monarch. Edward, however, was from his birth the heir to the throne. Details of his education are sketchy, but it seems that he had a tutor, probably from the age of 7 or 8. As a young prince his military education started around the same age, with his first suit of armour recorded in 1338. Preparation for high office started early in his life. When he was only 7 years old he was despatched to meet the two cardinals sent to try to prevent the outbreak of war in 1337 and escort them to the City of London in some splendour. He was appointed keeper of the realm in 1338, 1340 and 1340–42 during the absence of his father overseas. This was largely a ceremonial office and he had the support of advisers. Nevertheless, through this experience he was introduced to the responsibilities of government at an early age.

Edward, as the eldest son of the king, could potentially be used to secure important alliances through marriage. The first attempt to find a suitable bride began shortly after his first birthday when marriage to a daughter of the King of France was proposed, but nothing came of the proposal. In 1340 a proposed marriage with the daughter of John Duke of Lorraine and Brabant, a vehicle to secure the support of Brabant against France, also came to nothing. An attempt to forge an alliance with Portugal through a marriage between the prince and the king's daughter Leonor also failed, mainly, it seems, because of delays in communication. It is curious that an heir to the throne should not eventually marry for dynastic reasons and remain unmarried until the age of 31. Instead he chose for his wife the twice-married Joan Holland, a woman with a colourful past, known to posterity somewhat ironically as 'The Fair Maid of Kent'.

The prince's introduction to overseas service came in 1345 during an abortive expedition to Flanders led by the king. The king and the prince returned to England after only three weeks. His father's thoughts now turned to what was to be the Crécy campaign of 1346. Edward's first real taste of military life came during this campaign. The prince was knighted shortly after the landing in the Cotentin peninsula in Normandy in July 1346, participated throughout the campaign and was in the forefront of the fighting at the Battle of Crécy on 26 August 1346. The king marched on to lay siege to Calais. The siege was to last almost a year before the town surrendered. The prince's activities during the siege are unclear, but judging from records of reinforcements and supplies sent from his demesnes, it seems likely that he was present along with his father. Philippe VI dispersed his army shortly after the end of the siege. Edward III exploited the opportunity with raids into French-held territory. The prince led one such raid into the Artois region. The Truce of Calais followed in September 1347, which it was agreed would last until July 1348.

The Black Death swept across both countries in 1348 and 1349, killing between 30 and 50 per cent of the populations. The Truce of Calais was extended but low-level fighting continued, particularly in the south-west. The truce was repudiated by the French in August 1349.

On New Year's Day 1350 the Black Prince was involved in an exploit which prevented a plot to retake Calais by surprise. In late 1349 Geoffroi de Charny, the epitome of chivalry in France and author of *Le Livre de Chevalerie*, bribed Aimery de Pavia, captain of one of the gates of the citadel. The plan was for de Pavia to open the gates to the French, who would enter and seize the town. Aimery, however, told Edward III of the plot. The king crossed the channel with the Black Prince and a small force of men-at-arms. On the night in question the drawbridge was lowered, the gates opened and the portcullis raised. A number of men entered. The bridge was raised behind them and they were quickly overpowered. The overwhelming bulk of the French force was still outside. Some fled when it became apparent what was happening but de Charny drew up in battle order those who remained. They were caught between Edward III coming out from the town's south gate and the Black Prince coming from the northern gate. The French suffered 200 killed, with more drowned as they fled across the marshland. De Charny was among the prisoners taken. He was sent to England and eventually liberated against ransom in 1351. De Pavia paid the price for his treachery the following year. Having been captured by de Charny, he was taken to St Omer. He was tortured with red-hot irons and dismembered with a meat-axe.

Later in 1350 the prince experienced war at sea. In that period there was little difference between combat on land or at sea. Ships closed and grappled. Archers would be employed but success or failure would turn on hand-to-hand combat between men-at-arms. On 29 August a fleet of some forty English ships intercepted twenty-four larger Castilian ships, which had been raiding in English waters on behalf of the French, off Winchelsea. The Black Prince's ship rammed a Castilian ship but was also holed and began to sink. Fortunately the Earl of Lancaster had attacked from the other side of the Castilian ship and the Black Prince and his men were able to board Lancaster's ship as their own ship sank. The English carried the day, but with high losses.

Despite the excitement of events at Calais and Winchelsea in 1350, the truce was renewed. Edward spent the years of relative peace in England at court or his own residences at Kennington, Berkhamsted and Wallingford. He was involved only to a minor extent in matters of state, although present on such occasions as the appointment in 1354 of the Earls of Lancaster and Arundel as ambassadors to Avignon. The prince devoted a good deal of time during this period to the administration of his lands. In 1353 he spent two months in Cheshire between early August and early October. His *Register* during his stay shows a wide range of administrative acts. They include acts to remedy difficulties related to the Black Death and the administration of justice. In September, demonstrating a sense of justice, he gave personal judgment in favour of 'a poor woman, Ellen sister and heir of Adam le Walkere'. Adam had contracted to take on two mills at Macclesfield but owing to the plague there had been no revenues. Despite this, the Justice of Chester had enforced the due payment. The prince ordered a gift of 117s 6d (£1.88) to Ellen, to be paid from debts due to the prince from the estate of the said justice Sir Thomas de Ferrers.

In November, with the prince back in London, we see evidence of discontent and disorder in Cheshire. First, the prince gave orders on 7 November to establish the extent of 'great waste and destruction' and to determine the extent of the damage to the prince's interests. He expressed his displeasure that this matter was concealed from him during his visit to the palatinate. Of wider importance, on the same day he issued strict orders to the new Justice of Cheshire, Sir Bartholomew de Burghersh, to enforce ordinances for the keeping of the peace which had been issued in writing and proclaimed orally during the prince's visit to Cheshire. The prince ordered that the Justice of Chester seize those who had ignored his orders and take them to Chester castle to wait his punishment, which was to serve as an example to others. The *Register* entries show something of the character of the prince. King Jean of France was noted for his short temper and arbitrary approach to justice, often running roughshod over due process. The prince, however, seems to be measured in his judgments and it is also clear that he often acted on the advice of his council. The prince's *Register* also shows something of his taste for luxury, an example being the payment of the large sum of £200 to the jeweller Martin Parde.

This peaceful interlude in the life of the prince came to an end in 1355 as the truce, intended to expire in the summer, approached its end. There had been sporadic fighting in the south-west of France during the truce. However, since shortly after his appointment as King Jean's lieutenant in the Languedoc in November 1352, the Count of Armagnac had been making incursions into English-held territory. The actions of Armagnac were causing increasing concern to the Gascon nobility and in January 1355 a number of them came to London and urged Edward III to take the offensive in the south-west. They asked for men to be sent under the leadership of the prince.

The king agreed and preparations were set in hand to gather shipping and muster men. An indenture setting out the terms of service for the prince's expedition was signed by the king and the prince on 10 June 1355. The hope was that the expedition would leave port in late June, but in the event the habitual problems of the time – waiting for favourable winds and gathering sufficient shipping – delayed departure until 9 September. The fleet of 179 ships, drawn from thirty-five ports in England, arrived a week later on 16 September. The prince lodged in the archbishop's palace. At the beginning of October the prince set out with a combined Anglo-Gascon army, with a smattering of men from elsewhere in Europe, on a raid deep into the Languedoc, penetrating as far as Narbonne on the Mediterranean coast. By early December he was back in Gascony and most of the army dispersed for the winter. The prince spent the next months mainly in Bordeaux, while several of his senior commanders led smaller-scale operations to consolidate the success of the autumn and bring more Gascon towns and lords over to the English cause. By the summer preparations were in hand for a further campaign. The prince set off from Bergerac at the beginning of August on the *chevauchée* which resulted in the Battle of Poitiers. The events during the prince's *chevauchées* of 1335 and 1356 and the Battle of Poitiers are considered in detail in later chapters.

The prince and his army lodged on or near the battlefield after the Battle of Poitiers. The Black Prince is said to have entertained King Jean to dinner after the battle. During the dinner he demonstrated his loyalty and care for those who served him, leaving his guest in order to tend personally to the badly wounded Sir James Audley when he was brought in from the battlefield, raising his morale with the news of the capture of the king. It is said also that the prince waited on the king, and during dinner asked him: 'Fair cousin, if you had taken me today, as by the grace of God I have taken you, what would you have done with me?' The king did not answer, and out of courtesy the prince did not press the point.

Geoffrey Hamelym, a groom in the prince's chamber, was despatched with the tunic and bascinet of King Jean II as evidence of his capture, and a messenger sent with letters. The news was known in England by 10 October, when King Edward gave orders for the proclamation of the victory. On receiving the news Edward III is reported to have said: 'We take not pleasure in the slaughter of men, but we rejoice in God's bounty and we look forward to a just and early peace.'

Although a famous victory had been achieved, and, in modern parlance, the French command structure decapitated, the prince and his advisers would have been only too aware that a substantial part of the enemy army had escaped unscathed. In the event any concerns that they may have had on this score were misplaced, with the French apparently more worried about a possible follow-up assault on the town of Poitiers. Indeed, Froissart tells us that they watched from the gates and towers of the city all night, and the next morning armed all manner of men to help the defence. He attributes the prince's lack of interest in Poitiers, and indeed places on the route to Bordeaux, to the fact that the Anglo-Gascons were so charged with gold, silver, jewels and valuable prisoners that they had neither the time nor the need to attack towns and fortresses. However, despite the French preoccupations with Poitiers, an attempt to liberate the king could not be ruled out. This was a time for prudence, not dalliance. A return to Bordeaux without delay was advisable.

Before leaving, time was required to identify and bury the dead, at least those of higher social status, to tend to the wounded, and to arrange for the release on parole of those prisoners who were not to be taken to Bordeaux. The prince and his army moved only the short distance of 5km from the battlefield on the day after the battle. Two further days were required before the army started to move to Bordeaux on Thursday, 23 September. Once the march back to Bordeaux had started, however, no further rest days were taken, other than pauses following river crossings when the journey had almost been completed, until the 270km journey was ended eleven days later. The priority now was to ensure a safe passage rather than to spread destruction along the line of march, and they moved in one body, save for an advanced party of 500 men-at-arms under the command of the Earls of Warwick and Suffolk which went out ahead to reconnoitre and secure the way. According to Froissart they need not have been concerned since, on account of the disaster at the battle and the loss of so many nobles and the king, any men-at-arms along the route shut themselves up in castles.

On 30 September the army reached Libourne and the river Dordogne. The great adventure was now almost over. The army crossed the river on 1 October and made its way towards Bordeaux the following day. Meanwhile the prince waited in Libourne for preparations to be made for his and King Jean's reception in the city. About a fortnight later the prince crossed over the Dordogne and made his way to Bordeaux with the king. They were received with great celebrations and the prince and the king were lodged in the abbey of St Andrew.

With the prince back in Bordeaux with his prisoners, and with the news having reached London of his momentous victory, attention turned on the diplomatic level to capitalising on the advantageous situation in which King Edward found himself. The French were in disarray, with a crisis of leadership and governance. Both sides had an interest in securing peace: the English to press home their advantage, and the French to restore government, to stop the continuing military action of English troops under the Duke of Lancaster active in Brittany and Normandy, and to nullify the threat posed by the English forces in Calais.

The English negotiating team was led by the Dean of Chichester, William Lynne, and the Constable of Bordeaux, John Stretelee. They acted on behalf of King Edward, and, although members of his entourage were involved, the prince took no part in the peace negotiations. The negotiators were in contact with London throughout the winter, but serious talks started in early 1357 when the Dauphin Charles had re-established a modicum of control in France.

On 22 March 1357 a truce was signed, which would extend until 9 April 1359. The truce made provision for a cessation of hostilities and for the prisoners held by the English to go to England. King Edward had already put arrangements in hand for the return of the prince with his prisoners, and on the Tuesday after Easter, 11 April 1357, the prince set sail from Bordeaux for Plymouth. According to Froissart and Jean le Bel, the departure caused some consternation on the part of the Gascon magnates who are said to have felt uneasy that, since they had played such a large part in the capture of the king, they should see him leave for England. Froissart says that the prince had to pay 100,000 florins to put the Gascons' minds at ease, but there is no other evidence to support this contention. The prince and King Jean landed at Plymouth on 5 May. Shortly afterwards they travelled to London where the king was lodged in the Savoy Palace.

King Jean's character was marked by a strong temper and often arbitrary approach to justice riding roughshod over due process. His advisers had great difficulty reasoning with him when he was under the influence of his temper. The Black Prince himself was not averse to loss of temper, with a notable example during the Battle of Poitiers which I will discuss later. However, the difference between them was that the prince listened to his advisers and allowed himself to be restrained from the arbitrary killing of a prisoner. Reference to the Black Prince's *Registers* shows us not only a man with a sense of justice and due process as discussed above, but also a man who was generous to those who had served him well, not only the great and the good but men of low social status. The process of rewarding service in Gascony and at the Battle of Poitiers, dispensing justice and redressing wrongs started soon after the prince's return to Bordeaux and continued for several years.

Some of the acts in the prince's *Registers* were signed by councillors, but others were personally authorised by the prince. However, it is reasonable to assume that the tenor of the documents, even when not personally issued by him, reflect the policy and character of the prince. As one would expect, there were many awards to senior members of his entourage. Sir James Audley received the largest reward of all, being granted a huge annuity of £400 a year to be drawn from the issue of coins from the Cornwall stannary. This large award may in part be a reflection of the role he played at the battle. However, it is also possible that the award was recognition that he had fought to the end, was badly wounded and renounced any chance to take prisoners and reap the rewards of ransoms. The acts linked to service in Gascony and at the battle in the *Register* for England are predominantly grants to members of the knightly and yeoman classes. In the records for the Palatinate of Cheshire, however, we find the prince dispensing a large number of pardons to men drawn from the lower classes. Those awards that were made were also for those of the lower classes: grants of pasture and the taking of peat for life and allowances of oaks to be taken from the prince's lands for the repair of houses. There is also an example of justice being administered in response to a petition from Alice, the widow of a soldier killed at the Battle of Poitiers. He had given money to his brother to be paid to his wife but the money had been withheld. The petition was endorsed as true and instructions issued in favour of Alice for the wrong to be remedied. In Cornwall a servant and porter was recompensed for his good service, particularly at the battle, with profits and customs from the Saltash ferry.

Also in the Palatinate of Cheshire we see that the prince was prepared to go back on his judgment when presented with subsequent evidence. Ransoms were important to men of all ranks and, since half of the sum raised was due to the prince, the process always risked bringing men into dispute with the Black Prince. On 3 July 1357 an order was issued in the prince's name to arrest and imprison in Chester castle two men accused of having concealed a prisoner and denied the prince his share of the ransom. They were to be held until they had paid the share of the ransom due and satisfied 'the prince of the contempt done to him'. In February of the following year the prince, having been 'assured by Sir Bartholomew de Burgherssh [*sic*], to whom the said prisoner surrendered that the above suggestion was untrue', ordered that the men were to be released and any property seized to be restored to them.

The prince seems to have been largely involved with the administration of his estates while King Edward engaged in peace negotiations with King Jean. The negotiations resulted in two successive treaties, the First and Second Treaties of London, which were rejected when submitted for approval to the Dauphin and the Estates General in France. Frustrated by the failure to secure French agreement to the second treaty, Edward led an army to France in 1359 with the intention of being crowned in Reims, the traditional place for coronations of French kings. The prince commanded the rearguard during this short campaign. However, the principal protagonists in the peace negotiations were Jean and Edward III and thus events surrounding the negotiations and the associated Reims campaign are discussed in detail in the next chapter.

After the ratification and signature of the Treaty of Brétigny at Calais in 1360 the prince returned to England. Marriage followed quickly. His bride Joan, Countess of Kent, 'The Fair Maid of Kent', was a woman with a colourful past. When Joan was around 14 or 15 she secretly married Sir Thomas Holland. During Holland's absence at the siege of Calais in 1347 Joan was married to the Earl of Salisbury. Sir Thomas was not daunted by the prospect of a quarrel with the powerful earl and petitioned the Pope. Joan's marriage to Salisbury was annulled in 1349. In 1352 Joan became Countess of Kent on the death of her brother. When her husband Sir Thomas died in 1360 she was a rich, beautiful and highly eligible widow. The prince's behaviour in the matter could be considered less than honourable. One of his household knights, Sir Bernard Brocas, who had fought with the prince at Crécy and Poitiers, had asked the prince to act on his behalf in proposing marriage to Joan. Instead the prince asked for her hand in marriage for himself. Papal agreement to the marriage was required since the prince and Joan were related. This was quickly forth-coming and on 6 October 1361 the marriage was celebrated in Lambeth by the Archbishop of Canterbury.

In July 1362 the Principality of Aquitaine was created, comprising all those territories in the south-west ceded to the English under the Treaty of Brétigny. The Black Prince was appointed to govern the principality. The process of annexing the newly acquired territories was started by Sir John Chandos on 1 July 1362. The process was not an easy one. A number of the great nobles of the new principality, including Jean, Count of Armagnac, who had been the French king's lieutenant in the Languedoc during the prince's *chevauchée* of 1355, initially refused to recognize the right of King Jean to transfer them and their lands to a new sovereign. Similarly, Gaston Phoebus refused to render homage for Béarn, which he considered he held in full sovereignty. The province of the Rouergue and many towns were reluctant to accept English overlordship. Ultimately, however, without support from the French crown they had no choice but to do so. However, the discontent of towns and nobles sowed the seeds for dissent in the future.

The prince took a considerable retinue with him: 250 men-at-arms and 320 archers. It took time to find sufficient shipping and it was not until April 1363 that he was able to take up his appointment. It seems that the prince lived a lavish lifestyle while Prince of Aquitaine, with splendid banquets, considerable expenditure on jewellery and clothing, and hunting and hawking. The extent of his literary interests is difficult to gauge, but there were numerous book-owners and authors in his circle. It is clear, however, that music was always important to him and he took six minstrels with him to Aquitaine. A little less than two years after his arrival in Aquitaine the prince's first son, Edward of Angoulême, was born in March 1365.

Although France and England were ostensibly at peace, the war con-tinued by proxy through the civil war in Brittany. In addition, France was plagued by the ravages of the free companies of *routiers*, bands of demobil-ised soldiers and mercenaries fighting for their own personal gain. These were often described as English by the French but in fact drew in men from both nations. The *routier* bands were often of a substantial size. The Great Company led by the French knight Seguin de Badefol defeated a French army despatched by King Jean II and commanded by the Count of Tancarville at the Battle of Brignais in April 1362.

When Charles V came to the throne in 1364 there was a change of approach to the problem of the *routiers*. Instead of expending considerable resources trying to defeat them, why not divert them to another purpose? Under the cover of a plan for a crusade to drive the Moors from Spain, an army was gathered with the aim of replacing Pedro the Cruel, who was allied with the English, with his half-brother Henry the Bastard of Trastamara as King of Castile. The crusade was given papal blessing and funding at Avignon in November 1365. In this context it is not surprising perhaps that the prince believed the cover story and gave his blessing for some in his service to participate in the expedition. However, there was an Anglo-Castilian treaty of 1362 and on 6 December 1365 Edward III issued orders that Englishmen were not to fight against Castile. However, in addition to treaty obligations there was a good practical reason why it was undesirable for Englishmen to contribute to the overthrow of Pedro: with Henry on the throne Gascony would have an unwelcome enemy close to its southern frontier.

Despite this interdiction, there were English, notably the *routier* captain Hugh Calveley, and Gascon mercenaries fighting alongside the French in the campaign of early 1366 which resulted in the overthrow of Pedro and his replacement by Henry. Pedro made his way to Gascony. Under the terms of the treaty of 1362 England was committed to coming to Pedro's aid if Castile was threatened by invasion. Presumably this commitment was made on the assumption that Pedro would still be on the throne and would have an army at his disposal with the English providing reinforcements. The situation when the Black Prince met Pedro at Capbreton in August 1366 was of an entirely different complexion. Pedro had been driven from his throne and had neither army nor money to pay for one. If the Black Prince were to help him he would need to raise the money against the dubious prospect of Pedro repaying the cost once he had been restored to the throne.

There are conflicting accounts of the prince's attitude towards helping Pedro. On the one hand he is reported to have reacted with enthusiasm to the prospect of going to war in Spain in his support. This was said to have been against the advice of the majority of his counsellors. Another account says that he was cautious and hesitant. The prince and Pedro had little in common. The Black Prince was pious, chivalrous, treated his prisoners with respect and was a man of his word. Pedro, in contrast, was in alliance with Muslim Granada and had justly earned his epithet 'the Cruel'. He had ordered the murder of the Archbishop of Santiago, personally murdered one of his half-brothers, had maltreated and possibly murdered his wife and was renowned for his cruelty towards prisoners. As was to become only too clear, his word could not be trusted. On balance, it seems that the prince was a reluctant supporter of the plan to go to Pedro's aid. However, Edward III was strongly in favour, and whatever the prince's personal reservations his loyalty to his father would override any misgivings. Nevertheless, the prince did secure a concession from his father which shows something of his own values. He would undertake the expedition only if Pedro would swear an oath to support the Church, restore all property taken from the Church, drive all Muslims from his kingdom, take a Christian wife and renounce adultery. The king agreed, although probably neither he nor the prince had much confidence in Pedro abiding by his oath.

Measures had already been taken in England for support of Pedro as early as May 1366 with reinforcements ordered to Gascony after Pedro's deposition. In July the prince started to assemble an army. Also in July the prince opened negotiations with Charles, King of Navarre, whose support would be necessary to secure a safe passage across the Pyrenees. In early August the prince, Charles and Pedro met at Capbreton. They agreed in principle that the prince would lead an army into Castile in January 1367. The terms of the support for Pedro were agreed in the Treaty of Libourne signed on 23 September 1366. Charles of Navarre agreed to allow the prince's army to cross the passes of the Pyrenees which he controlled. In return Pedro would cede two of his provinces to Charles, giving his kingdom access to the sea. Charles would also receive a number of Castilian fortresses and 200,000 florins in cash. Pedro would also cede the Basque region of Viscaya around Bilbao to Aquitaine. Pedro was also committed to reimbursing the prince for the costs of the expedition. The risks for the prince were immense. Failure of the expedition or the refusal or inability of Pedro to meet his commitments would leave the prince with debts worth many times the revenue of his lands.

Charles of Navarre, as duplicitous as ever, entered into negotiations with Henry, agreeing to break the Treaty of Libourne and actively oppose the prince's passage across the Pyrenees. He surrendered two frontier castles as a demonstration of good faith. The news of Charles's betrayal reached the prince in Bordeaux in early January 1367. The prince took immediate action. Sir Hugh Calveley, who was still in Castile and close to the frontier with Navarre, having been there with his company during the previous campaign, was ordered to invade Navarre. He cut the roads between the Navarrese capital Pamplona and Castile, and Charles's advisers quickly brought him to his senses. At the end of the month Pedro, Charles and the prince met again and the Treaty of Libourne was confirmed.

At about the time that news of Charles's treachery reached him, the prince's second son Richard of Bordeaux was born. Around the middle of January the prince left Bordeaux, initially for Dax, where the army was assembling. In February 1367 the prince crossed the Pyrenees and entered Castile on a campaign which was to end with the defeat of Henry of Trastamara at the Battle of Nájera on 3 April 1367 and the restoration of Pedro to his throne. We will deal with the campaign and the battle later in considering the prince's military career. However, there were incidents concerning prisoners after the battle which show us something of the prince's character.

Many prisoners were captured; of particular interest were French captives who had been captured before and whose ransoms remained unpaid. Among these was Arnoul d'Audrehem, a marshal captured at the Battle of Poitiers. The prince accused him of breaking his parole. However, rather than acting arbitrarily, the prince was content to see the matter settled by a jury of twelve knights: four English, four Breton and four Gascon. Audrehem's defence was that he had taken up arms not against the prince but against Pedro, and thus had not broken his word. The jury found in his favour and the prince was content to accept their judgment. Pedro's attitude towards his prisoners was light years away from that of the prince. The Treaty of Libourne had provided for prisoners to belong to their captors, save for Henry. Pedro recognised among the prisoners a man who had deserted his cause the previous year. The man was a prisoner of a Gascon knight but Pedro killed him with his own hands. The knight was furious not just because of the loss of ransom but also because, under the code of chivalry, he was dishonoured by his failure to protect his prisoner. He complained to the prince, who in turn protested to Pedro. Pedro wanted to execute the Castilian prisoners to purge the threat to his hold on the throne and offered to buy the prisoners from their captors. The prince refused to countenance such indiscriminate slaughter and his only concession was to allow the execution of Henry's chamberlain, Gomez Carillo. In a fashion typical of Pedro's barbaric character, he was drawn through the army and then had his throat cut.

The battle over and restored to his throne, Pedro immediately started to try to back-pedal on the Treaty of Libourne, despite his three daughters being held as hostages in Aquitaine. He refused to make the territorial concessions and wanted to renegotiate the money due to the prince. The wage bill was rising every day and there was little sign of Pedro being able to pay his debts. Sums due were reassessed and agreed at the beginning of May. Pedro wanted to be rid of the prince, not least because he feared that elements of the prince's army, which was becoming increasingly discontented, would turn to support Henry, who remained at liberty. Thus, he attempted to raise money through loans and taxation. However, Pedro pleaded that he could not raise the money with the prince's army still on his territory. Whether this argument would have been persuasive in itself is open to doubt, but there was the looming threat of an invasion of Aquitaine by Henry. In August the prince's army started to withdraw. By now the prince had contracted the disease which was to incapacitate him progressively during the rest of his life and eventually lead to his premature death. We cannot be certain of the disease, but it has been suggested that it was a form of amoebic dysentery. Certainly dysentery was common on campaign in the period.

The prince's return to Aquitaine was quickly followed by discontent and indeed rebellion, which was in due course to lead to renewal of war with France. A number of reasons have been advanced for the rebellion. In the past Aquitaine had been a rich duchy, based largely on the wine trade. However, since the outbreak of war the production and export of wine had diminished significantly. To some extent this loss of wealth had been replaced by thriving businesses associated with waging war and increased revenues for the nobility through booty and ransoms. However, the cost of maintaining the prince's court only added to the problems of expenditure which exceeded revenues. There was also the perception that the prince was overly extravagant. The return from Castile exacerbated the financial problems of the principality, with Pedro's debt amounting to the enormous sum of £385,000. Without Pedro's money, payment for those who had contributed to the army was extremely problematic.

The ostensible cause for the rebellion was the taxation raised to meet these liabilities. However, the rate of direct taxation imposed was less than the direct tax imposed in 1364. Perhaps this rate of tax reflected the fears of the prince and his advisers over the reaction to the taxation within the principality. It has been calculated that it would have taken seventy-one years to raise sufficient revenue from the tax to meet Pedro's debt. Thus, even if the taxation proved to be a source of discontent, it was completely inadequate for its purpose. It has also been suggested that the anglicised administration of the principality caused resentment within the Gascon nobility. Finally, the prince was seen by some as unduly arrogant, although his attitude to subordinates seems to have been consistent with the norms of the age. All of these factors may have contributed to the brewing rebellion, but also many of those who owed allegiance to the prince because of the Treaty of Brétigny had never really come to terms with this. Among these men was the Count of Armagnac, erstwhile lieutenant of King Jean in the Languedoc, who was to prove to be the catalyst for the return to war. However, another factor, although entirely understandable in the context of the times, was the ransoming of Bertrand du Guesclin, captured at Nájera. This charismatic, talented and dynamic leader was appointed Constable of France in 1370 and was to be Charles V's principal instrument in the French recovery after the return to war.

The Black Prince was now suffering badly from his illness, experiencing periods of great lassitude and often bedridden. Jonathan Sumption argues that the disappointment of the aftermath of Nájera and the effects of his illness resulted in the prince lacking interest in governing, having an irascible temper and exercising poor judgement. In early 1368 Armagnac made a plea to the prince for exemption from the tax imposed after Nájera on the basis of his financial difficulties. He also argued that the Counts of Armagnac were free men and had never been obliged to pay taxes to either the King of France or the King of England. Whether or not a conciliatory approach on the part of the prince would have had any effect on the subsequent turn of events is arguable. However, he would brook no opposition and rejected Armagnac's case out of hand. He would not countenance any exemption for Armagnac and threatened the count with his complete destruction.

In May 1368 Armagnac was in Paris for the marriage of a Gascon lord, Arnaud-Amanieu d'Albret, to Charles V's sister-in-law Marguerite de Bourbon. D'Albret had accompanied the Black Prince in 1355 during his *chevauchée* in the Languedoc and fought against the French on the side of Charles of Navarre in 1364 at the Battle of Cocherel. Having changed sides, he became Constable of France in 1382. The month before, in April, Edward III's second son, Lionel Duke of Clarence, on his way to Milan, had been received in great splendour by King Charles. The marriage of this important Gascon noble into the French royal family and the reception of Clarence were examples of how on the surface relations between England and France were cordial and peaceful. However, below the surface Charles V was manipulating events in a manner which would inevitably result in a renewal of war.

While the Count of Armagnac was in Paris he filed an appeal against the recent tax imposed by the Black Prince. The appeal was addressed to the King of France. Charles did not respond immediately. If he were to accept the appeal, he would be in breach of the Treaty of Brétigny under which Jean had renounced sovereignty over Aquitaine. This would inevitably lead to war. Before taking such a step he needed to rally support. Meanwhile

Armagnac came under increasing pressure from the prince, with reports of men-at-arms being recruited to seize his lands and grant them to Olivier de Clisson. After six weeks, on 30 June 1368, Charles announced that he would hear the appeals of Armagnac and his son and any similar appeals that he might receive. Behind the scenes Charles V had been negotiating with a number of other Gascon lords who had also lodged appeals. He promised not to renounce sovereignty over Aquitaine as required by the Treaty of Brétigny without the agreement of the appellants. They agreed in return not to settle with either Edward III or the Black Prince without the agreement of King Charles. The appellants also agreed to fight for the King of France in those provinces adjacent to the Duchy of Aquitaine. Within the duchy the king agreed to come to the aid of the Gascon parties to the agreement if they were attacked by the prince.

After hearing about Charles's decision to receive the appeals of the Gascon lords, the prince was under no illusions about where events were leading. By August recruitment of men-at-arms and archers was proceeding apace in Cheshire and Wales and among the prince's retainers elsewhere in England. Edmund of Langley, Earl of Cambridge, and the Earl of Pembroke also set about raising men. There was alarm in London at the turn of events and in September ambassadors were sent to Paris to try to clarify what was happening. The Lord d'Albret, who had recently lodged his own appeal, took the opportunity to set out his grievances with the ambassadors. Albret had friends at court and Edward III wrote to the prince asking for an explanation. The prince was incensed and threatened to challenge anyone who took Albret's word against his.

As the clouds of war gathered, little support came from England for the prince to defend Aquitaine. The crown paid for the men of the Earls of Cambridge and Pembroke, but all other defence had to be paid from within the resources of Aquitaine. As the prince prepared for the coming war, Charles V fomented rebellion with encouragement to join the appellants and downright bribery.

On 16 November 1368 King Charles V issued a summons to the prince to answer for the appeals in Paris on 2 May 1369. The summons came at the worst of times for the prince. He had become seriously ill at the beginning of November and remained bedridden for some months. Chandos Herald tells us how the summons was received by the prince, and his response: 'the Prince, who was sick, when he had heard what was done, was mightily provoked ... Then he wrote back to the King of France in stern and frank tone, that willingly and certainly would he come at his bilding [*sic*], if God granted him health and life, himself and all his company, helmed to the head . . .'.

With the prince all but incapacitated, Sir John Chandos was recalled from Normandy to assist in the defence of Aquitaine. With the traditional recruiting lands in the hands of discontented lords, raising men locally was difficult. A small force of 250 men left England in November, but the Earls of Cambridge and Pembroke did not follow until February 1369. With so few troops, the prince and Chandos had little choice but to mount a static defence when war began, coming as it did before the prince was due to appear before Charles V. No doubt the early start to the war was driven in part by the obvious advantage of striking before substantial English reinforcements could arrive. In January 1369 French troops started to appear in the Rouergue, and many fortresses and towns were either taken or went over to the French. A French army, perhaps 4,000 strong, was gathering at Albi during January. In February Rodez, the chief town of the Aveyron, admitted the French army without resistance. Most of the province quickly surrendered to the French led by Raymond de Rabastens with the Count of Armagnac at his side. Within a month the English position in the Quercy had also almost collapsed. The situation continued to deteriorate and by the end of 1369 the Rouergue, Quercy and Agenais had all fallen to the French. The French objective for 1370 was to take the war to the heart of Aquitaine. Indeed, by the end of 1369 they had penetrated as far as Bazas, little more than 50km south-east of Bordeaux. The rapid collapse of the English position was in part due to inadequate forces, but it can hardly have been helped by the prince's incapacity. The petulant behaviour of the 22-year-old Earl of Pembroke, who refused to take orders from Sir John Chandos because he was simply a banneret and thus junior in rank to Pembroke, could not have helped. It is difficult to see a fit Black Prince tolerating such behaviour. Add to all this the deaths of three competent and experienced commanders – Suffolk in November 1369 at the ripe old age of 71, Sir John Chandos at the beginning of January 1370 after a skirmish with the French, and Warwick from the plague in March – and the lack of a well-coordinated defence is hardly surprising.

In the summer of 1370 the Duke of Berry struck south, encountering little opposition, and reached Limoges on 21 August 1370. Limoges, as was often the case in French medieval episcopal cities, effectively comprised two towns with suburbs between them. The larger and older town, known as the Château, was grouped around the château of the viscount and an abbey on high ground about 800m from the river Vienne. It was the main commercial centre of Limoges, had a population of around 10,000, was well defended by strong thirteenth-century walls with numerous towers and fortified gates, and had a strong English garrison. The smaller of the two parts was the *cité*. It was walled but fortifications were in a poor state of repair. It was under the jurisdiction of the Bishop of Limoges, with only a small number of men detached from the Château. The Château held out against Berry and remained loyal to the Black Prince. In the *cité*, however, the bishop, an erstwhile supporter of the Black Prince, presumably taking the view that the English cause was on the wane, decided that he would surrender and on 24 August submitted to the Duke of Berry. Perhaps for financial reasons, the French campaigns suddenly came to an end at the end of August, and only three days after he had accepted the submission of the *cité* Berry marched away, leaving Roger de Beaufort, Hugh de la Roche and John de Villemur to hold the *cité* with 140 men. Berry made no attempt on the Château before his withdrawal, leaving the *cité* with its small garrison isolated and vulnerable.

Retribution was not long in coming. John of Gaunt, who had landed in Calais in July, moved by sea to Bordeaux, arriving probably in mid-August with some 4,000 men. In early September he arrived at Cognac and joined forces with the Black Prince and the Earls of Pembroke and Cambridge. Fewer than three weeks after the departure of Berry, the Anglo-Gascon army arrived before the *cité* of Limoges. The Black Prince summoned the inhabitants to surrender with the customary warnings of the consequences of the town being taken by assault: the destruction of their homes by fire and sword, and, implicitly, the risk of their lives being lost. The citizens may now have been regretting their submission to Berry, but with his garrison installed in the *cité* there could be no question of immediate surrender. The Anglo-Gascons did not seem inclined to settle down to starve the population and the garrison into surrender. Thus, the inhabitants faced the unenviable prospect of the consequences of the town being taken by the besiegers. After five days of siege the *cité* fell to assault.

The sack of Limoges has gone down in history, thanks largely to the account of the chronicler Jean Froissart, as an infamous day in the life of the Black Prince. Froissart alleged that in the mayhem of looting, killing and burning that followed the assault, more than 3,000 people were killed and the whole *cité* was stripped of its goods and then left in flames. The casualty figures are improbable: even if refugees from outlying places are added in, this figure would have equated to almost the total population. Froissart is not known to have visited Limoges and no other source refers to a massacre on such a scale. Recent analysis points towards Froissart's account as being fanciful at best and at worst black propaganda intended to sully the reputation of the Black Prince. Another, more realistic, contemporary account talks about 300 civilians being killed, and a letter written by the Black Prince has come to light which recounts that 200 of the garrison were captured and, by extrapolation, it appears that some 100 men-at-arms and perhaps 200 civilians were killed. The Black Prince threatened to behead the bishop for his treachery, but in the event his life was spared and he was ransomed the following year.

The prince's health continued to deteriorate and during his absence from Bordeaux at the siege of Limoges he heard of the death from plague of his eldest son Edward of Angoulême. His fighting days were over. He decided to relinquish Aquitaine and in October handed over to John of Gaunt as Lieutenant for Aquitaine. In January 1371 he sailed for England with Joan and his 4-year-old son Richard. On his return to England he played a part in state and political life when his health allowed. In 1372 he escorted Constanza, daughter of the now dead Pedro the Cruel, to London for her marriage to his brother Gaunt. The English recognised Constanza as Queen of Castile, although Henry of Trastámara was now back on the throne, and Gaunt became pretender to the crown. Gaunt led a disastrous *chevauchée* in 1373 from Calais to Bordeaux, during which the French skilfully avoided pitched battle but all but destroyed his army through minor skirmishes and harrying of detachments of the army. Gaunt's poor leadership, notably with delays leading him to cross the rugged and inhospitable Massif Central in the depths of winter, was a major factor in the disaster. His conduct of this campaign drew serious criticism from the prince. Their relationship deteriorated as Gaunt began to harbour ever-growing ambitions at the expense of the interests of England. The Good Parliament of 1376, where the commons brought their complaints about the perceived corruption of royal officers and the disastrous conduct of the war in France, has been portrayed as the scene for the prince to support the commons in restraining Gaunt's ambitions. The prince may well have been in sympathy with the commons, but there is little evidence to suggest that he took a public stance which would have undermined the authority of his father and brother. Furthermore, although the prince was present for the opening, by early May he was so ill that he retired to Kennington. One of his last acts, however, was to support the commons' demands for the removal of the king's mistress Alice Perrers, who was seen as a malign influence on Edward III and the conduct of government. He arranged for the arrest and interrogation of a Dominican friar accused of employing his magical gifts to give Alice influence over the king. The result was that Alice was banished from the court.

The prince was not to recover this time. He was moved to Westminster at the beginning of June and he died on Trinity Sunday, 8 June 1376, a day which he had always held in particularly high regard. He was buried, according to his wishes, in Canterbury cathedral. His death was commemorated not just in England but also in France, where King Charles V held a service of remembrance in the Sainte Chapelle in Paris in the presence of many prelates, barons and knights. He was just one week short of his 46th birthday when he died. King Edward followed the prince the next year, leaving the prince's son, 10-year-old Richard of Bordeaux, to become the unfortunate King Richard II.

The death of the prince robbed England of one of the greatest warriors and leaders of the Middle Ages. He was a religious man and chivalrous within the standards of the time. No doubt he could be ruthless, if not necessarily cruel. One of his strengths was to gather round him competent and courageous men, but most importantly he sought and listened to their advice.

Chapter 2

King Jean II, 'The Good'

Jean was born to Jeanne de Bourgogne, wife of Philippe de Valois, Count of Maine, on Thursday, 26 April 1319 in the castle of Gué de Maulny, destroyed during the Hundred Year War in 1359, close to Le Mans. It seems that he was not a handsome baby, but the midwife tried to console his mother by assuring her that all babies looked frightful at birth. Judging by the portrait held in the Louvre, first impressions were perhaps correct. Setting his looks aside, it is unlikely that anyone saw a future for this first son of the count beyond that of succeeding his father as a high-ranking nobleman.

His grandfather Charles de Valois had been the second son of King Philippe III, but the crown had passed through the eldest son Philippe IV to his eldest son Louis X. However, an extraordinary series of events brought Jean's father to the throne as Philippe VI in 1328 when Jean was 9 years old.

Three years before Jean's birth Louis X had died in June 1316, at only 26 years old, leaving a daughter Jeanne and no male heir. This was the first time in the 327 years of the Capetian dynasty that a King of France had died without a male successor, and this left a quandary for the ruling classes. Charles de Valois laid claim to the regency, but the barons of France opted for Louis' brother Philippe to assume the role of Regent and Governor of France. Hopes for the future rested on the outcome of the pregnancy of Louis' queen, five months pregnant when the king died. All seemed to augur well when a son Jean was born on 20 November 1316. Alas, the infant King Jean I died five days later. Philippe seized the throne as King Philippe V. The coup was bloodless, but not without opposition from those who thought that the throne should pass to Louis' daughter Jeanne. To head off any real opposition, Philippe went to Reims and was crowned king, thus consolidating his position and creating the precedent that the throne could not pass to a female. This was enshrined in law in February 1317.

Philippe V was on the throne when Jean was born, but his reign was short-lived and he died in 1322 at the age of 28, leaving four daughters but no male heir. The precedent having been set, and the law confirmed

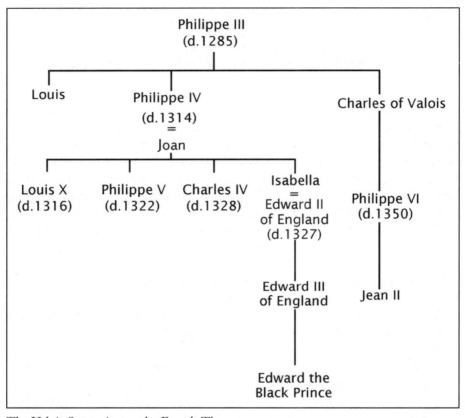

The Valois Succession to the French Throne.

that a female could not take the crown, the throne passed to the third of Philippe IV's sons, Charles IV. This third son of Philippe IV also died young and without a son in January 1328. History was repeating itself since he left a pregnant queen. The barons of France assembled at the beginning of February 1328, with English representatives, to consider the situation if the new baby were a girl. Charles IV in his last will and testament had expressed a preference for the crown to pass to Philippe de Valois, son of Charles de Valois and grandson of King Philippe III, in the event that Queen Joan gave birth to a daughter. However, he was not the only claimant. Philippe, Count of Evreux, was also a grandson of Philippe III through the king's youngest son Louis. And there was a third claimant: the 15-year-old King Edward III of England, who was descended directly from Philippe IV through his mother Isabella. The 22-year-old Philippe of Evreux was quickly discarded, judged to be too immature and lacking both

in character and ambition. The barons assembled at the Château de Vincennes could not countenance the prospect of the crown passing to an
English king, however strong his claim, particularly not to a callow youth
under the tutelage of his mother, even if she were a princess of France.
To eliminate Edward from the contest it was ruled that if a woman could
not inherit the throne, then by the same token the crown could not pass
through her to her son. There was plenty of precedent for women inherit-
ing titles to counties and duchies, but the crown was judged a case apart.
When on 1 April 1328 Joan gave birth to Blanche, Philippe de Valois
acceded to the throne of France as Philippe VI. The Capetian dynasty had
given way to the Valois, and as he approached his 9th birthday Jean was
catapulted from the prospect of being a second-rank noble to being heir to
the throne of France.

In this complex succession lay the seeds of problems for the future, both
for France and the future King Jean. The claim of Edward III to the
French throne was to be one cause of the series of wars now known as the
Hundred Years War, and English sovereigns maintained this claim until it
was finally renounced in the Treaty of Amiens in 1801. Closer to home,
the claim of the Counts of Evreux was to prove a major challenge for King
Jean II when he became king in 1350. Charles, who had succeeded his
father in 1343, was 18 when Jean acceded to the throne, and had become
King Charles II of Navarre in 1349. Despite marrying Jean's daughter
Joan in 1351 he was constantly plotting against the king and intriguing
with the English. Charles, appropriately nicknamed 'the Bad', was a thorn
in Jean's side and a major distraction during the war with England.

One of Philippe VI's first acts was to appoint a governor to oversee the
education of his son. He chose the Lord of Mareuil, a Marshal of France.
In his letter of appointment the king was careful to assure Mareuil that
this was not a demotion. He wanted his son's mentor to be constantly at
his side and not distracted by other affairs. Thus, Jean grew up with the
guidance of a soldier steeped in the traditional form of warfare which
emphasised the role of heavily armoured cavalry. In contrast, Edward the
Black Prince grew up watching the tactical innovations his father developed during the wars with Scotland before the outbreak of war with
France in 1337.

Childhood was brief in the Middle Ages and in April 1332, before his
13th birthday, Jean was named Duke of Normandy and Count of Maine
and Anjou. In July of the following year the 14-year-old prince married
Bonne de Luxembourg, youngest daughter of the King of Bohemia. Two
days after Jean's marriage, Philippe VI took the cross with the intention

of leading a crusade. In his absence the young Jean would be Regent of France and was thus knighted. By the thirteenth century chivalry had less significance than previously for many in its fullest religious and martial senses. However, for the King of Bohemia and his young son-in-law and godson Jean, it remained full of meaning. It was the sole means of obtaining honour in this world and life eternal in the next.

In June 1335 the 16-year-old prince fell gravely ill at Taverny, but by the first week in July he had recovered and walked on foot with his father 15km to the cathedral of St Denis to give thanks to God for his deliverance from illness. War broke out between England and France in 1337, with the initial theatre of operations in Flanders. In January 1338 Jean became a father with the birth of Charles, the future King Charles V, who was to be responsible for recovering his father's territorial losses. Charles was the first of Jean's children. Jean was already showing an unfortunate side to his character: a capacity for blind, inexplicable rage. However, another side of his character was also emerging: an innate ability to lead other men, coupled with great courage. Were these, taken together with his youth and lack of military experience, for which hunting and tournaments could not compensate, the characteristics of a commander of a large field army? It was of little consequence. It was unthinkable that a prince could not command. He certainly had the confidence of the nobility of Normandy for in 1339 they asked the king to appoint Jean commander of an army to invade England. Commitments were made to raise an army, but in the end the plan came to nothing.

The first years of war brought little military activity, despite Edward III expending considerable energy and treasure in attempting to rally Flemish and German lords to his cause. However, by early 1340 French raiding into Flanders had tried the patience of the Count of Hainault to breaking point and he allied himself with the English and made raids into northern France. In response, in April 1340 Jean was given his first military command. He was to lead an army into Hainault. The constable, Raoul d'Eu, and two marshals of France were sent with him to provide advice to the 21-year-old commander. The command was a considerable one, with 6,000 men-at-arms and 8,000 infantry. The campaign was one of widespread destruction, with a number of minor sieges. Jean was already showing a predilection for military engineering and siege warfare. The end of the campaign was a stand-off between Jean's army and that of the Flemish across the river Scheldt near Thun-l'Evêque. Meanwhile Edward III had sailed from England and defeated a French army aboard a fleet bottled up in the port of Sluys. Edward next set about a fruitless siege of Tournai with his Flemish allies that ended in stalemate and the Truce of Esplechin.

Jean had played no further part in the campaign in Flanders after his inconclusive confrontation with the Flemish army near Thun-l'Evêque. However, he was soon engaged again. This time he was despatched to Brittany in September 1341 as civil war broke out between rival claimants to the duchy: Jean de Montfort and Charles de Blois. Jean, in company with Charles de Blois, took Champtoceaux and Nantes. At Nantes an incident took place which some have attributed to Jean as an example of his violent temper and penchant for arbitrary cruelty. The incident in question was the decapitation of thirty prisoners and the catapulting of their heads into the town. When the town fell, Jean de Montfort was captured and sent to Paris as a prisoner. This might have been the end of the quarrel between the two claimants, but de Montfort's wife Jeanne took up her husband's cause. Brittany now became a new theatre of war between Edward III and Philippe VI as the English came to Jeanne's aid. First Walter Mauny arrived in May 1342 with a small force, in the company of Amaury de Clisson, a Breton who had gone to England to seek aid. He was followed in August by the Earl of Northampton and Robert of Artois with further men from England. Edward III came with reinforcements at the end of October. Once again the war settled into stalemate as the English attempted to take Vannes. Jean, Duke of Normandy's army came to within 30km of the English, but there was to be no battle. In winter conditions, suffering from mud and rain, neither army was in an enviable situation. The arrival of papal delegates gave both commanders a way out of the impasse. In January 1343 the three year Truce of Malestroit was agreed.

During the fighting in Brittany, Pope Benedict XII died in April 1342. It seems that the Duke of Normandy was temporarily relieved of his responsibilities in the duchy since he was despatched by his father to press the case for a French successor. He arrived too late to influence the election, but King Philippe's preferred candidate had been elected in any case. Pierre Roger, a former Archbishop of Rouen and adviser to Philippe VI, was crowned Clement VI in May 1342. It did not escape notice that the future King Jean had the honour of holding the reins of the new Pope's horse and sitting at his right hand at dinner.

Although Amaury de Clisson had taken Jean de Montfort's side and played a part in securing the help of the English for him, his brother Olivier had given his support to Charles de Blois. Olivier was taken prisoner by the English during a sortie from Vannes. On his release, following a prisoner exchange, he rejoined the household of Jean, Duke of Normandy. However, Jean's father believed Clisson to be guilty of plotting with the English during his captivity. He was arrested and arbitrarily executed by the king without due process. Subsequently a dozen Breton knights and squires were arrested for having been complicit with Olivier's crimes. Their trial before *Parlement* was interrupted and the king once more exercised his personal judgment and ordered their execution. This demonstration of arbitrary power must have had a profound impact on Jean, and he was later also prone to such extra-judicial action.

There was, however, a problem closer to home for the young Duke of Normandy. A quarrel had arisen between two Norman barons: Robert Bertrand of Briquebec, Marshal of France, and Godfrey of Harcourt. The quarrel erupted into a private war. Philippe VI, concerned about the impact of these events on his son's duchy, and judging this private war as illegitimate when France was at war with England, summoned Bertrand and Harcourt to appear before *Parlement*. When Godfrey failed to respond to two such summonses, he was banished from the realm and all his property was forfeit. The duchy was now divided into two camps. Three of Harcourt's minor supporters were captured fighting for the English, and accused, *inter alia*, with plotting to depose Jean as Duke of Normandy and replace him with Godfrey of Harcourt. They were executed at Easter 1344 by royal warrant and their heads displayed in St-Lô. This policy of repression did not have the desired effect of suppressing disaffection within the duchy. Many nobles resented this exercise of arbitrary power by the king in response to what they saw as a legitimate private war under feudal rules.

The Truce of Malestroit had envisaged peace talks starting in mid-1343 under the auspices of the Pope. The start of the talks was successively delayed because of the machinations of the English. Jean had been sent to Avignon as part of a high-ranking delegation, along with the Duke of Burgundy and the Chancellor of France. Edward III had sent only minor officials. In the face of successive delays and insubstantial talks with these functionaries, the two dukes returned to Paris in the summer of 1344. The talks finally opened in October 1344, but without Jean being present.

During his stay in Avignon Jean met Humbert II, ruler of the Viennois, a self-governing principality within the Holy Roman Empire in the southeast of modern France. The ruler of the Viennois was known as the Dauphin, a reference to the dolphin on his coat of arms. Humbert II had had the terrible misfortune to drop his 2-year-old son and heir André to his death from a window of his castle. The death of his wife without the birth of a further child and enormous debts left Humbert in a parlous state, and he had been touting the sale of his principality without success for several years when he met the young Duke of Normandy. His discussions with Jean rapidly bore fruit. On 30 July 1346 the transfer of the Viennois to France was agreed and took place formally in 1349. In effect Humbert sold his principality to France for a large sum of money and an annual pension. The title of Dauphin passed initially to Philippe VI's younger brother Charles, but on his death it was agreed that in future the title would be carried by either the eldest son of the king or by the king himself. The first such dauphin should, therefore, have been Jean, but he elected to pass the title to his son Charles, the future King Charles V. Henceforth the eldest son of the King of France was known as the Dauphin. However, there was much more to Jean's diplomatic coup than the acquisition of a new title. It represented a considerable expansion of the territory of France in a strategically important position.

By the summer of 1345 the war had been renewed. The Earl of Derby disembarked in Bordeaux and set out on a campaign which drove back the weak and dispersed French forces. Derby seized Bergerac in August, sending shock waves through the French court. The Duke of Bourbon was despatched as the king's lieutenant in the Languedoc to muster men. Jean was sent to Angoulême to take overall command of operations as the men from the Languedoc joined with those already available in the area. In October Derby inflicted a serious defeat on a superior French force at Auberoche, close to Périgueux. Although Jean, with a force again superior to Derby's, was only some 40km away, he did not pursue the Anglo-Gascon army. He dispersed his army for the winter and withdrew to Châtillon-sur-Indre, some 250km to the north. Thus, Derby and the Anglo-Gascons had a free hand for operations which continued throughout the winter and spring. In November Aiguillon, a small but strategically very important town on the confluence of the rivers Lot and Garonne, had fallen to the Anglo-Gascons. Retaking the town for the French was to be Jean's next challenge. The siege that he set in April 1346 was one of his major operations. Suffice it to say here that, although the town had fallen to Lord Stafford in a matter of hours, his siege lasted throughout the summer until he was forced to withdraw in August when ordered by his father to move north to join the army gathering to counter Edward III's campaign. Not only was his siege unsuccessful but also he arrived too late to participate in the fateful Battle of Crécy.

As the French withdrew, a curious incident occurred which is an example of Jean's sense of honour and chivalry. When Walter Mauny, one of the commanders of the Anglo-Gascon garrison of Aiguillon, realised why the French were withdrawing, he wished to join Edward III's army in the north. The Duke of Normandy issued Mauny with a safe conduct for him to cross France with twenty men. He also arrived too late for Crécy.

After Crécy, Edward III set siege to Calais, which he was to take after almost eleven months. Jean was present with Philippe VI's army which set out on an unsuccessful attempt to relieve the town just before its capitulation in August 1347. A truce followed which was to last initially for a year. In the event, although there was sporadic fighting in several theatres, it was extended until 1355, when war returned with a vengeance. In the meantime both realms had been ravaged by the Black Death. Jean's wife Bonne of Luxembourg was among the victims of the plague, dying in September 1349. Five months later he married again. The new Duchess of Normandy was Joan, Countess of Auvergne, whose husband had died at the siege of Aiguillon.

In August 1350 Philippe VI died and Jean acceded to the throne as King Jean II. Jean acquired the nickname 'The Good', reflecting renown for his courage. He acceded to a realm which had been devastated by the Black Death and had been plunged into economic crisis by the loss of a large proportion of its population. The currency had been devalued and there was unrest in the countryside.

In October 1350 the new king demonstrated his penchant for the arbitrary exercise of justice and power. Raoul de Brienne, Count of Eu and Constable of France, had been captured by the English in 1346 and passed the subsequent four years in captivity in England. He was released on parole to return to France to raise the considerable ransom demanded by Edward III. He arrived in Paris on 16 November 1350, no doubt expecting a warm welcome from his erstwhile friend King Jean. Instead he was arrested, charged with treason and summarily executed the next day. His crime was that, as part of his settlement with Edward III, he had sold the castle of Guines to the English king. On the face of it this was an entirely reasonable transaction within the norms of the time for settling a ransom. However, Guines was strategically important as it stood on the border of the Calais Pale and Jean saw its disposal as an act of treachery. The execution sent shock waves throughout France. The nobility were shocked by the lack both of mercy and of due process, something the king's favourite, 24-year-old Charles of La Cerda, known as Charles of Spain, was suspected in some quarters of having encouraged. Furthermore, in appointing Charles as the new constable and showering him with favours, Jean sowed the seeds for further discord. There was general discontent among the aristocracy about the appointment, but more serious was the enmity created between Jean and the young King of Navarre. Among the favours bestowed upon Charles of Spain was the grant of the County of Angou-lême. By right this county belonged to the Kingdom of Navarre. The 18-year-old King Charles of Navarre, known as Charles the Bad, who had been crowned in the summer of 1350, was understandably aggrieved. He left his realm in the hands of his youngest brother Louis and went to plead his case at the court of King Jean. A deep and lasting hatred rapidly developed between the two Charles, a hatred which was to have serious repercussions for Jean in the following years.

In early 1351 the new constable married into the royal family by taking as his wife the great-niece of King Jean, Margaret of Blois. This only served to intensify the King of Navarre's hatred for Charles of La Cerda. However, beyond this quarrel at the heart of his court Jean faced serious financial problems. In England it had been recognised and accepted for some while that the king alone did not have the resources to wage war and parliamentary subsidies were a well-established means of funding the recruitment and support of royal armies. The French nobility, however, clung to their belief in the feudal principle of raising armies through the king's vassals and any subsidies required should come from his revenues. Reform had started during the reign of Philippe IV at the beginning of the century with appeals made to the Estates General for the levy of taxes. In February 1351 Jean called the Estates and set out his case for subsidies. Delegates argued that it was obvious that the king had sufficient resources for his needs. Nevertheless, taxes were grudgingly approved, albeit these were only temporary and hedged about with constraints. The sum granted fell well short of the king's needs, and Jean resorted to devaluation of the silver currency. Jean was to resort to this expediency many times as he faced a continuing fiscal crisis throughout his reign. Jean appreciated that the French system for raising and maintaining armies was archaic and inefficient. Shortly after the *ordonnance* for devaluation of the currency, he issued a second *ordonnance*, in April 1351, this time instituting military reforms.

Until Jean's reforms French armies were largely recruited through the *ban* and the *arrière-ban*. The former was the mobilisation of the nobility, and the latter called upon their vassals to rally to the crown. This was essentially a feudal system, although knights, men-at-arms and squires did receive wages. The system had a number of weaknesses: an absence of hierarchy and organisation which resulted in a lack of discipline, fraud for payments to phantom soldiers and double-counting of payments for horses, and freedom for men to leave the battle without dishonour if they did not like the turn of events. These weaknesses had been evident at Crécy, with an ill-disciplined attack on the English contrary to the wishes of King Philippe. Jean's reforms were limited but he had clearly recognised the need to make changes. Wages were increased and extended to archers, shield-bearers and infantry. Horses were to be marked and their descriptions recorded, and inspectors appointed to audit muster rolls for both men and horses. Men-at-arms were required to select a captain and companies were formed of between fifteen and eighty men. Separate companies of infantry and archers were formed. Captains of companies were required to serve under commanders of the divisions, normally the van, centre and rearguards, and these in turn were subordinate to the constable, the two marshals and the master of archers. Men could no longer leave the battle without the permission of their captain, and captains required the authority of their divisional commander before doing so.

During 1351 Jean made a royal progress through his realm. The objective was, through contact with his subjects, to heal some of the divisions in France. On his way back north towards Paris he paused to summons an army to retake St-Jean-d'Angely, which had been in English hands since 1346. He played no part in the ensuing siege, watching events from afar at Poitiers, save to arrive for the surrender in August. In September the truce, which had been honoured more in the breach than the observance, was renewed for one year.

Jean now turned his attention to further reform. This time he founded a new order of chivalry, the Order of the Star. Jean was a man who was driven by a strong sense of honour and chivalric values, although as we have already seen with his treatment of the Count of Eu, and shall see again, this came into conflict with his violent temper and perhaps his sense of the sacred status of kingship. No doubt Jean took some inspiration from Edward III's recently formed Order of the Garter, and his belief in the concepts of honour and chivalry would have reinforced his motivation for forming a comparable order. However, underlying the order was his perception that French knights had fallen from their once pre-eminent place in European chivalry. He wanted to reverse this trend, which he attributed to a lack of training, experience and inclination. He hoped to generate the enthusiasm for war which he saw among the lords and knights serving Edward III. Thus, despite the ceremony and pageantry of the order, the extension of Jean's military reforms was an important strand in the foundation of the Order of the Star. Jean's reforms were the first steps in a series of reforms by successive French kings throughout the

Hundred Years War which played a significant part in the ultimate defeat of the English.

While Jean had been occupied with administrative reforms, the quarrel between Charles of Spain and the King of Navarre had been festering and was soon to explode with a vengeance. The King of Navarre, who in 1352 had become Jean's son-in-law through marriage to Joan of Valois, had meanwhile gone to his lands in the County of Evreux in Lower Normandy with his brother Philippe. He had thus left Charles of Spain a free hand in Paris and perhaps this bred complacency on his part. On Epiphany day in January 1354 Charles of Spain set out for Normandy to visit his cousin the Countess of Alençon. He clearly had little concern for his security and was travelling with only a small escort. He stopped for the night at an inn in a village near l'Aigle about 45km south-east of Evreux. His passage through the county did not escape the notice of Charles the Bad, who set out at dusk with a troop of knights and men-at-arms. At first light they came to the inn. Charles the Bad prudently kept his distance, while his brother Philippe with other men burst into the room of Charles of Spain and murdered him with multiple sword blows.

King Jean was stunned by the news. For several days he seemed incapable of reacting and then exploded with anger. He cried that he should never have given his daughter in marriage to such a wretch as Charles of Navarre and swore vengeance. Navarre was, of course, alive to the risk that he ran of Jean's summary judgement. He wrote to those who might support him and also to the king's council. He accepted responsibility for the death of the constable, explaining that he was justifiably reacting to wrongs and outrages that he had suffered at the hands of Charles of Spain. In a letter on 11 January to the inhabitants of Reims he wrote that the death was necessary in view of the bad advice given by Charles to the king. He was pained by the thought that the king might for the moment be troubled by the death of the constable, but took comfort from the belief that when the king had had the chance to reflect he would experience great joy at the justice meted out by Charles of Navarre. He wrote also to the Pope, the Holy Roman Emperor and other princes to explain his actions and to attempt to transform himself from a murderer into a dispenser of justice. To hedge his bet should this public relations exercise fail, he also plotted to regenerate the war between England and France by proposing an alliance with Edward III. However, Navarre was adept at double-dealing and this was no more than a stratagem to achieve his objective of reconciliation with King Jean. Jean's advisers pressed him to come to terms with Navarre. Jean had no wish to break the truce with England and saw the sense in not driving Navarre into the enemy camp. The Treaty of Mantes of February 1354 between the kings of Navarre and France resolved a number of territorial issues and made concessions to Navarre, including an additional payment for the dowry of his queen. Navarre, having received a royal pardon for the murder of Charles of Spain and gained important concessions from Jean through the Treaty of Mantes, backed out of his proposed alliance with the English.

However, the affair was by no means over. Two of the participants in the murder of Charles of Spain, John and Louis of Harcourt, were full of contrition and revealed to King Jean that two of his close associates, the Cardinal of Boulogne and the Grand Chamberlain, Robert of Lorris, had been complicit in the death of the constable. The king exploded in rage. The cardinal was sent to Avignon in disgrace and the chamberlain was banished from court. Notwithstanding the pardon given to Navarre, Jean set aside his notions of honour and chivalry to dispense with due process and resolve to rid himself of Charles and his two brothers. The plan was to seize them during a banquet and have them assassinated. The Navarre brothers were warned of the plot and escaped. Charles fled to Avignon where French and English delegates were present for a further attempt to secure peace under the auspices of the Pope. Thus, Navarre had the chance to plot once again with the English. Jean declared Navarre a rebel, suspended the Treaty of Mantes and set about seizing the lands and castles of the Navarres. This effort met with mixed results with a number of towns and strongholds holding out and refusing to allow King Jean to take possession. However, despite this resistance, Normandy remained calm on the whole, and Jean seems to have been satisfied with that and turned his attention to the peace talks under way at Avignon. Pope Innocent VI continued to press for peace, but in the face of decreasing interest on the part of the English.

The King of Navarre was at the heart of the problem. Despite his evident bad faith in his earlier agreement with Edward III, he had started meeting the Duke of Lancaster to plot an alliance once again. He proposed to recognise Edward III as King of France and to dismember France to the advantage of himself and the English. The military plan was for Charles to mobilise an army in Normandy and seize Cherbourg in preparation for the arrival of an English army. Charles, however, was, as usual, playing a double game and his main objective seems to have been to manipulate a reconciliation with King Jean if he could do so on favourable terms. No doubt aware that Jean had intelligence of events in Avignon, he sent a messenger to the king in early 1355 to assure him of his loyalty.

He admitted the contacts with Lancaster but said that he only made them so that he could better serve King Jean.

There was little prospect of the peace talks succeeding, and the best that could be achieved was an extension of the truce from 1 April to 24 June 1355. The continuing problem of Charles of Navarre now took second place to preparations for war. Jean faced the perennial problem of a lack of funds. He turned to the time-honoured stratagem of devaluation, the twenty-fifth in less than five years, this time masked by the issue of a new coin, the *mouton d'or*, so called because of the image of a sheep on its face. As he tried to raise funds for the renewal of war, intelligence indicated to Jean and his advisers that the English would indeed land in Normandy. The province was ill prepared. Not only was it subject to the machinations of Charles of Navarre, but also its military governor had been sent to Picardy some eighteen months before and not replaced. Jean decided to appoint his 17-year-old son, the Dauphin Charles, as his lieutenant in Normandy. In March 1355 the dauphin departed for Rouen to assume his responsibilities.

It was clear that the military situation was dire: garrisons were weak and there was no field army ready for mobile operations. Substantial sums would be required to rectify this situation and the Estates of Normandy were summoned by the dauphin to meet at Rouen at the end of April. By early May agreement had been reached to raise a series of taxes over a three-month period to fund 2,000 men-at-arms. The tax revenue was lower than expected, but by June the measures taken had borne some fruit and the dukedom was in a better state of preparation, with men placed on coast watch throughout Normandy. Meanwhile in London three cam-paigns were being planned: Edward III in Normandy, Lancaster in Brittany and Edward the Black Prince in Gascony.

Charles of Navarre arrived in Cherbourg in early July 1355 along with 2,000 men who had been shipped from the port of Capbreton in English Aquitaine. While Lancaster sent messengers to try to keep Charles the Bad to his word, King Jean sent negotiators to attempt to patch things up with Navarre. The result was the Treaty of Valognes of 10 September 1355 which was designed to resolve all the differences between King Jean and his errant son-in-law. As the historian Jonathan Sumption has written: 'between more reasonable individuals than Charles and his father-in-law, it might have done so'. It did nothing of the sort. Furthermore, once again the duplicitous Charles had broken his promised alliance with the English. Without the support of Navarrese troops in Normandy, Edward III's expedition had to be cancelled.

The public reconciliation between Jean and his son-in-law brought the king some respite in his troubles at home, his advisers telling him that a bad treaty was better than a good war. Thanks to the Treaty of Valognes, Jean had seen the threat of an English landing in Normandy dissipated, at least for the time being. In this happier situation he was overwhelmed by feelings of good will towards the King of Navarre. He was so confident of having resolved his differences with Charles that, as was to become clear, he imprudently gave his son the dauphin into his care. The two Charles were very different in character. The young prince was quickly seduced by the charm and flattery of the King of Navarre.

Despite the abandonment of Edward III's planned landing in Normandy, Jean still faced a direct threat to his realm with the Black Prince landing in Bordeaux only three weeks after the Treaty of Valognes. The immediate objective of the Black Prince was to carry the war to the south in the Languedoc to relieve the threat to Aquitaine posed by Jean, Count of Armagnac. The prince's Anglo-Gascon army set out from Bordeaux on 2 October 1355. Jean, however, could not be sure initially that the Black Prince would not strike north and Poitiers seemed a likely target. He set in hand a range of measures to protect the town. Lancaster's expedition to Brittany had been postponed until the spring of 1356, and Jean no longer faced the threat of war on three fronts. Nevertheless, although Edward III would not now land in Normandy, he switched his objective to northern France. On 2 November he marched out of Calais at the head of an army about 5,000 strong. As he marched south he met Jean de Boucicaut, a prisoner of the English crown on parole to raise his ransom. Under the terms of his parole he could not fight the English, but he was able to bring Jean II intelligence of the strength and disposition of Edward's army, reporting that the army was weaker than might have been expected. However, Jean was not much better placed than Edward. Troops were dispersed in a number of towns around the perimeter of the Calais Pale. A field army was gathering at Amiens and he had the cavalry of the dauphin and the newly reconciled King of Navarre at his disposal, but recruitment during October had been disappointing. Furthermore, the proclamation of the *arrière-ban* when Edward had landed had brought only small contingents of infantry which were late in arriving. The situation was such that Jean did not wish to risk facing the English in battle. His men withdrew as the English advanced, removing stores and destroying crops as they did so. The English reached Hesdin, about 50km south of Calais, around 6 November. The supply position for Edward's army was becoming difficult. In view of the haste of putting together the expedition, resupply arrangements were not what they should have been, and Jean's scorched earth policy left little to be taken from the land. Jean marched north from Amiens on 8 November but as he approached, Edward withdrew towards Boulogne. Jean followed at a safe distance. Three days later the English re-entered the Calais Pale. Jean skirted the perimeter of the Pale to St-Omer, 30 km south-east of Calais. The English started to embark for home and Jean discharged his army on 15 November.

While Jean had been preoccupied with events in Picardy, the Black Prince had spread havoc in the Languedoc, burning, destroying and pillaging a wide swathe of one of the richest regions of France. He had reached the Mediterranean coast at Narbonne and by the time Jean's army in the north dispersed, he was returning to Aquitaine. Within two weeks he was back in English-held territory and disbanded his army for the winter. Jean, Count of Armagnac, was the king's lieutenant in the Languedoc. He had a significant army at his disposal and had shadowed the prince throughout most of the *chevauchée*. There had been occasions when there had seemed to be some prospect of battle, but in the event the Anglo-Gascon army returned home unmolested. Writing on 18 December 1355, King Jean acknowledged that the French army was several times greater than that of the Black Prince and expressed some frustration that the Anglo-Gascon army had not been brought to battle. However, his dissatisfaction seems to have stemmed from his view, or at least from the view given to him, that the Anglo-Gascon army had been able to elude battle, rather than that the Count of Armagnac had avoided battle.

At the beginning of December the Estates General, summoned by Jean, assembled in Paris to consider the peril facing the realm. The assembly was incomplete, with most of the representatives from the Languedoc absent, preoccupied with the aftermath of the havoc wrought by the Black Prince in the preceding two months. After the events in Picardy and the Languedoc, the Estates were under no illusions about the grave situation before them. A huge subsidy of 5,000,000 livres *tournois* was agreed, sufficient to support an army of 30,000 men for a year. With the general levy of men through the *arrière-ban*, this would give Jean some 90,000 men under arms. In addition, there were the militias available for the defence of towns. Such a large sum required a range of extra taxes. In return for a subsidy on such a scale the king accepted the demand of the Estates for special measures both for the raising and dispensing of the money and also the abolition of certain royal practices.

In the intervening months since the Treaty of Valognes Charles of Navarre had been working on the malleable young dauphin to undermine his loyalty to his father. He insinuated that the king clearly did not love him since he had not so far given him the dukedom while King Jean had been granted the duchy by his father when he was only 13. In his endeavours Navarre was ably assisted by Robert le Coq, Bishop of Laon. It was suggested that not only did Jean manifestly not love his son but that he also nurtured a hatred for him. Le Coq told the young dauphin that his father plotted to assassinate both him and Charles of Navarre. Also it would be a service to God to throw down this weak king. A voyage to Germany for the King of Navarre and the dauphin to enlist the support of the Holy Roman Emperor, Charles IV of Bohemia, was planned to start on 7 December 1355. Hardliners in the party seem to have wished to raise an army in Germany to overthrow the king and then to assassinate him, while others appear to have been opposed to the idea of regicide. Where the dauphin stood is unclear. In the event King Jean got wind of the plot and elected to nip it in the bud. The day before the planned departure, Jean summoned his son to see him. The dauphin confessed all. Contrary to his normal behaviour, Jean reacted calmly, thanking Charles for his honesty.

Far from punishing the dauphin, Jean decided to reward him with sumptuous gifts and the grant of Normandy in appanage to allow him to govern as duke and draw on its revenues in his own right. He had previously hesitated to do so, concerned as he was by Charles's lack of experience and apparent lack of aptitude. However, Charles had had time to get to know Normandy and had performed well enough in the recent campaign in Picardy, and the time seemed right to increase the dauphin's responsibilities, extend the influence of the Valois dynasty and, perhaps most importantly, try to neutralise the influence of the King of Navarre by bringing order to the duchy. There was concern within the Navarrese camp over reprisals, but King Jean issued letters patent on 6 January 1356 which pardoned all involved. In the months that followed, the duplicitous King of Navarre renewed contact once again with the English and tried to persuade the dauphin to revive his visit to Germany. In March and April 1356 the Estates of the Languedoc met and agreed a subsidy for King Jean's pursuit of the war, but on condition that the dauphin was despatched to the south to take command personally.

The dauphin never made it to the Languedoc that year. Once again the king's intelligence was good and he was aware of Navarre's plotting. Jean was furious that, having given Normandy to his son, the duchy still seemed to be in a state of anarchy and that the King of Navarre was flouting his pardon. He was exasperated at once again being drawn into the web of intrigue of Navarre and distracted from the other affairs of state. Towards the end of March Jean was in Artois to become godfather to the first-born of John of Artois. John revealed to the king a plot by the King of Navarre to seize King Jean during a visit to Normandy, imprison him and then kill him by poisoning. The plan was to share the realm between Navarre and Edward III. Jean could not contain his anger and desire for revenge. Learning that the dauphin was to hold a banquet in Rouen for the nobility of Normandy and the aldermen of the city, the king decided to make the most of this opportunity to catch the plotters together.

On 5 April the king, accompanied by his second son Louis, Duke of Anjou, his brother Philippe, Duke of Orléans, Marshal d'Audrehem and 100 men-at-arms, burst into the banqueting hall at the height of the festivities. The king strode forward and seized Navarre crying: 'Stand up, traitor, you are unworthy to sit at the side of my son. On the soul of my father, I shall neither drink nor eat while you live.' Colin Doublet, a squire to the King of Navarre, seized a carving knife and pointed it at King Jean's chest. Jean released his grip on Navarre and ordered that he, his squire and another plotter, Friquet de Fricamps, be taken from the hall. The dauphin tried to intervene to stop the king but to no avail. Navarre tried to plead his innocence, also with no effect. The king turned on his son when he tried once again to intervene, pleading that the king had dishonoured him in his own home: 'Be quiet, Charles, you do not know what I know. These men are evil traitors as will soon become clear.' The king assaulted a further plotter, John of Harcourt, striking him with a formidable blow between the shoulders. He was also taken away, along with others party to the plot. Once again Jean rode roughshod over due process. Four men, including John of Harcourt and the unfortunate squire of the King of Navarre, lost their heads that day. For unknown reasons Navarre and Fricamps were spared summary execution.

King Jean took immediate steps to punish others thought to be complicit in the plotting against him: the possessions of the Harcourts were seized and Evreux invested by royal troops, and castles and towns seized from plotters. Fears spread among those with split loyalties to the Kings of Navarre and France that previous pardons would be cast aside by Jean and that they would suffer from his fury. Normandy was in turmoil and Jean's advisers persuaded him that it was unsafe to remain in the duchy and that he must return to Paris. On 24 April 1356 Jean arrived in the capital with his prisoners. Charles of Navarre was imprisoned in the Châtelet. He does not seem to have been tortured. Fricamps was less fortunate, revealing in the process names and details concerning the murder of Charles of Spain, the negotiations between Lancaster and Navarre, the planned expedition to Germany and the recent plot. Having revealed all, Fricamps succeeded in escaping and disappeared into thin air. Navarre was moved successively to the castles of Crèvecoeur and Arleux near Douai in the north of France, Jean seeming to step back from the grave measure of summarily executing a king. Perhaps his anger had cooled sufficiently for his sense of the sacred nature of kingship to overcome his desire for revenge. Following the events in Rouen, extravagant rumours flew around: Charles would be tortured, executed in secret or perhaps encased in a coat of lead and left to die. Talk of the king's injustice in proceeding against the plotters without due process was again widespread, as with the earlier case of the Count of Eu. Anger mounted, with support growing for Charles despite his treachery. The king banished Godfrey of Harcourt for life, but this punishment was more moderate than might have been expected in view of the enormity of his crimes. He also wrote to his son in a conciliatory tone to calm the duchy, reassuring the duke that he would not set aside previous pardons and if need be these could be reissued. Jean was taking account of popular sentiment and trying to eliminate internal unrest while the war with England continued.

Despite these efforts at reconciliation, Normandy remained a threat to the stability of the realm. The King of Navarre's brother Philippe remained at large and was fomenting revolt and renewing contact with the English to try to bring about the king's release. Philippe's emissaries were welcomed with open arms by the English and in May 1356 Edward III launched a vigorous diplomatic campaign in favour of Charles, denying that there was an alliance between Navarre and England, and condemning Jean as disloyal to his subjects, dishonoured and unworthy of knighthood.

This period of Jean's rule was overshadowed in every activity by the events at Rouen and their aftermath. Jean set out to calm tempers and counter Edward III's campaign by publishing a document to justify his action. The sealed letter purported to show that Navarre had been in league with the English, along with Harcourt and others, to kill the king and the dauphin, seize the throne, and cede Aquitaine and Normandy to Edward III in full sovereignty. Nevertheless, the situation continued to deteriorate across the realm. In the Languedoc the promised arrival of the Duke of Normandy was awaited with impatience. Charles was, however, too preoccupied with events in Normandy to leave for the south. To try to assuage the south, Jean decided to send another of his sons, 16-year-old Jean, appointed as Count of Poitiers, Lieutenant of the Duke of Normandy beyond the Loire and all the Languedoc. His progress was hardly encouraging and two months later he had only reached Bourges, and by then events had changed and the Black Prince was on the march again.

Notwithstanding Jean's preoccupations with the Normans and Navarrese, he could not neglect preparations for the renewal of war with the English, including the raising of subsidies. Despite the difficulties in the duchy the Estates of Normandy voted a subsidy for the repair of fortifications and to raise men-at-arms. However, Philippe of Navarre was still plotting to free his brother. He had a twin-track approach: negotiation and appeal to King Jean while also turning to Edward III for assistance with the support of several Norman barons. He was open in his challenge to Jean, even addressing a letter to him in insulting terms as 'Jean of Valois who calls himself King of France'. A violent reaction could perhaps have been expected, but Jean seems to have been relatively impassive, perhaps feeling that after all he held the trump card with Charles in prison and he had the strength to crush the rebellion if need be.

Initially, Jean limited himself to ordering the forfeiture of all towns and castles held by the Navarrese. Philippe had no intention of complying and organised resistance with Harcourt's help. Jean had no alternative but to respond with force and summoned an army to assemble at Chartres on 1 June 1356. Despite all his bravura, Philippe knew that he could not hold out against the king alone and called for urgent help from England. The Duke of Lancaster was despatched to Normandy and landed on the Cotentin peninsula in early June. He brought with him initially a small advanced guard but eventually the English contingent amounted to around 500 men-at-arms and 800 archers. These numbers were augmented by Bretons and Navarrese to bring his total force to around 2,400 men.

In the third week of June Lancaster set out on a *chevauchée* towards the Seine, driving French besiegers away from Pont-Audemer and taking the castle of Conches from the king's supporters. The next target was the castle of Breteuil and the dispersal of the French besieging force. Jean left Chartres, 65km distant, and headed for Breteuil to intercept Lancaster. However, by now Lancaster was on the move again, initially heading almost directly towards the king. On reaching Verneuil-sur-Avre he seems to have received intelligence of the approach of Jean's host. He did not have the strength to face the French in battle and turned west to withdraw towards the Cotentin. Nevertheless, the two armies came into contact near l'Aigle on 8 July. Lancaster deployed his men in the forest of Tuboeuf, a little to the east of l'Aigle, and tried to entice Jean to pursue him into a narrow gorge. Jean was not to be persuaded, well aware of the dangers in such a situation, even against the smaller numbers of Lancaster's army.

He challenged Lancaster to open battle. He in turn was not to be tempted and slipped away to the west. Instead of pursuing Lancaster, Jean decided to return to Chartres to demobilise his army, but en route he elected to restart the siege of Breteuil castle, which had been resupplied by Lancaster and left in the hands of a resourceful commander called Sanchez Lopez. We shall return to Jean's conduct of the siege later. Suffice it to say here that he devoted considerable resources and efforts to the siege. It started in mid-July and a first assault was attempted on 10 August. At about this time news reached Jean that the Black Prince had left Bergerac on 4 August and was moving north. The siege of a minor castle should perhaps have been considered insignificant compared with the threat posed by the Anglo-Gascon army now heading towards the centre of his realm. However, Jean had invested too much in terms of resources and honour to easily abandon the siege. A second assault was planned but, with further news of the advance of the Black Prince, Jean elected to buy the castle from the garrison. Around 20 August the garrison opened the gates and marched away to join Philippe of Navarre.

Jean could now turn his attention to the Black Prince. He demobilised contingents which were judged inapt for the coming campaign and summoned a new army to gather at Chartres on 1 September. While awaiting the assembly of his army, Jean despatched reconnaissance forces south of the Loire to establish the movements of the Black Prince. The prince was heading towards the Loire with the hope of joining forces with the Duke of Lancaster, who had set out from the Cotentin to reinforce the Anglo-Gascon army. This was not to be and on 9 September Jean crossed the Loire at Blois in pursuit of the Black Prince. Ten days of manoeuvring followed before the fateful Battle of Poitiers on 19 September 1356, and the capture of Jean.

The prince's priority was to get his important captive to safety and he moved quickly to return to Bordeaux. He arrived at Libourne on 30 September and waited for a fortnight for preparations to be made for an appropriate reception in Bordeaux. Jean was lodged in comfort in the abbey of St Andrew, free to communicate with the dauphin acting as regent. In March 1357 a truce was agreed. The Truce of Bordeaux was to last until April 1359 and provided for the cessation of hostilities and the transfer of prisoners to England. Importantly for the dauphin, the English disavowed further support for the Navarrese.

On 11 April 1357 Jean boarded the *Sainte-Marie* at Bordeaux, along with numerous other prisoners captured at the battle, on his way to London. The *Sainte-Marie* reached Plymouth on 5 May. On 24 May, riding a white courser, the French king entered London with the Black Prince. The prince rode behind the king on a modest black hackney, probably to emphasise the eminent rank of his captive. The occasion was accompanied by much pomp and theatre from the moment the prince and Jean were met by the mayor and leading citizens on their approach to London. As they passed through the city, they were escorted by 1,000 mounted men and crowds of Londoners thronged the streets. Members of the guilds and companies dressed in their rich livery were drawn up in his honour, and the prince was met by the Bishop of London at St Paul's churchyard. He and Jean then moved off towards the Duke of Lancaster's Savoy Palace, which was to be Jean's residence. He was accompanied by many of his household to ensure his habitual comforts. He was allowed almost total liberty and was able to hunt with his son Philippe, the future Duke of Burgundy. He also devoted a good deal of his leisure to his love of books, and was a frequent visitor to Queen Isabella, Edward III's mother, at Hertford.

On the diplomatic front, negotiations now turned to securing a permanent peace. In June the Cardinal of Périgord, who had been involved in the negotiations in Bordeaux, and the Cardinal of San Vitale arrived in England to join the renewed discussions. These dragged on until eventually, at Windsor in May 1358, Jean ratified the peace treaty known as the First Treaty of London. The terms of the treaty set Jean's ransom at the enormous sum of 4,000,000 gold *écus*, of which the first instalment of 600,000 was to be paid before his release. Edward agreed to drop his claim to the French crown in return for the transfer to the English crown of great swathes of France in full sovereignty, which amounted to around one-third of France. The first payment of the ransom was due by November 1358, but despite strenuous efforts on Jean's part, the money could not be raised. This was perhaps unsurprising since the dauphin was facing considerable unrest, particularly in Paris, with Charles of Navarre meddling unhelpfully yet again, having escaped from prison in November 1357.

With the expiration of the Truce of Bordeaux fast approaching, Edward increased the pressure. In December arrangements were made for Jean to move from the comfort of the Savoy Palace to the more austere Somerton castle in Lincolnshire. This transfer was put in abeyance until July 1359, but nevertheless Jean was now held in the Savoy without the freedom of movement that he had enjoyed hitherto. On 18 March 1359 it was agreed to extend the Truce of Bordeaux until 24 June 1359. Jean was presented with a revised treaty, the terms of which were much more severe than those of the preceding year, known as the Second Treaty of London, ceding even more territory and in effect restoring the Angevin Empire of Henry II. The ransom was reduced to 3,000,000 *écus*, but a bond of a further 1,000,000 would be forfeit if payment was not made by 24 June 1360. A first payment of 600,000 *écus* was due on 1 August 1359. Jean signed the draft on 24 March. In France the Estates General were summoned to consider the Treaty. They met on 25 May 1359. They judged that the terms were displeasing to all the people of France, and that they were neither feasible nor acceptable. They advised the regent, the Dauphin Charles, to make war on England.

Edward III was furious and held Jean responsible. Jean was initially transferred to the castle of Hertford, vacant since the death of Queen Isabella in August 1358, with a much reduced household. In July the anticipated move to Somerton was put into effect and Jean was kept under close surveillance. He was to remain in Somerton until March 1360, when he was transferred to the Tower of London to be closer to the seat of power in anticipation of renewed peace negotiations.

Meanwhile the renewal of the war had become inevitable, and in 1359 Edward III mustered the largest army that ever went to France during his reign. It was 12,000 strong and organised in three divisions led by the king, the prince and the Duke of Lancaster. By early November the army had crossed the Channel to Calais. The objective was clear to all. The king would go to Reims and be crowned and anointed as King of France.

When the army approached Reims it became apparent that the English were not going to be welcomed with open arms, and that the fortifications and defence of the city had been well prepared and the storehouses stocked. In mid-December the English army started a blockade. Early in the siege an attempt was made to take the city by storm, but the attack was repulsed and not repeated. By early January a shortage of supplies for Edward's army was causing concern, and on 11 January the king had no alternative but to lift the siege. He departed towards Burgundy and then swept round to the north-west to approach Paris. During this period he hoped to entice the French to face him in battle, but the dauphin was too smart to fall into this trap. On 7 April the army drew near to Paris and until 12 April ravaged the suburbs in the hope of drawing the French out. This was to no avail and, since there was no prospect of Edward sustaining an effective siege of Paris and supplies were running short, the army set out for Chartres on Monday, 13 April. Disaster then struck. After weeks of warm weather a great thunderstorm broke, bringing high winds and driving rain which turned to sleet and hail with the temperature dropping below freezing. On this day, which became known as Black Monday, men and horses died of exposure, others were killed by the effects of the storm, and much of the baggage sank into mud and was abandoned. Although his military position was by no means desperate, Edward interpreted these events as a sign from God that it was time to settle, and he decided to resume negotiations for peace.

These talks started in the village of Brétigny on 1 May 1360. With so much ground work done before, terms were rapidly agreed and sealed on 8 May. The terms of the Treaty of Brétigny were essentially those of the First Treaty of London agreed between Edward and Jean almost exactly two years before. Edward was to hold in full sovereignty all the provinces in the south-west which his ancestors had held. He was also to hold the County of Ponthieu, Montreuil and Calais. However, the ransom for Jean was reduced to 3,000,000 *écus* and was to be paid in six annual instalments. Jean was to renounce the territories by 29 September and in exchange Edward would renounce his claim to the throne of France.

The English returned to England and the two kings ratified the terms of the treaty on 14 June 1359 at the Tower of London. Jean now started to raise the first instalment of his ransom. He was allowed his previous liberty and preparations were made for his return to France. He left London on 30 June and on 6 July arrived at Dover, where he dined in the castle with the Black Prince before embarking for Calais two days later.

Jean found France in a parlous state and it was clear that raising his ransom would prove far from easy. By the time Edward and Jean arrived in Calais in October for what should have been the formal ratification of the treaty, only two-thirds of the first instalment had been raised. In addition, the detailed negotiations for the mutual renunciations were proving diffi-cult. It was decided to make these renunciations the subject of a side-agreement and they were removed from the main treaty, which was signed in the Church of St Nicolas in Calais on 24 October 1360.

Edward III and Jean now spent several days together. Edward was reconciled with the Count of Flanders and Jean put to one side his differ-ences with Charles of Navarre. Jean then set off on foot to cover the 30km to Boulogne on pilgrimage to Notre-Dame de Boulogne. He was accom-panied by the Black Prince.

Jean now took power back from his son. Among his first acts was the enactment of new taxes to raise his ransom. In return he promised a strong currency. He then turned his attention to the companies of demobilised soldiers spreading havoc throughout the realm. The situation was not helped by the continuing presence of castles still occupied by English troops, contrary to the Treaty of Brétigny. The Black Death also returned and Jean lost his second wife, Jeanne de Boulogne, to the disease in September 1361. Two months later Jeanne's son from her first marriage with Philippe of Burgundy, Philippe of Rouvres, Duke of Burgundy, also died. He died intestate and without issue. There were two claimants to his lands: Jean himself and, once again, his *bête noir*, Charles of Navarre. Jean acted quickly and annexed Burgundy to his realm. In April 1362 he suffered a set-back in his campaign to rid France of the *routiers* at the Battle of Brignolles, where a royal army was crushed by the Great Company. It might have been expected that Jean would now focus his resources and efforts on bringing peace to the country. However, instead he turned his thoughts to leading a crusade, perhaps in the hope of a glorious campaign which would efface the disaster of Poitiers.

In August 1362 he set off to Avignon, arriving just in time for the death of Innocent VI. His successor Urban V was enthusiastic for a crusade. On Good Friday 1363 Jean took the Cross and was appointed to lead a crusade, the departure of which was fixed for March 1365. Jean saw the crusade as a means of reconciliation within Christendom and was delighted when Philippe of Navarre agreed to put past differences aside and join the expedition. Edward III was, however, deaf to his appeal. As plans proceeded for the crusade an unexpected turn of events threw all into disarray.

A number of captives from Poitiers, including four royal princes (Jean's brother the Duke of Orléans, two of his sons, Louis I, Duke of Anjou, and Jean, Duke of Berry, and the Duke of Bourbon) were hostages for the fulfilment of the terms of the Treaty of Brétigny. They were becoming increasingly discontented with their captivity and the princes entered into negotiations with Edward III to, *inter alia*, cede land and castles to Edward and facilitate payment of the ransom for which instalments were already overdue. The agreement reached became known as the Treaty of the Lilies. In return for their agreement to the treaty, the captives were moved to Calais and allowed considerable freedom, including absence on parole for up to three days. In September 1363 Louis broke his parole and did not return to Calais.

Jean was scandalised by his son's dishonourable behaviour. He summoned the Estates General to meet at the beginning of December. Initially the proceedings were devoted to preparations for the crusade: nomination of the regent, creation of a permanent army of 6,000 men-at-arms to counter the companies of *routiers*, and the levy of a permanent tax to be devoted to defence. A permanent army had to wait until the next century, but we can at least see that Jean recognised the need for reform in the

French military system. At the end of proceedings Jean delivered a bomb-shell: he would return to England to take Louis' place and erase the shame of his son's behaviour. Contemporary commentators, who did not take his decision at face value, attributed various motives to Jean: to persuade Edward III to join the crusade, to negotiate the freedom of the remaining hostages, to deliver in person 107,000 *écus* which, although less than the first annuity, was a sign of good faith, to conduct business with Edward for the sale of wine and horses, to profit from the good life of banquets, hunting and tournaments, or simply to escape the trials and tribulations of governing his realm.

On 3 January 1364 Jean landed at Dover and on 15 January arrived in London. He lodged once again at the Savoy Palace. Discussions between the two kings made no progress concerning the crusade. However, more importantly the risk of the renewal of the war which had been present in late 1363 due to the non-payment of ransom instalments was set aside. Furthermore, Edward III agreed to allow the royal princes to return to France with Jean when he left for home.

In early March 1364, however, Jean took to his bed. The precise nature of his illness is unclear, but he did not recover. He received the last rites and drew up his will on 7 April 1364. He died the following day. His embalmed body lay in state in St Paul's and a memorial service was held in the presence of King Edward and Queen Philippa before the corpse was conducted to Dover by Edward III for return to France. On 1 May the funeral cortège entered Paris. He again lay in state before being interred in the cathedral of St Denis on 8 May 1364. He had died at the age of 45.

Jean is one of the least revered of French kings. Perhaps this is not surprising in view of his defeat at Poitiers, his volatile temper and often arbitrary exercise of justice, despite his strong sense of honour. However, he was to a great extent a victim of the system he inherited. He recognised the need for reform but the changes he effected were minor. It was for his son and great-grandson to bring about the reforms that would finally drive the English from France. As we have seen, he also had to cope with serious internal dissent. In Shakespeare's *Richard II* Thomas Mowbray, Duke of Norfolk, says: 'Mine Honour is my life; both grow in one: take honour from me, and my life is done.' Jean's sense of honour was undoubtedly an important part of his character, but this overriding sense of honour could lead to dubious decision-making, such as at the siege of Aiguillon and the Battle of Poitiers.

PART TWO

THE PRINCIPLES OF WAR, COMMAND AND LEADERSHIP IN THE HUNDRED YEARS WAR

Modern armies devote a good deal of training of their officers to the principles of war and leadership. These matters, although not formalized in the same way as today, were equally important in the Middle Ages. Ancient texts on the conduct of war were widely known and used, and young men of rank would receive training in military matters from an early age. As we have seen, it is likely that the Black Prince had a tutor from the age of 7 or 8 and Jean II also had a mentor during his youth. Much of their education would have been devoted to the skills of combat, but they were also being prepared for the command which would come naturally with their rank. They would also accompany their fathers on campaign from a young age to gain experience. The recognition of the importance of experience in the conduct of war can also be seen in the assignment of seasoned and successful commanders to accompany the Black Prince on his first independent command in France in 1355–6. Before examining the conduct of war by Jean II and the Black Prince, let us take a look at the principles of war, both ancient and modern, and leadership in the Middle Ages.

Chapter 3

The Principles of War

Sun Tzu, a sixth-century BC Chinese general and strategic theorist, wrote the commonly quoted *The Art of War*. There was much in common between the wars of the period of Sun Tzu and those of the Black Prince and King Jean II, in the sense that movement was on foot and horseback, weapons were essentially those of close combat supplemented by the bow, and although gunpowder artillery had made its appearance in Europe by the mid-fourteenth century, siege artillery was still predominantly mechanical. Thus, the writings of Sun Tzu seem an obvious framework for comparing the generalship of the Black Prince and King Jean. However, although there is much that is useful in *The Art of War*, it is a series of aphorisms rather than a coherent concept. It does not, therefore, lend itself as a structure for comparing these two medieval commanders, although there are aspects which are of value when examining their careers. The following discussion is by no means an exhaustive analysis of the usefulness of *The Art of War*, but gives some examples of the application of Sun Tzu's treatise to the conduct of operations by the Black Prince and King Jean.

Sun Tzu highlights the importance of logistics, advising that supplies should be brought from home and supplemented by forage, which was particularly important for the success of raids penetrating deep into enemy territory, characteristic of Edward III's strategy based on the *chevauchée*. He also emphasises the importance of seeking victory over the enemy as opposed to conducting long campaigns for their own sake. This was exemplified in the battle-seeking strategy of *chevauchées* during the reign of Edward III. Sun Tzu also points out the importance of surprise: 'Appear at points which the enemy must hasten to defend; march swiftly to places where you are not expected', which is once again a fundamental element of the *chevauchée*. A further principle for Sun Tzu when considering the art of manoeuvre was that to seize an advantage where speed is of the essence, it may be necessary to separate a flying column from the baggage train. Sun Tzu goes on in the same section to point out the importance of knowledge of the country in which the army is operating.

There are a further number of Sun Tzu's axioms which are relevant to the fourteenth century: the dangers of attacking uphill, pursuit of an army simulating flight, falling for bait offered by an enemy, and interference with an army returning home. He also emphasises the importance of leaving a surrounded army an escape route.

Whether or not Sun Tzu was read or used in the fourteenth century is not clear. However, there is evidence that *The Epitome of Military Science*, written by the Roman general Vegetius in the late fourth century or early fifth century AD, was widely known. The work is a comprehensive document embracing recruitment, training, the structure and organisation of the ancient Roman legions, logistics, pre-battle strategy and strategy and tactics in combat, fortification and sieges, and naval warfare. It was in effect a handbook covering the range of military activity from the organisation of armed forces, through strategy and doctrine to tactics in the field. N.P. Milner, in the introduction to his translation, explains how there were a number of translations into vernacular languages, often with adaptations made to reflect the age of chivalry. Some of the content, such as that relating to the organisation of the legions of ancient Rome, would have been of little more than historical interest and the sections which were reproduced were those considered particularly relevant. It is believed that King Henry II and King Richard I, the Lionheart, had copies of the treatise and it had been translated into French by 1284. It is probable that both the Black Prince and Jean II would have been well acquainted with its contents during their education.

Vegetius sets out at some length the general rules of war. In these rules he emphasises, *inter alia*, the importance of doing what benefits the commander and not simply reacting to the actions of the enemy, which can only be to the opponent's advantage. He appreciates the value of bravery, which he judges to be of more value than numbers, but he also believes that opportunity in war and choice of terrain can both be of greater value than bravery. Vegetius, in contrast to Sun Tzu, favours the use of famine, raids and terror to subdue the enemy rather than battle where fortune can have too great an influence. Battle should only be joined, he believed, either under great necessity or when the occasion is advantageous. These principles, in particular enticing the French into combat in conditions advantageous to the English, are in essence those of the *chevauchée*. He sets out the importance of maintaining reserves, surprise and logistics. Vegetius recognises the importance of consulting widely on possible courses of action, but he cautions a commander against bringing too many into his confidence once he has decided on the action he is going to take.

There is much in his work which can be applied to the conduct of war in the fourteenth century. He explains the importance of the procurement and storage of fodder and grain, both for armies on campaign in the field and for towns and fortresses. Techniques for crossing rivers are explained. In discussing pre-battle strategy he sets out the factors to be considered when judging whether to engage the enemy, advises the commander how to take account of an army which is unaccustomed to fighting or newly recruited, the deployment of men and the positioning of reserves behind the line. He also, in common with Sun Tzu, explains the importance of allowing the enemy an escape route: not to allow them to avoid defeat but to allow their pursuit and destruction once they have been routed. On the other hand, he sets out the principles of disengaging from the enemy if the battle plan cannot be effected. Guidance is also provided for commanders on how to react to a partial or total rout of his own army.

At first sight it may seem anachronistic to examine military operations against modern principles of war. However, the current principles of war for the armed forces of the United Kingdom are almost timeless. The ten principles also have the advantage of being concise and coherent.

Selection and maintenance of the aim is the master principle of war for the British armed forces. A single, clearly defined, commonly understood and unambiguous aim is the key to successful military operations.

The second principle emphasises the importance of maintaining morale to enable a positive state of mind derived from inspired political and military leadership, a shared sense of purpose and values, well-being, feeling of worth and group cohesion. Commanders must give those under their command an identity, self-esteem, and a sense of common purpose and achievable aims.

Offensive action, the third principle, is the way a commander seeks to gain advantage, sustain momentum and seize the initiative. This was the essence of the *chevauchée*, with deep penetration of enemy territory forcing the French to react to the enemy's manoeuvring rather than take the initiative.

Security has a broad sense in modern warfare. It embraces the provision and maintenance of an operating environment that gives freedom of action to achieve objectives, and enhancement of freedom of action by limiting vulnerability to hostile activities and threats. Sound security also denies critical information to the enemy. However, it was equally important to medieval armies. The *chevauchée* was vulnerable to enemy harrying of scouting and foraging parties and if, as in the case of the Crécy campaign, the French were in close pursuit this could present a serious risk.

Surprise has been throughout history an important element of successful warfare. The modern interpretation is that it is the consequence of confusion induced by deliberately or incidentally introducing the unexpected. Surprise is built on speed, secrecy and deception and, when successful, it achieves results disproportionate to the effort expended. There is an adage attributed to the Prussian Field Marshal Helmuth von Moltke the Elder, the architect of the Prussian victory over France in 1871, that 'you will usually find that the enemy has three courses open to him, and of these he will adopt the fourth'.

Concentration of force in modern warfare involves decisively synchronising and applying superior fighting power to realise intended effects, when and where required. It was equally important to medieval combat. The failure of Sir John Talbot to apply this principle at Castillon in 1453 contributed to his defeat and the final expulsion of the English from Aquitaine.

Economy of effort is judiciously exploiting manpower, materiel and time in relation to achieving objectives. Economy of effort implies the balance of available resources, given acceptable risk, against a commander's priorities.

Flexibility is the ability to change readily to meet new circumstances. Plans must be sufficiently flexible to respond to the unexpected and to empower commanders with maximum freedom of action. This requires understanding of the superior commanders' intentions, flexibility of mind, rapid decision-making, good organisation and good communications.

The penultimate principle for the modern British armed forces is co-operation. This embraces teamwork and a sharing of dangers, burdens, risks and opportunities in war.

The final principle is that of sustainability. In essence this means ensuring that measures are taken to ensure that fighting power and freedom of action are maintained. The importance of this principle has been recognised throughout history, even if expressed in different terms, and is reflected in the treatises of Sun Tzu and Vegetius. The importance of sustainability was also clearly appreciated in the age of chivalry. It is evident in the preparations made by Henry V for his Agincourt campaign of 1415, and there were numerous occasions when sieges during the Hundred Years War were abandoned because of an inability to sustain the besieging force. Sustainability of the army on the march in enemy territory in the fourteenth century required a blend of supplies taken with the army, as well as foraging and looting. However, in the English case, with their reliance on archers, sustainability also included an effective system for manufacture and resupply of arrows, bows and bow strings.

Chapter 4

Command and Leadership in the Hundred Years War

The *Oxford English Dictionary* defines generalship as the skill or practice of exercising military command. In essence it is the combination of the exercise of high command and leadership. Command in the Hundred Years War was seen as an innate quality for those of high birth. It was expected that military command was a natural consequence of nobility. Looking back from the twenty-first century, this may seem to be nothing more than arrogance. However, we should see it in the context of the concept of the three estates of medieval society. The first estate comprised the clergy, those who prayed; the second consisted of the nobility and knights, those who fought; and the third embraced the peasantry, those who worked. The responsibility of the second estate was to protect both the clergy and the peasantry, with the king holding the ultimate responsibility to defend his subjects.

In practice the boundaries between the estates were blurred. Members of the clergy frequently took up arms, notable examples being the Archbishop of Sens and the Bishop of Châlons, respectively captured and killed at the Battle of Poitiers while fighting for the French, and the English army led by the Bishop of Norwich in Flanders in 1383. Furthermore, indentured, paid contract service, rather than feudal obligation, meant that some of the English knightly class were content to stay at home and manage their estates rather than go to war. Also, drawing solely on nobility and knights would not provide sufficient men for military service so that the peasantry could not avoid being drawn into the armies of the period. Also, with the growing importance of commerce, merchants and the bourgeoisie, this hierarchy was beginning to break down. Nevertheless, the concept that it was the duty of the nobility and knights, and above all the king, to protect the other estates was deeply rooted in society. It is also worth remembering that the presumption that high birth and wealth presupposed the right to lead remained central to the recruitment of officers in the British army until the reforms of Edward Cardwell, Secretary of State for War, abolished the purchase of commissions and promotion in 1871.

Despite the pre-eminence of noble birth in command appointments, there were examples of men of exceptional ability achieving high office during the Hundred Years War, but even these men came at least from the gentry. Sir John Chandos, a close companion in arms of the Black Prince, was Lord of the Manor of Radbourne in Derbyshire. His ability led him to occupy positions of great importance, including Constable of Aquitaine and Seneschal of Poitou and, due to his successes, he was rewarded with the viscountcy of St-Sauveur in Normandy in 1361.

Contemporaries of the Black Prince and Chandos included two other men from the lower gentry who gained fame and command: Sir Hugh Calveley and Sir Robert Knolles. Sir Hugh Calveley was the youngest son of a member of the gentry in Cheshire and, in common with many in such a position, he followed a military career. His career progressed steadily and he fought under Chandos at the Battle of Auray. After the end of the War of the Breton Succession he joined the Free Companies and subsequently fought in Spain. Initially he fought on the side of Henry of Trastamara but subsequently served alongside the Black Prince in the defeat of Henry at the Battle of Nájera. With the renewal of war, he went on to attain high office as Governor of Calais and as Admiral of the West.

Sir Robert Knolles was a companion in arms of Calveley. Son of a burgess or yeoman, he fought in the War of the Breton Succession and at the Battle of Nájera. He went on to obtain command, and in 1370, after the renewal of war, he landed at Calais in command of an army of 3,000 men. His campaign was beset with difficulties, which demonstrated the challenge faced by a man of relatively low birth in keeping the loyalty of subordinates of higher birth. In the words of Jonathan Sumption, some of his captains 'at least in their own estimation, were better-born and better formed in chivalry'. He was wary of a set-piece battle with the French, contrary to the wishes of some of his captains, and decided to withdraw to Brittany. His army disintegrated, with three divisions remaining in the vicinity of Le Mans as Knolles withdrew. The remaining elements were dispersed and defeated in detail at Pontvallain and Vaas in December 1370. Sir John Minsterworth, one of the most virulent of Knolles' opponents amongst his captains, returned to England and laid the blame for the failure of the campaign at Knolles' door. The King's Council ruled against Knolles and he forfeited the lands that had been given to him as his fee for raising his army and 10,000 marks that he was believed to have gained from the campaign. He was subsequently exonerated, in part due to the protestations of the Black Prince, but he was never to regain the land and money that he had forfeited.

On the French side, perhaps the most remarkable example of a man not from the top rank of nobility but gaining high military office was Bertrand du Guesclin. Born into minor Breton nobility in 1320, du Guesclin quickly established a reputation for his prowess, and most importantly earned the respect of the senior French nobility during the War of the Breton Succession and, *inter alia*, victory at the Battle of Cocherel against Charles of Navarre in 1364. He was captured at the Battle of Nájera fighting against the Black Prince and ransomed. He continued to fight in Spain until returning to France in 1370. He was held in high regard by King Charles V, and on his return he was appointed Constable of France. In this senior position he was largely responsible for the French recovery and driving the English out of the territory gained in the first phase of the war and under the terms of the Treaty of Brétigny.

Rank, in terms of birth rather than appointment, was not without its problems, as seen with the difficulties experienced by Robert Knolles. On the renewal of war in 1369, the 22-year-old Earl of Pembroke refused to serve under Sir John Chandos. Chandos was a resourceful, experienced and successful commander. In view of the sickness of the Black Prince, at this time Prince of Aquitaine, Chandos had been appointed Seneschal of Bordeaux in 1369 to counter the French incursions into Aquitaine. Notwithstanding Edward III's personal appointment of Chandos, Pembroke considered it beneath his dignity to take orders from a mere gentleman. However, there were examples of men of nobility serving under men of lower social rank. Turning once more to Sir John Chandos as an example, at the Battle of Auray in 1364, during the War of the Breton Succession between Charles de Blois, supported by the French, and Jean de Montfort, supported by the English, de Montfort was content to allow Chandos to command the Anglo-Breton army.

Unfortunately high rank did not always bring military competence. On 22 March 1421 Henry V's brother Thomas, Duke of Clarence, was defeated by a predominantly Scottish Franco-Scottish army. Clarence, an impetuous and rash commander, attacked the French and the Scots at Baugé, against the advice of the Earl of Huntingdon and Sir Gilbert Umfraville, before he had gathered all his army. However, as a duke he trumped an earl and a mere knight, and he attacked a force of between 4,000 and 5,000 Scots and 1,000 French troops with about a third of his own force, some 1,500 men. The result was a disaster, with many English killed and most of the survivors captured. Clarence was among those killed in the mayhem.

The importance of status is evident in the request of the Gascon barons in 1355 to send the Black Prince to take personal command of the planned expedition to Aquitaine. The prince had served with distinction at Crécy in 1346, but nonetheless he had never had independent command and was an unknown quantity as a commander. Similarly, after the 1355 *chevauchée* the Estates of Languedoc stipulated that taxes raised for the war in 1356 would be retained for the defence of the Languedoc and would be contingent upon King Jean II sending the dauphin to take command in the south. Astute rulers, however, appreciated that successful command depended also on military competence. If necessary this would be ensured by providing the commander with experienced and respected advisers. In the case of the Black Prince's expedition of 1355–56, King Edward III was careful to ensure that his eldest son, respected but as yet untried in command, was accompanied by men of considerable military experience and ability.

The responsibility of command goes hand-in-hand with leadership, but how should we consider leadership at the time of our two protagonists, Jean II and the Black Prince? Good leadership is easy to recognise but much harder to define. Countless words have been written, and continue to be written, on the definition and practice of leadership. The British Army Leadership Code elaborates seven behaviours which contribute to good leadership: to lead by example, to encourage thinking, to apply reward and discipline, to demand high performance, to encourage confidence in the team, to recognise individual strengths and weaknesses, and to strive for team goals. This code sets out to pull together what has worked throughout history. Some of the code is expressed in modern terms which do not easily translate into the Middle Ages, although leadership by example, the application of reward and discipline, the encouragement of confidence and, although not formalised as such, the striving for team goals can be recognised in the period. Field Marshal Sir William Slim, commander of the British Fourteenth Army in Burma in the Second World War, described leadership as 'that mixture of example, persuasion and compulsion which makes men do what you want them to do. If I were asked to define leadership, I should say it is the "Projection of Personality". It is the most intensely personal thing in the world, because it is just plain you.' This definition certainly seems timeless.

In an age of hand-to-hand combat, example through personal courage was a particularly important element of leadership. King Jean II earned his epithet 'the Good' because of his renown for personal courage, which was certainly demonstrated at the Battle of Poitiers. Perceived lack of courage, and by inference failure to lead by example, could bring disgrace. The English defeat at Patay in 1429 was variously attributed to the rashness of Sir John Talbot and the cowardice of Sir John Fastolf, in part a model for Shakespeare's Falstaff. Fastolf was exonerated after thirteen years and restored to the Order of the Garter from which he had been suspended following the defeat. He went on to serve with distinction in France, but his reputation was for ever tainted.

However, successful leadership required much more than personal bravery. Indeed, courage on its own could lead to disaster. Sir John Talbot rode into battle at Castillon in 1453 unarmed, honouring his oath (given on his release by the French in 1450) not to take up arms again against the King of France. No one could doubt his courage, but his example was not enough and his rash leadership was a major factor in his army's defeat and his death.

Reward and discipline were certainly important elements of leadership in the Middle Ages. Reward could come in many forms: advancement in rank, the shares of booty between men and their captains codified in indentures, and grants and annuities made for exceptional service such as those we see in the *Register* of the Black Prince after Poitiers. Discipline could be set out for particular campaigns, such as Edward III's orders to respect the property of the Normans during his Crécy campaign, even if these orders were to little avail. During the Black Prince's *chevauchée* of 1355 the order was given that the men were to bear the red cross of St George. This was later enshrined in the first known English Ordinances of War of Richard II for the war against Scotland in 1385, which instructed that: 'everyone ... of our party, shall bear a large sign of the arms of St George before, and another behind, upon peril that if he be hurt or slain in default thereof, he who shall hurt or slay him shall suffer no penalty for it'. Henry V was a firm disciplinarian, hanging a soldier, represented by Shakespeare as the unfortunate Bardolph in *Henry V*, who had stolen from a church contrary to the orders of the king to respect Church property. On the eve of Agincourt, in order that the normal clamour of camp life should not mask the noise of French movement, Henry V gave strict orders for silence throughout the English army. This order was to be enforced by harsh penalties: gentlemen would forfeit their horses and equipment, and archers and others of lower rank would have their right ear cut off. Harsh punishments were hardly exceptional in the Middle Ages, but discipline itself would not be sufficient to lead an army to success and Henry V was clearly an inspirational commander and, of course, success breeds success.

Taking Field Marshal Slim's definition, persuasion also had a part to play and both the Black Prince and Henry V are said to have addressed their men on the eve of battle at Poitiers and Agincourt respectively. Loyalty among those who serve is a strong indicator of the leadership of the commander, and records show that men frequently engaged with the same captains. Clear objectives set out by Edward III for his campaigns and that of the Black Prince in 1355–56 equate to the team goals of the modern British code, and it is clear that these were communicated to and well understood by senior subordinates.

The leadership demonstrated by King Jean and the Black Prince at the Battle of Poitiers provides interesting contrasts. Jean may have been respected for his courage, but he was unable through his leadership to exercise control over his subordinates and the start of the battle was un-coordinated as a consequence. In contrast, the Black Prince was not only astute enough as a commander to recognise a critical moment in the battle but was also capable through his leadership to rally his men and lead them to victory. Good leadership, in the Middle Ages as in all ages, required that commanders had the ability to draw on the experience of those around them, to take decisions and to persuade their men to accept these decisions whatever misgivings they may have had.

PART THREE

THE PRINCIPAL CAMPAIGNS OF KING JEAN II AND THE BLACK PRINCE

In examining the generalship and leadership of the Black Prince and Jean II I have limited the scope to their principal campaigns. For the Black Prince these were his expedition in France of 1355–56 with his *chevauchées* of 1355 and in 1356, which culminated in the Battle of Poitiers, and the Battle of Nájera of 1367. The most important campaigns for Jean examined here were his sieges of Aiguillon in 1346 and Breteuil in 1356, and his pursuit of the Black Prince and the subsequent confrontation with the prince at Poitiers.

Both of course were influenced by their other experiences. In Jean's case these included his participation in the early years of the war in Flanders and his stand-off with Edward III in the inconclusive English expedition in the north of France in 1355. Jean, although he was not present, would also have drawn lessons from his father's defeat at Crécy in 1346, and these were instrumental in his military reforms of 1351. The Black Prince was present during the Crécy campaign and in the forefront of the fighting as nominal commander of the vanguard during the battle. However, perhaps the most important lesson that he would have drawn from this campaign was the importance of maintaining the aim. After crossing the Seine at Poissy, Edward III was racing north to cross the Somme with Philippe VI in hot pursuit. Speed was of the essence but valuable time was wasted when men of the Black Prince's division attacked the village of Vessencourt close to Beauvais. The men were stopped from assaulting Beauvais itself but not before they had wasted further valuable time setting fire to suburbs, churches outside the walls, and adjoining villages and farms. This diversion from Edward's objective incurred the king's wrath and to set an example twenty men were hanged. Despite this exemplary punishment, and contrary once again to the express orders of the king and the despatch of sergeants to stop the attacks, further time was wasted sacking and burning the town and castle of Poix as the army approached the Somme. The absence of such incidents during the *chevauchées* of 1355 and 1356 illustrates not only that the prince had drawn the appropriate lesson from this experience but also that he and his senior commanders were able to maintain the aim through discipline and leadership. The prince was also present at the siege of Calais and would have seen the challenges of resourcing and sustaining a siege.

Chapter 5

The Siege of Aiguillon
1346

The Prelude

Edward III's preferred method of waging war was the wide-ranging *chevauchée*, but he had also to secure the borders of his lands in Aquitaine. This meant holding towns and fortresses. By 1345 the borders had been progressively pushed back by the French and if the duchy were to survive it was necessary to bring places back into the allegiance of Edward III. That summer Henry of Grosmont, the Earl of Derby, was despatched to Gascony to remedy the situation. He took Bergerac and pressed on north to try to take Périgueux. Derby did not have the resources for a close siege and elected to take a number of fortresses in the vicinity of the town as a means to cut off supplies. The blockade did not have time to become effective before Louis of Poitiers, despatched by Jean, still at this date the Duke of Normandy and now the king's lieutenant in the Languedoc, relieved the town and set about retaking the surrounding fortresses which had fallen to Derby. One such fortress was Auberoche, but here the tables were turned when on 21 October 1345 Derby fell upon and defeated the besiegers. Although Jean still had under his command an army larger than that defeated at Auberoche, he decided to abandon the campaign and disbanded his troops at Angoulême on 4 November. This decision had far-reaching consequences as Henry of Grosmont, Earl of Derby, who on 22 September 1345 had succeeded to the earldom of Lancaster and become the most powerful and wealthy of Edward III's vassals, turned his attention to the Bordelais.

At the beginning of November 1345 the Earl of Lancaster moved up the Garonne to La Réole. The town had a weak link: the lack of loyalty of the population to the French. On 8 November a diversionary attack was launched at one end of the town which drew off the garrison while the gates at the other end of La Réole were opened to allow Lancaster's men to enter the town. The men of the garrison managed to escape being trapped on the ramparts and withdrew into the castle. The castle held out for some weeks before terms were negotiated. A truce would be maintained for

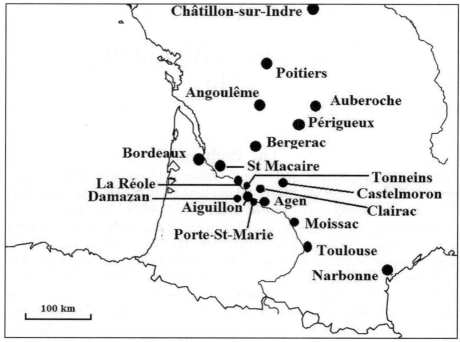

The Aiguillon Campaign, 1346.

five weeks and the commander would surrender and the garrison would be allowed to depart with safe conduct if relief did not come within that period. Notice of the terms was sent to Jean with a request for a relief force to be sent. However, Jean, having disbanded his army, was 350km away in his winter quarters to the north at Châtillon-sur-Indre and relief did not arrive. The garrison surrendered early in January 1346 and marched away under safe-conduct.

Following the success of the Earl of Lancaster at La Réole, part of the English army returned home and the Gascons dispersed until the start of campaigning the next spring. The English who remained set about raiding and taking towns and fortresses, mainly in the Garonne valley and to the north. In the Agenais many lords who had been uncertain about where their best interests lay came across to the English side, and in December the English opened a campaign in the area to extend their influence. By March 1346 the English were predominant in the region through a combination of conquest and defections. The French had been reduced to a handful of strongholds at Port-Ste-Marie, Agen, Moissac and Castelmoron. Among the places to fall was Aiguillon, a strategically important town at the confluence of the Garonne and the Lot. The surrender was probably the result of secret arrangements made in advance, since the inhabitants turned on the garrison when Lancaster arrived. The importance of Aiguillon passing to the English was not lost on the French and during 1346 they attempted to retake it.

With the approach of the spring of 1346 came fresh energy on the part of Jean. He left his winter quarters at Châtillon-sur-Indre and moved south for a campaign planned to restore French fortunes in Aquitaine. With him as he marched south were the Count of Burgundy and Duke of Athens and numerous other nobles, as well as the great military officers of state: the constable, both marshals and the Master of the Royal Archers. Meanwhile the Duke of Bourbon and the Bishop of Beauvais were gathering at Toulouse an army drawn from the Languedoc. During March the two armies came together in the Quercy, 120km or so to the east of Aiguillon.

The Siege

The duke's declared objective was to retake La Réole downstream on the Garonne. However, the French would need the rivers for resupply and the English held Aiguillon upstream and St-Macaire downstream of La Réole. Jean appreciated that retaking La Réole meant that he must secure the Garonne for communications. Aiguillon was the key to freeing up use of the Lot and the Garonne to enable a successful move against La Réole. On 1 April 1346 the vanguard of the French army arrived before Aiguillon and the *arrière-ban* was proclaimed in the south the following day to rally more men for the campaign. Jean arrived during the second week of April with his principal advisers. At its peak the strength of the army that Jean had at his disposal was possibly the largest ever gathered by the French for war in the south-west and has been estimated as being between 15,000 and 20,000 strong. It included 1,400 Genoese mercenaries and a siege train with five cannon.

Despite its strategic importance, Aiguillon was a small town with defences that left something to be desired. It had been formed over the years by two communities growing together. To the north was Lunac-d'Aiguillon, an ancient Gallo-Roman town surrounded on a rectangular pattern by crumbling brick walls. In the north of Lunac, overlooking the confluence of the Garonne and the Lot was the seigneurial castle. This had brick and stone walls about 10m high. There were gates in the northern, eastern and southern walls. To the west, where the Garonne flowed against the walls, there was a postern gate. The castle had the river

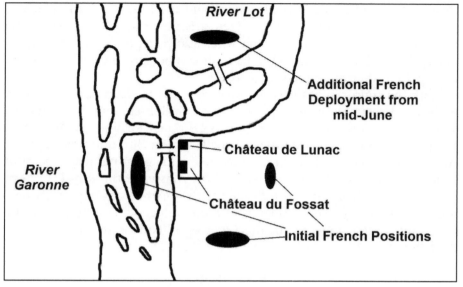

The Siege of Aiguillon, 1 April to 20 August 1346.

Lot and a branch of the Garonne to protect the northern and western walls. A moat, fed by the rivers, protected the south and east. A short distance to the south was Le Fossat d'Aiguillon, another seigneurial castle, and a small village which had developed around the fortress. The two parts of the town had grown together and work had started on modern walls in a rectangular form about 250m by 150m to enclose the town in its entirety. Unfortunately the work had never been completed and the gaps had to be filled with barrels filled with stones. There was a bridge to the west over the Garonne and a further bridge over the Lot a little north-east of the town.

Within the town were some 600 archers and 300 men-at-arms, led by the seneschal, Ralph Stafford, and Hugh Menil. Among the garrison were also two distinguished soldiers: Walter Mauny from Hainault and the Gascon Alexander de Caumont. Lancaster, who had been at La Réole for the winter, withdrew to Bordeaux initially to reassemble his army and muster companies gathered by the Gascon lords. Reinforcements from England were promised, mainly archers, and some men arrived during the summer. Conscious of the importance of Aiguillon, Lancaster had strongly garrisoned Damazan, 6km to the west of the town and the Garonne, and Tonneins, 11km to the north. Aiguillon had fallen to the Anglo-Gascons the year before in a matter of hours. The scene was now set for a siege that would last throughout the summer to the increasing frustration of Jean, who swore that he would not withdraw until the town had fallen.

Initially the French took up position on the island between the two branches of the Garonne to the west and on the plain to the south and east of the town. They set about digging trenches and constructing earthworks to their rear to protect against a surprise attack and a recurrence of the disaster at Auberoche the year before. This left access to the town open to the north. It also left the garrison control of the Lot and islands to the north of the town to shelter their flotilla of boats. For Jean to deploy troops to the north without ensuring rapid communications between the three elements would be to risk attack and defeat in detail of parts of the army without the means to concentrate all of the besieging forces. The English garrisons of Tonneins and Damazan close to hand made this threat more acute. One of the first actions of the French was to take control of the bridge at Clairac, 8km upstream on the Lot. They also built a wooden pontoon bridge over the Garonne downstream of Aiguillon. This was carried out over several weeks by some 300 men, defended by Genoese crossbowmen. Despite this protection, the garrison made determined efforts to prevent the construction of the bridge with frequent sorties and assaults launched from barges to attack the bridge and its builders. The bridge was destroyed twice before it was finally completed late in May. The French then stretched a chain across the Garonne to prevent river-borne communications. With the French holding Port-Ste-Marie upstream on the Garonne and Clairac upstream on the Lot, then, in theory at least, the town was cut off from reinforcement and resupply by river. This should, in turn, have given the French free use of the rivers for their own ends, but that proved to be far from the case.

On 16 June 1346 two large barges coming down the Garonne from Toulouse laden with supplies for the besiegers were intercepted and captured by the garrison. Two raiding parties set out from the town: one in small boats from close to the castle of Lunac and the other across the bridge over the Garonne. The second of these comprised around 100 men-at-arms led by Alexander de Caumont. Although they succeeded in passing through the French lines and achieving their objective, the withdrawal of the raiding party to the town proved to be a disaster. The French reacted vigorously and both sides threw reinforcements into the fighting developing on the bridge. The French advanced across the bridge. The portcullis was dropped to prevent them entering the town, with the result that the raiding party was trapped outside. There were numerous casualties and Alexander de Caumont was captured. It seems strange by modern standards that the French should release such a celebrated soldier. However, the ransom of prisoners was first and foremost a commercial transaction and in return for a large sum, much of which was advanced by the Earl of Lancaster, de Caumont was back with the Anglo-Gascons in a matter of days.

Meanwhile Edward III was planning his great expedition which would culminate in the Battle of Crécy in August. When news of Jean's advance towards the Garonne reached England, it seems that Edward was considering taking his army to Aquitaine. The indenture between Edward and Lancaster stated: 'the king has agreed that if it shall happen that the said earl is besieged or beset by so great a force that he cannot help himself unless he is rescued by the king's power, then the king is bound to rescue him in one way or another, provided that he can be rescued easily'. Of course, Lancaster was not in Aiguillon, moving initially from La Réole to Bordeaux and then returning to La Réole to direct support of the besieged town. However, there can have been no doubt that if Aiguillon were to fall, Lancaster would be beset by a great force and the terms of his indenture would apply. It is possible that Edward was initially planning to go to Gascony to bring relief directly to Lancaster, even though the terms of the indenture would not require the king's personal presence. However, he kept his cards very close to his chest and it may be that his eventual landing in Normandy was his objective from the start. The landing in Normandy had the primary objective of bringing Philippe to battle. Nevertheless, it is possible that there was a deliberate strategy of the indirect approach with the secondary objective of the landing in the north being to relieve the pressure on Lancaster, judging correctly that his invasion would compel Philippe to recall Jean to join the royal army gathering to counter the English *chevauchée*.

Despite their success in taking the barbican gate in mid-June, the French were making little progress in bringing the siege to a successful conclusion. At some point Lancaster had returned to La Réole with his army. He kept pressure on the besiegers by harrying French lines of communication, foragers and messengers. Notwithstanding their vastly superior numbers, fieldworks and barriers, the French were unable to seal off the town. There were numerous examples of supplies reaching the town by stealth, and at least one case of a detachment from Lancaster's army fighting their way through the French lines with victuals. Perhaps in response to Lancaster's success in getting supplies and reinforcements into the town, in mid-June Jean moved his headquarters north of the Lot between Aiguillon and

Tonneins. He also somewhat belatedly appears to have launched attacks on the islands used to shelter the garrison's flotilla. As was often the case with a prolonged siege, the besiegers, perhaps ten times more numerous than those within the walls, found obtaining food an increasing problem. The strong English presence in the Périgord and downstream of Aiguillon on the Garonne restricted the scope for foraging. Purveyors were sent as far afield as Béarn, 160km to the south, and to the hills of the Aubrac, more than 300km away to the east, to requisition cattle. The area around Toulouse was also stripped of food and wine for the besieging army.

The besiegers tried to break the deadlock with an assault on the castle of Lunac. The plan was to make the attack from three siege towers mounted on barges. The attack was a complete failure. One of the barges carrying a tower was struck by a stone thrown from a trebuchet; it capsized and sank, taking with it the tower and all the crew of the barge. The attack was abandoned and the other towers withdrawn. To try to exploit his numerical superiority Jean launched successive assaults over a period of five or six days with his men working in shifts around the clock. The hope was that this incessant fighting would exhaust the defenders. It was to no avail. Jean then brought siege engines from Toulouse and procured a number of cannon, but he met with no greater success. After some four months of siege Jean finally appreciated that he did not have the means to take Aiguillon by force. At long last he realised that it was time to try to reduce the town by famine. However, with events unfolding in the north it was too late to be effective.

With the arrival of Edward in Normandy on 12 July 1346, and with a further Anglo-Flemish army in Flanders under the command of Sir Hugh Hastings, it was apparent to Philippe VI that the most serious threat that he faced was now in the north. It seems that elements of Jean's besieging force were withdrawn early in the summer, since shortly after Edward III's arrival in Normandy the French constable and at least one of the marshals were in the north involved with countering the English landings. Indeed, it seems that the constable was recalled to take command of the defence of Harfleur on the Seine estuary when the English fleet was believed to be on the point of departure.

Jean had continually suffered from attacks on his lines of supply. A particular problem was posed by frequent attacks by Gaillard de Durfort from his castle at Bajamont, some 30km east of Aiguillon, on French river supplies on the Garonne. On 18 July Jean decided to act and despatched 2,000 men to counter Durfort's attacks. However, the orders given to the detachment were simply to contain the castle garrison and starve it into surrender. The garrison came out from the castle and inflicted a humiliating defeat on Jean's men.

Philippe recalled his son to join his army to counter the English invasion. Jean was reluctant to leave before he had brought the siege to a successful conclusion and he quarrelled with his advisers and dragged his feet. He was more concerned, it seems, about his loss of honour than the threat to the realm, and with the hope of saving his dignity he sent a mission which on 13 August met with Lancaster, now in Bergerac, to offer a truce and suspension of the siege of Aiguillon. The earl was every bit as well informed of events in the north and saw no incentive to agree to the French proposals. Jean prevaricated but ultimately had no option but to obey his father's orders and he lifted the siege a few days later on 20 August. The French departed in haste and left their camp, equipment and horses in the safe-keeping of some local men, who were quickly overwhelmed by men of the garrison. Jean could not cover the 780km to Crécy-en-Ponthieu before the battle six days later and Philippe VI was deprived of a valuable contingent of men largely because of the resilience of the garrison in Aiguillon, Lancaster's shrewd management of his forces, and Jean's pride.

There was an interesting episode at the end of the siege which shows us something of Jean's character. In the rout of the local French levies at the end of the siege prisoners were taken and the garrison learnt of events unfolding in Picardy. Walter Mauny wanted to join the fray and, in exchange for remitting the ransom of a friend of Jean's captured in a skirmish, received a safe-conduct to cross France with twenty men and join Edward III's army. Jean's sense of honour and his concept of the code of chivalry had prevailed over pragmatic military judgement.

Jean's Generalship

In 1340 Jean, in his first military command, with an army 10,000 strong, attempted to take the town of Valenciennes in the County of Hainault. His army had advanced quickly into Hainault, outstripping the speed of his supply train, and moved along the Scheldt valley. Jean compounded his supply problems by leaving three strong castles along the Scheldt in enemy hands. He had barely arrived outside Valenciennes when an unexpected sortie by the garrison dispersed his army in a chaotic rout. Jean then belatedly turned his attention to the castles left in his rear.

When Jean set out to take La Réole six years later he had at least learnt the lesson that for a siege army it was essential to have secure lines of communication. In besieging La Réole he would need to use the Garonne for resupply, and he appreciated that he needed to take Aiguillon before turning his attention to the primary objective. However, he did not apply the same logic to the siege of Aiguillon and left the Anglo-Gascon garrisons in Damazan and Tonneins, both of which served to assist in resupplying Aiguillon and disrupting French supplies. By leaving these towns in enemy hands he failed to provide security for his siege force. Similarly, it was only late in the siege that he turned his attention to the castle of Bajamont, which also threatened his supply lines. When he did so, his measures were half-hearted: he limited the mission of the detached force to containment, which inevitably would have meant a loss of troops from his main force over a protracted time if it had not been defeated soon after its arrival. Selection of a more aggressive aim and concentration of a larger and sufficient force to achieve the aim would have minimised this risk.

It is a laudable characteristic in a commander to maintain his aim. However, during the siege of Aiguillon Jean appears to have lost sight of the fact that his primary objective was La Réole and not Aiguillon. Instead of Aiguillon being a means to an end, it became the end itself. Lancaster, although disposing of many fewer men than Jean, by skilfully supporting Aiguillon with resupply and disruption of Jean's lines of communication was able to keep Aiguillon in Jean's sights.

Jean initially relied on siege engines and superior numbers to assault and take Aiguillon. As a consequence he neglected properly to blockade the town and only resorted to attempting to starve the garrison into submission more than four months after the start of the siege. Certainly closing off all access with the numerous channels of the Garonne and the many islands in the river did not make the task straightforward. Nevertheless, it was only in mid-June that he even deployed men north of the Lot to close the direct road from English-held Tonneins to Aiguillon. One of Jean's biographers remarks that he had a great interest in military engineering and siege engines. Unfortunately, this seems to have been at the expense of a thorough appreciation of the task before him. His failure to take Aiguillon stemmed from poor tactics, the absence of an effective blockade until late in the siege, the unchallenged presence of Anglo-Gascon garrisons in the immediate vicinity, and the limited effectiveness of logistic support requiring his army to search further and further afield for supplies as the siege progressed.

However, the seeds of this unsuccessful siege and the absence of Jean and his army from the Battle of Crécy perhaps lie in Jean's decision to disband his army in early November 1345. By eschewing offensive action he left the initiative with the Anglo-Gascons, which led to the fall of La Réole and Aiguillon. We do not know why Jean disbanded his army and withdrew to the north for the winter. Perhaps he was short of the means to sustain his army throughout the winter. If he had been able to maintain a presence in the south-west, he could perhaps have relieved the two towns and prevented them falling into Anglo-Gascon hands. If he had done so he would, in all probability, have been able to join his father with at least a substantial part of his force to participate in the Crécy campaign.

Chapter 6

The Black Prince's *Chevauchée* in the Languedoc 1355

The Strategic Background to the *Chevauchée*

When Edward III came to the throne England had a population approximately one-third of that of France. France was also wealthier than England, with the French king potentially able to raise three or four times as much in taxation as the English king. The English also had the disadvantage of external lines of communication. They needed to use the sea for reinforcement and logistic support from the home base, with all the challenges of finding shipping and the vagaries of the weather with which to contend, while the French enjoyed the inherent advantages of internal movement over land. Overall, the English did not have the capacity to wage a war of conquest and occupation, but they could carry the war to France through the *chevauchée* and, as a secondary but important consideration, keep the war away from home. As Christine de Pizan, writing in 1410 as a court writer for King Charles VI of France, declared: 'It is better to trample another country than to allow one's own to be trampled underfoot.' The *chevauchée* allowed the English to exert the maximum pressure from the available resources, and to choose the area of operations.

In the right circumstances the *chevauchée* could entice the enemy to do battle and encourage allies, but a key aspect was pillaging. Some of this was necessary to supply the needs of the army, but in addition there would have been the looting of movable wealth by troops. Not only did this diminish the resources of the French king's subjects available for taxation, but there was also the prospect of considerable personal gain, despite the general principle reflected in indentures that half of the spoils would be surrendered to the retinue commander of the man concerned and half of that figure to the king, or in this case the prince. The hope of personal enrichment was a strong recruiting incentive.

A critic of the prince's 1355 *chevauchée*, French historian Henri Denifle, unwittingly put his finger on the military objectives of such operations:

'They proposed above all to pillage and to ravage one of the richest parts of France, from where the king drew his greatest resources for waging war.' In other words, the *chevauchée* was an instrument of economic warfare which reduced the potential of the enemy to wage war.

Preparations

The fragile truce between France and England was due to expire in April 1355. In January senior Gascon nobles, including Jean de Grailly, holder of the ancient feudal title peculiar to Gascony of the Captal de Buch, who was to be a loyal supporter of the Black Prince and Edward III until the end of his days in a French prison, came to England to argue that when the truce expired Edward should take the offensive in the south-west. What fighting there had been during the truce had not gone particularly badly but neither had it gone well, and there was concern over raids being made on Aquitaine by Jean, Count of Armagnac. Jean of Valois had come to the throne in 1352 on the death of Philippe VI, and Armagnac was King Jean's lieutenant in the Languedoc. The Gascons were looking not only for military support but also for leadership from the king's son. Edward held a Great Council in April which, *inter alia*, agreed that the Black Prince should go to Gascony with an army and the Earls of Warwick, Suffolk, Salisbury and Oxford. An indenture with the king appointed the Black Prince:

> to go as his lieutenant to Gascony with 433 men-at-arms and 700 archers, 400 mounted and 300 on foot, as his own retinue, and with the men-at-arms and archers in the companies of the earls of Warwick, Suffolk, Oxford, and Salisbury, Sir John de Lisle and Sir Reynold [Reginald] de Cobham, who are to go with the prince to the said parts.

This was an experienced team of advisers for the prince. Thomas Beauchamp, Earl of Warwick, who was 41 or 42 in 1355, had fought on several of Edward III's campaigns since 1339 and had been in the prince's division at Crécy. Robert Ufford, Earl of Suffolk, had also fought alongside the prince at Crécy, and at 57 he brought considerable experience. John Vere, Earl of Oxford, was of similar age to Warwick, with military experience in Scotland, Flanders and Brittany. He had also fought in the prince's division at Crécy. Salisbury, at 28, was only two years older than the prince. They had a sometimes uneasy relationship but they had been knighted together when they landed in France in 1346 and they had fought alongside each other at Crécy. Cobham, amongst the older heads at 60 years of

Edward the Black Prince as a Knight of the Garter. Illustration from the Bruges Garter Book. (*Wikipedia*)

The tomb of the Black Prince in Canterbury Cathedral.
(*Josep Renalias/Creative Commons*)

(*Above left*) Fourteenth-century portrait of Jean II by an unknown artist. Held in the Louvre, Paris. (*Creative Commons*)

(*Above right*) King Jean. (*Wikipedia*)

Franc à cheval of Jean le Bon, 1360. (*Wikipedia*)

stiges of the ramparts of Aiguillon, dating back to Roman times.
oto issue de l'Atlas des paysages de Lot-et-Garonne – François Bonneau et associés – CD47)

stiges of Breteuil castle. It was built in the twelfth century by Henry II of England and
nolished in 1378 after being retaken for the French by Bertrand du Guesclin.

The Battle of Poitiers – This photograph was taken after t driest summer for fifty years. The Miosson was little more than a minor stream but in w weather it can be a much mo significant river. The bridge replaced an earlier structure washed away by the river in flood in 1982. The land in the foreground would be susceptible to flooding in suc conditions. Beyond the road the right, where grass has no been planted, marsh plants a evident even in dry weather. (*Peter Hoskins*)

The Battle of Poitiers – Baker's 'broad deep valley', with the river Miosson in the middle-ground and the road running up the hill towards the prince's position near the Croix de la Garde. (*Peter Hoskins*)

The Battle of Poitiers – This hedge has been allowed to grow to more than 3 metres, c 10 feet, in width. Such hedges would be formidable obstacle (*Peter Hoskins*)

(*Above*) The Battle of Poitiers, as depicted in Froissart. (*Wikipedia*)

(*Left*) A reconstruction of a belfry, or siege tower, as favoured by Jean II, at Tiffauges castle. (*Peter Hoskins*)

(*Below*) The arms of war of the Black Prince. The white label of cadency, a horizontal bar with three downward points, differentiates the prince's arms from those of his father and shows that he is the eldest son.

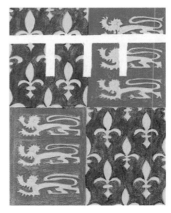

The church of St Vigor in Quettehou where the Black Prince is believed to have been knighted at the start of the Crécy campaign in July 1346. (*Peter Hoskins*)

The formidable defences of the *cité* of Carcassonne, which were sufficient to deter an attack by the Black Prince in 1355. (*Peter Hoskins*)

The Battle of Nájera – The bridge across the Najerilla looking towards the town and the high ground behind which trapped the fleeing Spanish army. (*Peter Hoskins*)

The Battle of Nájera – The flat ground on which the battle was fought. (*Peter Hoskins*)

The Battle of Nájera – The high ground on the approach to the battlefield looking north from the road between Navarette and Nájera. (*Peter Hoskins*)

The funeral procession of King Jean. (*Wikipedia*)

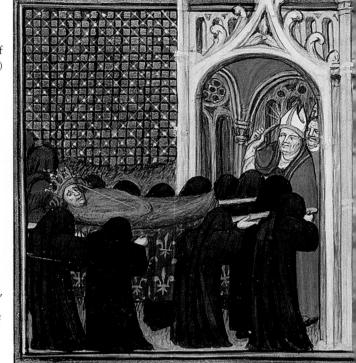

The thirteenth-century north door, known as the Valois door, of the basilica of St Denis in Paris – the final resting place of a number of French monarchs, including King Jean II. (*Peter Hoskins*)

age, and de Lisle, 37, had also been at Crécy. With the prince went three other veterans of Crécy who were to play a major part in the coming events: James Audley, 40; Bartholomew de Burghersh, around the prince's age; and John Chandos, 40 to 45. At the core of the force which the prince was to take to France was a group of experienced men, used to living and fighting together and alongside the prince. Their comradeship would be reinforced over the months ahead, and would stand the army in good stead. The force that would leave with them numbered around 2,600, comprising approximately 1,000 men-at-arms, 1,000 mounted archers, 300 to 400 foot archers, and 170 'Welshmen', who were most probably foot-soldiers or pike-men, a specialist arm provided by the Welsh.

The indenture between the king and the prince was dated 10 July and was signed in London. However, preparations had been put in hand some while earlier to gather the expeditionary force at Plymouth, with the first request for ships being issued on 10 March 1355, even before the arrival of the Gascon nobility, as Edward III began to plan for the renewal of hostilities. In Cheshire orders had been issued on 26 June for 300 archers to be sent to arrive in Plymouth by 'three weeks from Midsummer'. The prince arrived in Plymouth by 30 July, but by then it was clear that for want of sufficient shipping, and due to contrary winds, an immediate departure would not be possible. The English crown, however, had an efficient administration which was capable both of resolving the problems of shipping and furnishing the men and supplies for the prince's expedition at the same time as preparing the expeditions planned for Lancaster and the king. In the event the Black Prince's fleet sailed for Aquitaine on 9 September and arrived in Bordeaux eleven days later on 20 September.

The prince's expedition was part of a broader plan: an army under Edward moving out from Calais, a second in Normandy under the Duke of Lancaster, and the third with the Black Prince in Gascony. There was indeed a *chevauchée* by the king in Picardy in late October and early November 1355. Both King Edward and King Jean were apparently willing to do battle but vied for advantage in terms of place and time. In the event Edward returned to England and Jean discharged his army without battle. Plans for operations by the Duke of Lancaster that year were postponed, and he was not to land in Normandy until June 1356. Meanwhile the Black Prince had launched his first *chevauchée* in early October 1355 and was wreaking havoc in the Languedoc.

On 21 September 1355 King Edward's letters patent were read in the cathedral of St-André in Bordeaux to an assembly of the lords, senior clergy and prominent citizens of Gascony and Bordeaux. The prince pledged to be a good and loyal lord and to respect the rights of the citizens. In return he received the homage of the lords and citizenry. This large assembly was followed by a council of war of the most prominent lords. The prince expressed his outrage at the activities of Jean, Count of Armagnac, who had taken a leaf out of the English book and had been making a series of successful and disconcerting raids into Aquitaine. It was decided that the war should be carried into Armagnac's territory, and that the *chevauchée* should start in two weeks' time. This decision for a prompt departure appears to have taken some by surprise, but it was already getting late in the season for campaigning and the expedition would need to start soon to reduce the risk of being caught by winter weather. In addition, there would be an advantage if the Anglo-Gascon army could set off before the French had the chance to organise their defences. The prince's broad objectives set out in his indenture with the king were to restore and reinforce English control in Gascony and reassure the Gascon nobility of the king's commitment to the Duchy of Aquitaine. First and foremost this was to be achieved by demonstrating English power, with the territory of the Count of Armagnac as the first target. If the French forces in the Languedoc could be brought to battle, so much the better. As the military historian Lieutenant Colonel A.H. Burne put it, this could be achieved in two ways: 'by advancing straight toward him or, if he did not react to that, by devastating his country, until he was forced to take action in its defence'.

The two weeks left before departure on the *chevauchée* were devoted to unloading stores and horses, the purchase of further horses, and advances of money to be made to leaders. In view of the timescale, the Gascon nobility, who provided rather more men than those who came with the expedition, must have been mustering men and gathering supplies well in advance of the arrival of the Black Prince. Equipment also had to be gathered at the supply depot at St-Macaire upstream on the river Garonne near Langon for resupply as the army advanced.

With preparations complete, the Black Prince set out from Bordeaux on 5 October with the 2,600 men of his English and Welsh contingents who had voyaged from England, the men raised by the Gascon nobles and a smattering of German and Spanish lords. The overall strength has been estimated at between 6,000 and 8,000. With troops from such a range of countries, the common soldiers must have found communicating with one another a challenge with a mixture of Welsh, English, French and Gascon languages being spoken. However, Anglo-Norman French was still the language of the English nobility, and the senior elements of the army, with French as a common language, would not have faced the difficulties of the lower ranks.

The fighting men were supported by a large number of non-combatants. There would have been carpenters, farriers, bowyers, fletchers, smiths, armourers, cooks, bakers, saddlers and carters, among others. It has been estimated that in some cases during the fourteenth century the non-combatant element of an army could be as great as the strength of the fighting men. Even for a highly mobile operation such as a *chevauchée*, a complement of non-combatants of 50 per cent of the fighting strength would not be unusual. Thus, the overall strength of the army with its accompanying non-combatants was probably in the region of 10,000. In addition there were the animals.

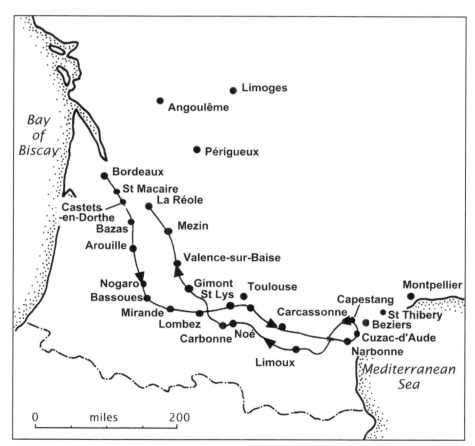

The Black Prince's *Chevauchée* in the Languedoc, 1355.

It is not possible to establish definitively how many horses were taken on the *chevauchée*, but it is useful to have some idea of the number simply to illustrate the scale of the operation and the logistic challenges faced by the Black Prince in feeding and watering the accompanying horses. As a rule of thumb we can say that in this period knights, esquires and men-at-arms typically took four, three and two horses respectively on campaign, and mounted archers would take at least one horse. Whether or not the knights, men-at-arms and esquires took as many horses on this particular *chevauchée* is not known, but one estimate places the number of horses transported to Gascony at 6,500 and horses were also purchased in Gascony. Overall, a figure of 13,000 horses for the use of combatants and non-combatants may not be far off the mark. On top of that there was the logistic train. Allowing for pack animals and horses to pull carts, there were probably a further 1,000 horses in the baggage train, carrying provisions, bows and arrows and other supplies for a total of around 14,000 horses to be fed and watered. Finding sufficient forage and water for them would be a daily preoccupation over the weeks ahead. It was also probably a determining factor on occasion for the length of the day's march and the duration of halts. However, the prince and his advisers were well aware of the importance of sustainability, and, other than some minor difficulties during the return march to Bordeaux, were able to sustain the Anglo-Gascon army even when deep in enemy territory.

The Advance to the Mediterranean

The army initially followed the course of the Garonne, taking on supplies which had been shipped down river to St-Macaire and turning south and leaving the river behind at Castets-en-Dorthe. When the army passed through the town of Bazas, about 20km south of Castets-en-Dorthe, and still 60km from enemy territory, the order was given that all in the army were henceforth to bear the red cross of St George. Whether or not it was standard practice at the time for English armies to wear the cross we do not know, but, as we saw above, by 1385 it had been enshrined in the Ordinances of War of Richard II, the prince's son, which instructed that: 'everyone ... of our party, shall bear a large sign of the arms of St George before, and another behind, upon peril that if he be hurt or slain in default thereof, he who shall hurt or slay him shall suffer no penalty for it'. Clearly there was much concern to avoid casualties from what we now euphemistically call 'friendly fire'.

The first significant test for the prince's army was the two days' passage through the Landes. Nowadays this is a thinly populated area largely given over to forest with packets of arable land. However, before the Landes were reclaimed from the sands in the nineteenth century, this area was much more hostile for the traveller and considered almost a desert. We get an idea of how unpleasant this area was at the time of the Black Prince's passage from the author of the *Pilgrim's Guide* writing in the twelfth century:

> Then, for travellers who are already tired, there is a three days' journey through the Landes of Bordeaux. This is a desolate country lacking in everything: there is neither bread nor wine nor fish nor water nor any springs. There are few villages on this sandy plain, though it has honey, millet, and pigs in plenty. If you are going through the Landes in summer be sure to protect your face from wasps and horse flies which are particularly abundant in this region. And if you do not watch your feet carefully you will sink up to your knees in the sea sand which is found everywhere here.

Despite these conditions, the measures taken to ensure the supply of the army allowed the Landes to be crossed successfully in two days. After clearing the Landes the army approached Arouille, just inside enemy territory in the County of Armagnac; here banners were unfurled and the army was split into three divisions. The vanguard was commanded by the Earl of Warwick, with the office of constable, and Sir Reginald Cobham, the marshal. The main body was commanded by the prince, and the rear-guard was under the command of the Earls of Suffolk and Salisbury.

The nature of the campaign would now change: provisions would be seized from the enemy and not purchased, pillaging and burning would begin, and there would be the ever-present risk of hostile action. From now on the army would generally advance in three columns on a broad front, which made for easier foraging and provisioning as they started to live off the land. It also enabled destruction to be extended across a wide area, so maximising the destructive potential of the army. But the divisions were generally close enough to come together quickly if needed for defence or a set-piece battle. The army was now on the threshold of action for the first time as it embarked on the offensive phase of the *chevauchée*.

The Black Prince's army entered enemy territory near Arouille on 11 October. The next few days resulted in the destruction of a number of small towns. Around 16 October the army came to Nogaro. This was the first town since the start of hostilities which it seems was well protected and garrisoned. During the *chevauchée* as a whole the prince did not spend precious time and risk valuable resources on sieges. Success did not hinge on reducing every town on the line of march. A demonstration that the King of France and his lieutenant in the Languedoc, the Count of Armagnac, were powerless to stop the Anglo-Gascon army would convey a sufficiently powerful message and Nogaro was left untouched. After the departure from Nogaro the destruction continued, with the exception of the small town of Bassoues – despite there being many examples on the *chevauchée* of the destruction of church property – which belonged to the Archbishop of Auch. The army was now approaching the boundary of the County of Armagnac, having left a wide trail of destruction through-out the 'noble, beautiful, and rich' lands of the Count of Armagnac. Many, including perhaps the count, may have expected the prince to turn back from here having inflicted retribution on the count for his hostility to the English crown. But this was not to be, and on 21 October the army reached Mirande, the chief town of the County of Astarac. It was fortified and well garrisoned, and once again the prince maintained the approach of not wasting resources on attacking strongly defended places.

From Mirande the march continued towards Toulouse, with the pattern of widespread destruction continuing but with a further example of a well-protected town, Lombez, being left untouched. Much of the itinerary since leaving Mirande had involved crossings of minor rivers flowing from the Pyrenees into the Garonne, which runs through Toulouse. On 26 October the army reached St-Lys, 25km west of Toulouse. Now a significant chal-lenge lay ahead if the army were to continue towards the Mediterranean: the crossing of the rivers Garonne and Ariège.

Sir John Wingfield, writing after the return to Bordeaux, summarised the tactical position:

> our enemies had broken down all the bridges on the one side of Toulouse and the other, save only the bridges in Toulouse, for the river goeth through the midst of the city. And the Constable of France, the Marshal Clermont, the Count of Armagnac, were, with a great power, in the said city at that same time. And the city of Toulouse is very great and strong and fair and well fenced.

Sir John was correct in describing Toulouse as well fenced. It straddled the river, but both parts were walled and the ramparts, having been rebuilt in 1347, were modern. The bridges connecting the two parts of the city were protected by the walls at both ends. The chronicler Jean le Bel tells us that the army of the Count of Armagnac, with the Constable of France, Jacques de Bourbon, and Marshal Clermont had four times as many men-at-arms as the prince. He also had some mercenary troops and local militia. The reported numbers may have been inflated, and many of Armagnac's men are likely to have been inexperienced and poorly trained. They may not have been a match for the Anglo-Gascon army in the field, but they could be expected to give a better account of themselves in defence of the ramparts. In addition to the bridges in the vicinity of Toulouse having been broken, other major crossings for 160km downstream, as far as Tonneins, were in enemy hands.

Against this tactical background the prince's options were: to attempt to take the city by assault, to lay siege, to try to draw the French into battle, to strike in a different direction without crossing the Garonne and Ariège, to turn for home, or to force a crossing of the Garonne and Ariège rivers near Toulouse and continue to advance into French territory.

Toulouse, as the regional capital of Languedoc and owing allegiance to the French crown, was a very important commercial and political city. It was one of the great medieval cities of France, probably with a population in excess of 30,000. To take the city would be a great triumph. However, an assault would have been a very risky enterprise which would almost certainly have resulted in heavy casualties even if successful. A siege would have been even less attractive. The army did not have siege equipment, and an army such as this, living predominantly off the land, had to keep moving. Spending more than a few days in any one place would lead to serious logistic problems. The army of Edward III besieging Calais, a city with perhaps a quarter of the population of Toulouse, had been much larger than that of the prince and could be resupplied across the Channel. Even so, the siege had lasted eleven months. The Anglo-Gascon army would not have been adequate to ensure a tight blockade of a city the size of Toulouse. With the prince stationary the French would have time to marshal greater forces, and the Anglo-Gascon army would reduce in strength and effectiveness through the inevitable toll that would be taken by the disease, desertion and battle casualties associated with medieval sieges. The approach of winter would only exacerbate these problems.

What of the next option, to attempt to draw the enemy into battle outside the city? The prince and his advisers would not have been overly concerned about the odds. They had an army that had been together on campaign now for three weeks, and many had been present when they had defeated the French at Crécy despite being heavily outnumbered. If the right circumstances could be found, then they would have no need to fear battle.

The next option, of striking in a different direction, was not a practical choice. The only way to turn was to the south towards the Pyrenees, but they would quickly enter the territory of the Count of Foix, who was an ally. Turning for home would not have been an unreasonable course to take. They had already achieved a great deal in laying waste the territory of Armagnac and Astarac, and no doubt they had already collected a good deal of booty. They could be home comfortably by mid-November before the winter set in.

To take the final option and cross the rivers would be risky, particularly if the French opposed the crossings. However, many present had made opposed river crossings before, at Poissy and Blanchetaque during the Crécy campaign, and to take the campaign beyond the Garonne would be to break new ground and inflict a shock on the French. Lancaster had been as far as Toulouse in 1349, but an English army had never before penetrated beyond the river Garonne. Although risky, this course of action had the advantage of being likely to be unexpected. It had the potential, through its audacity, to throw the French into disarray and change the strategic situation overnight, and the inhabitants to the east of the rivers Garonne and Ariège would be feeling secure behind these great rivers and would be ill-prepared to meet an invading army.

The prince, in choosing to continue to move east, took the French by surprise and his army was able to cross the rivers Garonne and Ariège unopposed. One area of uncertainty, however, is whether or not the prince sought battle before crossing the rivers. There are differing accounts from Baker and Jean Froissart of what happened over the next few days, with Froissart giving us two differing versions. In summary, it seems possible that the army may have been arrayed for battle before the river crossings; certainly it is most unlikely that the army was drawn up for battle after the crossings, where the ground would have been much less suitable. The prince, in his post-campaign letter, simply stated: 'we came to a league's distance of Toulouse, where the said Count of Armagnac and other great men of our enemies were gathered; and there we tarried two days. And from thence we took our march and crossed in one day the two rivers of Garonne and Ariège.'

Whether or not the army was arrayed for battle in the hope of tempting the French out from the safety of the walls of Toulouse is, therefore, uncertain. However, we do know that, having arrived at St-Lys on Monday, 26 October, the army paused in the vicinity of Toulouse on Tuesday, and on Wednesday, 28 October crossed the Garonne and Ariège rivers and stopped near Lacroix-Falgarde, on the far bank of the Ariège.

Sir John Wingfield, in reporting that the crossing of the Garonne was made at a ford, gives an indication that this was not a straightforward

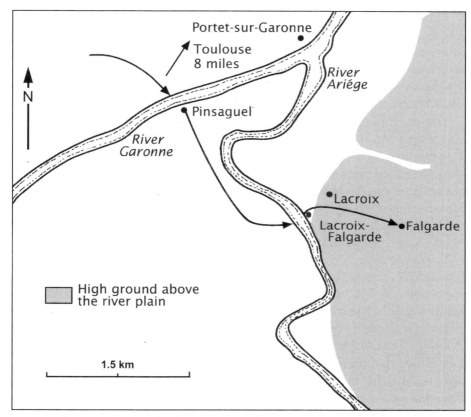

Crossing the Garonne and the Ariège, 28 October 1355.

operation: 'And there was never a man in our host that knew the ford there, yet, by the grace of God they found it.' The chronicler Baker reinforces this by describing the crossings as follows: 'the army crossed the river Garonne, swift, rocky, and very frightening; and on the same day they also crossed the Ariège, even more dangerous than the Garonne, and went downstream to Toulouse. No horse had previously crossed these rivers.' The prince attested to the difficulty of these crossings when he reported, in a somewhat understated way, that: 'we took our march and crossed in one day the two rivers of Garonne and Ariège, one league above Toulouse, which are very stiff and strong to pass, without losing scarce any of our people; and we lodged the night a league the other side of Toulouse'. Sir John Wingfield also describes the crossings as having been made a league from Toulouse, and Baker states that the night's halt at Lacroix-Falgarde was 1.5km from Toulouse.

The distances quoted by the prince, Wingfield and Baker are incorrect. The crossings could not have been closer to Toulouse than the confluence of the two rivers, since otherwise only the Garonne would have needed to be crossed. This means that the crossings were made at least 10km from Toulouse, or just over two leagues. Similarly, Baker is woefully inaccurate since Lacroix-Falgarde is 12km and not 1.5km from Toulouse.

The most likely place for the crossing of the Garonne is about 1.5km upstream from the confluence with the Ariège at a ford near Pinsaguel. The crossing of the Ariège almost certainly took place somewhere on the 3km stretch of river between the confluence and Lacroix-Falgarde. The crossing of the Ariège is not much more than 1.5km from the ford at Pinsaguel, and in effect the crossing of the two rivers should be seen as one operation, with leading elements having crossed the Ariège while some troops were still waiting to cross the Garonne.

There are no records of how the crossings were made. However, when Edward III crossed the Seine and the Somme in 1346 and Henry V forded the Somme in 1415 archers and men-at-arms were sent across to secure a bridgehead. In view of the possibility of Armagnac's men being in the vicinity, it would have been prudent to follow this practice to protect the crossing of the main body of men and the baggage train. Once it had been established that there were no French troops defending the Garonne, then presumably the bridgehead would be established beyond the Ariège. Vegetius provides advice on how to cross wide rivers. He advocates two lines of cavalry forming a corridor wide enough to allow the baggage train and those on foot to pass. The upstream line serves to break the force of the waters and the lower collects any on foot who may be swept away. Since the crossings were clearly hazardous but casualties low, it is quite possible that the prince followed this practice. On the Agincourt campaign Henry V and his senior commanders personally supervised the fording of the Somme to ensure a disciplined crossing.

The fact that at least one of the passages seems to have been made at a ford makes the absence of defensive forces even more surprising. Perhaps, if Baker is correct and 'no horse had ever previously crossed these rivers', Armagnac just did not consider the crossings to be possible. However, even if unopposed, the passage of two major rivers in close proximity to a large French army was a remarkable feat. The army was across the rivers, Toulouse had been bypassed, and Armagnac had been caught off guard. The crossings were indeed audacious and opened up a new phase of the *chevauchée*.

Having crossed the rivers, the army moved on the next day. The way was now open to the Mediterranean (or the Greek Sea as it was known to the English at the time). The region beyond the Garonne and Ariège was wealthy and the most productive grain-producing area in France. No doubt the inhabitants felt protected by the rivers, and the villages and small towns in the area were poorly defended: soft targets in today's parlance. The pickings would be rich for the army, and the economic and psychological impact on the Languedoc would prove to be profound. The Prussian military theorist Carl von Clausewitz wrote: 'If the enemy country is rather loosely knit, if its people are soft and have forgotten what war is like, a triumphant invader will have no great difficulty in leaving a wide swathe of country safely in his rear.' This was to prove to be the case for the Anglo-Gascon army as it advanced towards Narbonne. Poorly defended towns were taken by storm and mills destroyed as the army progressed.

The prince moved on to Carcassonne on Tuesday, 3 November. Carcassonne then, as now, consisted of two parts: the *bourg* built on flat ground to the west of the river Aude and the *cité* on a hill on the far side of the river. The *bourg* was poorly defended with earth walls, while the *cité* was strongly fortified with a double curtain wall built of stone, much as it is today; towering over the surrounding countryside, it would have been an impressive sight for the approaching army.

The still-existing stone *Pont Vieux* was the only connection between the two parts. The eastern end of the bridge is only about 250 metres from the walls of the *cité* and troops crossing the bridge would be exposed to missiles projected from the walls. In view of the river, the location of the bridge and the strength of the fortifications, it is no wonder that the prince left the *cité* well alone and concentrated his efforts on the *bourg*. Baker describes Carcassonne as extremely wealthy, well built and larger within its walls than London. Sir John Wingfield was closer to the mark in describing it as being bigger, stronger and fairer than York.

The army rested for two days, a truce was arranged, and envoys sent to the *cité* to arrange peace. The clergy of the *cité* sent a letter to the prince pleading 'that the *Bourg* is not burnt or that another new damage be added to that which it has already suffered'. In addition, the townspeople are said to have offered the enormous sum of 250,000 gold *écus*, around 50,000 pounds sterling, to spare the *bourg*. The letter from the clergy appealed to the prince's charity and gentleness, his nobility and religious sentiments, his sense of justice, his support for the church and above all his mercy. It finished with a call for the prince to respond favourably to the offer of the citizens of the *bourg*:

> If your Excellency refuses us this grace, by necessity the houses will be burnt, the churches abandoned and divine services cease. We do not believe that a heart as noble and as religious as yours could consent to this. Poor wretches that we are, we dare to make this humble plea to your Excellency, because we are persuaded of your clemency, that you love Jesus Christ and his servants, that you and yours seek only to defend and support the Church and to search for justice.

The plea of the clergy may have touched his heart and the ransom may have been tempting, but they had no practical effect. The prince, or at least members of his army, had not been averse to taking ransoms in the past. However, here was a different situation. Carcassonne, as a large and rich city, gave the prince an excellent opportunity to send a powerful message to the inhabitants of Languedoc consistent with the mission set by his father: they were deluded in continuing to be loyal to King Jean; he was a usurper and not their rightful lord; and what is more he was powerless to exercise his duty of kingship to defend them. The prince rejected the offer of the ransom, saying that he 'did not come for gold, but for justice, not to sell but to take cities'.

Baker describes the outcome: 'Since the citizens continued to fear the French usurper [King Jean], did not wish to obey their natural lord, or indeed did not dare to because they expected the usurper to take his revenge, the prince therefore ordered the *bourg* to be burnt, but the religious houses were to be spared.' Baker's account ends by reporting that the town was set on fire on Friday, 6 November and that the army then left, with the prince receiving reports later that the *bourg* had been burnt to ashes.

Froissart talks of the prince reviewing the possibility of taking the *cité* but concluding that there was more to lose than to gain. A nineteenth-century description of the defences shows what a formidable challenge it would have represented:

> Wall on wall, and tower on tower rise in imposing strength and forms to frowning heights along the side and summit of the ridge-like hill. A party that attacked and even gained a lodgement near the outer gate must first have crossed a wide, wet fosse around the barbican, while under double raking fires. It must then penetrate a long and narrow passage stretching up the hillside and enclosed between strong walls,

joined to alternate sides of which, at right angles, are cross walls. Advance through these would be like threading wards inside a lock. If any party gained the top of this long passage, it must then turn sharply to the right, and, in an oblong court surrounded by strong walls and swept by raking and by downward fires, next storm a parapet to gain the outside of the lowest of three gates, and those no farther than the outer line of the main defences. Then, in even more confined and dangerous positions it must carry the other two gates.

Not content with the inherent physical strength of the *cité*, the French had recently paid close attention to the defence of Carcassonne. A royal order had been issued in 1336 for the maintenance of a professional company of crossbow men and another in early 1355 required that the state of defences throughout the Carcassonne *sénéchaussée* must be attended to. The *cité* did, however, have a weakness: a dependence on deep wells for its water supply. This had been a major factor in its fall in similar circumstances in just a fortnight in 1209 during the Albigensian Crusade. However, to have relied upon this to bring the *cité* to its knees and settled down for a siege of even relatively short duration would have handed the initiative to the French, and would have been inconsistent with the approach adopted throughout the *chevauchée*. The prince's decision to move on and leave the *cité* could not have been a difficult one to take. Conscious once again of the importance of maintaining his aim and not wasting resources on attacking strongly defended places, the prince, his army having set the *bourg* ablaze, took his leave of Carcassonne on Friday, 6 November.

On 22 November, only two weeks after the destruction of the *bourg*, King Jean wrote to the people of Carcassonne explaining at length why he had been detained in the north to counter a threat from Edward III, saying how deeply affected he had been by the events at Carcassonne, expressing his desire for nothing more than to avenge the wrongs done to the people of the town, and promising to send his son with a great army. He wisely gave himself some leeway with this promise, adding the caveat that the despatch of the prince and his army will be 'God willing'. He finishes with an appeal for the continuing loyalty of the people. The tone of the letter gives a strong impression that Jean was deeply concerned by the impact of the *chevauchée* on the cohesion of his realm and the loyalty of his people.

The destruction of towns continued as the army marched towards the Mediterranean, reaching the large and prosperous city of Narbonne on Sunday, 8 November. Narbonne was built on low, flat ground, and potentially offered a softer target than Carcassonne. It promised rich rewards for the army. Narbonne was similar to Carcassonne in so far as it consisted of a *cité* and a *bourg* separated by a branch of the river Aude. Both parts were walled and the walls of the *cité* surrounded the cathedral, a castle for the bishop and a strong tower for the viscount. There were three bridges between the *cité* and the *bourg*, two of stone and one of wood. Only the central bridge, le Pont Vieux or Pont des Marchands, passed directly between gates in the walls of the *bourg* and the *cité*. The *bourg* was larger and better built than the *bourg* at Carcassonne. The prince described Narbonne as 'a noble city, of fair size, greater than Carcassonne'. For the time, Narbonne was indeed a large town with 30,000 inhabitants.

The inhabitants, or at least the women and children, had fled to the *cité*, and no doubt taken with them as many of their movable riches as they could. The defence was in the hands of Viscount Aimeri of Narbonne with 500 men-at-arms and a significant number of local levies. The Anglo-Gascon army took lodgings in the empty *bourg*, with the prince himself being accommodated in the Carmelite convent.

The choice of this convent for the prince's accommodation was risky. It was within easy range of stone-throwing engines, which were shooting from within the *cité* throughout the night and the following day, resulting in a number of wounded. The defence of the *cité* was vigorous and effective, and on Tuesday, 10 November the prince's army withdrew from Narbonne, setting the *bourg* alight as it departed. The army left in some disorder, with the townsmen being sufficiently confident to sally forth and plunder and destroy two of the prince's carts. They did so by falling upon the Anglo-Gascon army at a vulnerable time as the men crossed the river in a number of places. As the people of Narbonne watched the departure of the army they may well have reflected upon, and given thanks for, the wisdom and resolution of their consuls a few years before. Construction of the cathedral of St-Just and St-Pasteur had started in 1272 and came to a halt in 1344. Completion of the transept and the nave would have required part of the walls of the *cité* to be demolished. The consuls, seizing on instructions from King Philippe VI in 1344 to put the defences of the province in order, were adamant that they would not permit this demolition, and protracted discussions between the town government and the clergy ensued. The consuls petitioned the *viguier royal de Béziers*, and, despite an appeal from the Archbishop of Narbonne, their case was upheld. The result was that the transept and nave were never completed and, most importantly for the people of Narbonne, the city walls were intact in

November 1355. Once again the Black Prince had not compromised his mission by wasting resources on attacking a strongly defended place.

On the way north from Narbonne the army had to cross the Aude, and this probably happened near Cuxac-d'Aude, 7km north of Narbonne. Cuxac was fortified and escaped destruction, but it was the scene of one of the less savoury episodes, at least by modern standards, during the *chevauchée*. Prisoners taken at Narbonne either found the means to pay ransoms or were put to death under the town walls in view of the inhabitants, perhaps in part to serve as a lesson to the local people of the power of the invader, the inability of King Jean to defend his people, and of the consequences of resistance. It also shows that, despite his general adherence to the values of chivalry, the prince was not averse to the use of cruel means to support his objectives.

Although some elements of the army may have ranged as far as Béziers and St-Thibéry, the deepest penetration into the Languedoc for the bulk of the army was probably Capestang, 20km north of Narbonne. Capestang stands at the northern end of the lake which bears its name. Today the lake is marshy for much of the year, covered in water in winter, and can be almost dry in summer, but in medieval times it was part of a salt-water lagoon. The production of the precious commodity salt from the lagoon had made Capestang a rich town, and with 4,000 inhabitants it was more populous than today. This wealth enabled the town authorities to enter into negotiations with representatives of the Anglo-Gascon army for a ransom to save the town. Capestang was protected by walls and a substantial castle and the defences were, it seems, enough to encourage the army to negotiate a ransom in preference to an assault. Whether the consuls were negotiating in good faith is open to doubt. They may only have been stalling for time on the assumption that the prince would move on if he could not take the town quickly, and they broke off the negotiations when it became known that a militia army was approaching from Avignon. They may also have been aware that at long last the Count of Armagnac, albeit with some timidity, had emerged from cover and was close by with his army.

The Return to Gascony

At Capestang the prince had several options. Even with the news of the advancing army from Avignon he could have continued to move northeast towards Montpellier and face this army. However, he and his advisers needed to consider the strategic situation, the goals to be achieved by continuing to advance further, and the approaching winter season.

From a strategic point of view, with the evident caution of Armagnac, they might have been able to meet and destroy the army coming from Avignon separately before the two French armies joined forces. However, they would have had to consider that there was the possibility that they would be trapped in an unfavourable tactical position between numerically superior forces. The chronicler Jean le Bel claims that total French forces were three times as numerous as those of the prince, while one source puts the strength at the incredible figures of 11,000 men-at-arms and 115,000 men raised from the common people. Whatever the figures, it would be better to avoid meeting the French as a combined force. It may well have been that the militia army would have been raised for a limited period and only for local defence. If this were so, then turning to move away from Montpellier and Avignon to face Armagnac, as the prince did, would neutralise their contribution without the need for battle. It would also allow him to concentrate his forces on the more important target of Armagnac, the constable and the marshal.

What was to be achieved by going further northeast? More of the same, of course, but a great deal had already been accomplished and the message given to the people of the Languedoc had been a powerful one. The inhabitants of Montpellier had already destroyed suburbs outside the city walls in anticipation of the arrival of the prince's army, and had sent much of their wealth to Avignon, Aigues-Mortes and Beaucaire for safekeeping. The Pope had also taken fright and sent two bishops to try to head off the prince near Narbonne and encourage him to negotiate with the French. There was nothing to be gained for the prince in doing so and he declined.

Finally, to continue towards Montpellier and Avignon would have taken the army further away from Gascony when it was already late in the year for campaigning. At Capestang they were three weeks' march from home, and by the time they got to Avignon, still a week's march away, they would be doing well to get back by Christmas. In the meantime autumnal rains could make many rivers that were minor obstacles in October much more challenging on the return and turn roads into mud. In sum, consideration of the strategic situation, what remained to be achieved, and the impact of the likely deterioration in weather conditions all pointed in the same direction. It was time to turn for home. However, this was a change of direction, not of method. Burning, looting and destruction continued as the order of the day. In addition there was still the possibility of bringing Armagnac, the constable and the marshal to battle and victory in such an encounter would add another dimension to the success of the *chevauchée*.

Furthermore, to remain stationary and either try to negotiate the surrender of Capestang or take the strongly defended town by force would
have been inconsistent with the prince's conduct of the *chevauchée* to date.
Operations outside Capestang were broken off and the army turned west
to return to Aquitaine.

On 12 November the two armies were in close proximity. A local guide
of the Constable of France had been taken prisoner and examined, and it is
likely that the prince had sound intelligence on the location of the French.
In his letter to the Bishop of Winchester, written after the return to
Bordeaux, the prince wrote:

> and by reason that we had news from prisoners and others that our
> enemies were gathered together and were coming after us to fight us,
> we turned again to meet them, and thought to have had the battle in
> the three days next following. And on our turning back towards them,
> they turned again towards Toulouse. So we pursued them in long
> marches towards Toulouse.

The prince's army took a difficult route across the mountains, leaving
Carcassonne on the right. The rearguard deviated from the route of the
bulk of the army to destroy and pillage the wealthy town of Limoux. It was
a more heavily populated town in the fourteenth century than it is today.
With a population of 15,000, it was more populous than Carcassonne and
approximately half the size of Bordeaux and London. It was wealthy due
to cloth manufacture, dressing of furs, tanning, viticulture and the growth
and milling of grain. It held a substantial fair each year spread over fifteen
days either side, somewhat ironically in the circumstances, of St George's
day. The town straddled the river Aude, as it does today, with the greater
part of the town to the west of the river. To the east of the river were
suburbs which were not fortified. The two parts were linked by two
bridges.

The suburbs and religious house to the east of the river were quickly
pillaged and set on fire since, on this occasion, religious property did not
escape the destruction wrought on the rest of the town. Beyond the
suburbs was the town itself. There is conflicting evidence as to whether or
not the town was fortified but, irrespective of the state of the defences,
when news of the approach of the army reached the townspeople they fled
into the surrounding hills and remained there throughout the following
winter. Without a determined garrison walls would in any case have
served little purpose, and the result was the destruction and looting of
Limoux.

Destruction was widespread as the army marched towards Gascony. However, care was taken as the prince's army crossed the territory of Gaston Phoebus, the Count of Foix, that his possessions should not be damaged. Keeping the count sweet was entirely consistent with the prince's broad objective of reinforcing Edward III's position in Gascony. The prince met and rode with Phoebus as he advanced to the Garonne with the objective of cultivating friendly relations.

The last significant barrier before the return to friendly territory was the Garonne. The crossing of the river gives us a glimpse of the prince's tactical sense. Although the river here is only about half the width that it is where they crossed on their way east, it remains a formidable obstacle. The boats that were normally kept here to ferry people across the river had been removed. Heavy rain was proving a problem, and there was urgency in getting across the river before conditions deteriorated further. The rear and middle-guards forded the river at Noé in conditions which seem to have astonished the local population. Fortunately there was a bridge at Carbonne 5km upstream. In view of the river and weather conditions it was essential to secure the bridge for the passage of the baggage train. Vehicles inevitably slowed the progress of the army and the vanguard with the prince accompanying the baggage train was some time behind the other divisions approaching the river. With the French army close at hand – indeed, as the prince was to learn next day, they were only 10km distant – there was no time to lose if a defended crossing were to be avoided. It is strange in view of the close proximity of the Count of Armagnac that he took no action either to defend the crossing points or to break the bridge at Carbonne. The prince took advantage of this situation. The rearguard accepted the surrender of the castle at Noé, having crossed the river, while the middle-guard moved up the river and, to the amazement of the local people, crossed back over the Garonne 5km upstream to take the village of Marquefave. They then crossed a third time to take Carbonne by assault from the river side, which was not walled, before the arrival of the prince. With the rearguard at Noé protecting any approach from Toulouse and the town and bridge of Carbonne secured by the middle-guard, the prince crossed safely with the vanguard and the baggage train.

On Thursday, 19 November the army took advantage of fine weather to rest for the first time since leaving Narbonne. They now had no major obstacles between them and a return to friendly territory, and the march would regain a more measured pace interspersed with days of rest once more.

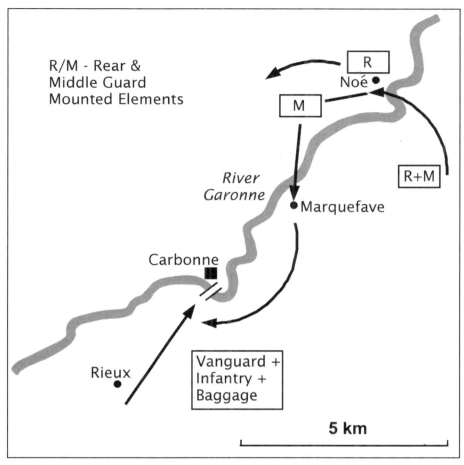

Crossing the Garonne at Carbonne, 18 November 1355.

On Friday morning the prince's army moved out from camp and was drawn up in battle order to face the French army. The stand-off between the armies took place to the north-east of Carbonne, downstream from the town and towards Toulouse. The prince reported that he had sent forward a number of lords with men to reconnoitre the position of the French. There are varying accounts of what followed. However, it seems that there was some skirmishing, with casualties inflicted upon the French and some prisoners taken. The upshot was that the French withdrew and thus avoided the risk of battle. As we saw above, King Jean acknowledged that the French army was several times greater than that of their opponents and expressed some frustration that the Anglo-Gascon army had not been brought to battle. The prince must also have been frustrated with every such encounter.

Following the withdrawal of the French, the prince's army moved off in their pursuit. Armagnac had clearly been either anticipating withdrawing in front of the prince or preparing for the worst if engaged in battle, since the prince reported that the French had broken down the bridges over the river Save during the night before the arrival of the Anglo-Gascon army. He also stated that the army camped within sight of the French camp-fires across the river. The prince sent men forward to repair the bridges over the Save and the army continued its pursuit of the French. Battle was anticipated in the vicinity of the town of Gimont, but when scouts were sent out they discovered once again that the French had withdrawn.

The chronicler Le Baker argues that this constituted a technical victory for the prince, in that after a persistent pursuit by the English with several opportunities for battle, the French had consistently avoided combat with the Anglo-Gascon army. Either Armagnac did not have the confidence to join battle or else considered that, with the Anglo-Gascon army already heading for home, the risks outweighed any potential advantage to be gained through battle.

Gimont was well fortified with walls, ditches and an external perimeter road to give a clear area away from the walls. The prince had to decide whether to attempt to take Gimont with the French inside or to continue on the way home. He took counsel and the assessment was that the town was too large and too strong to attack, and so the army moved off once more towards Gascony on Tuesday, 24 November. Once again the prince had maintained his approach to the campaign and avoided a potentially costly assault.

Although in general the logistics of the *chevauchée* were efficient, there were occasions when water was a problem, particularly for horses. One such occasion came shortly after leaving Gimont when, because of a lack of water, the horses were given wine to drink, with the result that on the Wednesday they were drunk and unsteady on their feet, resulting in the loss of many of them.

As the army moved back towards Gascony they passed Valence-sur-Baïse, a good-sized *bastide* founded in 1274 by the Count of Armagnac. The town sits on high ground on the eastern bank of the river. It was well protected by walls sitting on rock cliffs which enhanced their effectiveness, and the town would have been a very difficult nut to crack. Neverthe-less, earlier in the expedition this town belonging to Armagnac, if poorly garrisoned, might have attracted the attention of the army. Its escape at this stage of the *chevauchée* demonstrates perhaps that the priority was now on returning safely to Gascony rather than wreaking further destruction and plunder.

On Saturday, 28 November the army reached Mézin, leaving the lands of Armagnac behind them. The campaign was to all intents and purposes over. Banners were furled to indicate the end of hostilities and many of the Gascon troops were allowed to disperse. Four days later the prince entered the town of La Réole. The prince had led his army on a march of almost 1,000km deep into French territory and back in less than two months. He had not brought the French to battle, but the effects of his campaign were profound and remain seared in the memory of the region to this day.

However, the return to Gascony in early December 1355 did not mean that the prince had time to waste before the next campaigning season. He retained the initiative throughout the winter and operations were launched by relatively small forces under the command of the Captal de Buch, and the Earls of Suffolk, Oxford, Warwick and Salisbury, Sir John Chandos and Sir James Audley. Their objectives were to secure the frontier of the duchy, to extend the king's influence by bringing more Gascon lords back into allegiance to Edward III, and to counter any residual threat from the French who were still at large. Over the winter he also prepared for operations the following year by sending to England for 600 further archers, bows, arrows and bow strings to replenish stocks.

The Results of the *Chevauchée*

Before examining the generalship of the campaign, let us take stock of the results of the *chevauchée* of 1355. The achievements of the prince in the closing months of 1355 were measured by the historian Clifford J. Rogers against the objectives of a *chevauchée* drawn from a letter of Edward III to King Philippe VI during the Crécy campaign: 'to punish rebels against us and to comfort our friends and those faithful to us ... to carry on the war as best we can, to our advantage and the loss of our enemies'. Even without battle with the French, the prince could judge the *chevauchée* a success measured against the other objectives. The punishment of Jean, Count of Armagnac, and the comfort to friends were evident for all to see, and the economic, psychological and military results short of a battle had, without question, been to the advantage of the King of England and to the loss of the King of France.

There was also the psychological impact on the inhabitants of the Languedoc to be considered, which, as the historian H.J. Hewitt indicates, was considerable and enduring:

> Mentally and morally unprepared to bear with fortitude the horror, misery and grief inseparable from war, they had seen their great bridges broken down, their suburbs razed, their cities burnt, their valuables stolen and, in many instances, their fellows killed. The swift-moving, devastating power moved on unresisted, irresistible, spreading havoc wherever it went. Winter found them mourning, bewildered and fearful for the morrow.

Sir John Wingfield, a key member of the prince's household, writing to the Bishop of Winchester at Christmas 1355, reported: 'And, by the help of God, if my lord had wherewithal to maintain this war and to do the king's profit and his own honour, he would easily enlarge the marches and would win many places; for our enemies are sore astonished.' Sir John was, of course, a partial witness, but there is no doubt that in ranging as far as the Mediterranean and cutting a wide swathe of destruction with total immunity the prince had inflicted a great shock on the French, particularly to the east of the Garonne.

The *chevauchée* of the past two months had laid waste the lands of Armagnac, and in going beyond Toulouse had brought fire, pillage and destruction to parts of France that had previously been spared the direct ravages of the war. From the Anglo-Gascon viewpoint, the immediate benefits were evident in the form of considerable financial rewards with booty and ransoms to be collected from prisoners taken.

Of great importance was the financial impact on the French king's ability to wage war. The direct impact was the reduced tax base of the region as a result of the devastation caused during the *chevauchée*. In his letter to the Bishop of Winchester at Christmas Sir John Wingfield gave his assessment that the devastated area normally accounted for more than half of the revenue raised in France for King Jean. This was certainly an exaggeration, but there can be no doubt that the impact was very considerable. In addition there were secondary effects, which, although not apparent in December, would become so when King Jean tried to marshal his resources for the coming year's campaigning. As early as the end of October 1355 the first signs of what was to come had surfaced when the council in Millau, well away from the route of the *chevauchée*, resolved to allocate the major part of their tax resources to restoring the town's defences. Other towns in the Languedoc followed the lead of Millau.

When the Estates of Languedoc met in March and April 1356 to consider the King's request for raising taxes, things were to go from bad to worse. They agreed a subsidy, but it was conditional on the arrival of the dauphin to defend the Languedoc. It was only to be used for fighting in the south-west, and collection would cease if the dauphin withdrew for operations elsewhere. Raids by the Anglo-Gascon lords into the Languedoc and the Rouergue in the spring of 1356 did nothing to improve the situation and Jonathan Sumption describes the overall effect as being that 'the work of tax collectors and recruiting officers was paralysed'. The financial situation was not a rosy one for Jean, with the Estates of Languedoil in the north also deciding to retain subsidies for the defence of the areas in which the taxes had been raised.

   Nevertheless, despite the heavy financial impact, the French forces in the south-west had not been brought to battle. Furthermore, territory had not been conquered and castles had not been taken and garrisoned. However, the lack of concrete results in terms of conquered territory and garrisoned castles was the norm rather than the exception for a *chevauchée*, the key instrument of war for Edward III. Taking and holding territory had not been the prince's objective. The lack of a set-piece battle was not for the want of trying on the part of the prince, with his likely preparation for battle near Toulouse and during his pursuit of the French during his return to Gascony, and with his willingness for battle near Carbonne and Gimont. Overall the campaign had been a considerable success for the prince.

Generalship

The success of the campaign reflects the skill of the prince as a commander. He kept his aims firmly in mind. He did not allow himself to be diverted from his objectives by becoming bogged down with attacks on tempting targets which he recognised as being beyond his resources. Other than on a few occasions when the availability of water was problematic, the logistics to sustain the campaign cannot be faulted. An element of maintaining this sustainability was keeping the army on the move rather than wasting time and resources on fruitless sieges for which his army was not equipped. A spin-off of this continual movement was that the prince retained the initiative. The prince's *chevauchée* was characterised by offensive action and the exploitation of the element of surprise, epitomised by his bold stroke in crossing the Garonne and Ariège near Toulouse to carry the war to a region to date untouched by the Hundred Years War. However, his appreciation of the importance of offensive action and the element of surprise were exploited from the outset by his decision to move quickly once he had arrived in Bordeaux to minimise the opportunities for the French to muster larger forces to counter the *chevauchée*. The twentieth-century strategic thinker Basil Liddell Hart wrote that 'calculated risk guided by skill is the right way to interpret the motto *l'audace, l'audace, toujours l'audace*'. The prince and his advisers were prepared to take calculated risks and demonstrated consummate skill in crossing the rivers. The prince also demonstrated flexibility with the decisions taken near Capestang in deciding the best course of action and the route to follow for the return to Gascony. Although his initial crossing of the Garonne and Ariège shows us an audacious commander prepared to take calculated risks, his subsequent crossing of the Garonne on the return route had the hallmarks of a prudent commander employing skilful tactics to ensure the security of the most vulnerable elements of the army. In sum, the prince, in concert with his senior advisers, had conducted an exemplary campaign and demonstrated considerable military skill.

Chapter 7

Normandy and the Siege of Breteuil 1356

The Duke of Lancaster's Normandy Campaign

Following his successful *chevauchée* in the autumn of 1355 the Black Prince struck north in the summer of 1356 on the campaign which was to result in his victory at Poitiers in September of that year.

Meanwhile the long-running quarrel between Charles, King of Navarre, and King Jean came to a head in April 1356 when Charles was arrested by the king and imprisoned. Charles, who was also Count of Évreux in Normandy, had been negotiating, albeit duplicitously, with the English for several years and following his father's arrest his son Philippe turned to England for help. As a consequence the Duke of Lancaster arrived in Normandy in June and, together with English troops already in Brittany and a number of Navarrese, mustered around 2,400 men. This small mounted force caused disproportionate problems for the French with a limited campaign which diverted resources and effort from the recruitment of the army destined to fight the Black Prince at Poitiers in September.

The impact of Lancaster's fast-moving campaign was such that Jean decided he had to take matters in hand himself rather than leave it to the Dauphin Charles, Duke of Normandy, who had command in the duchy. The speed of Lancaster's army, moving as fast as 50km a day on some occasions, posed problems for the French. Lancaster's objective was to bring help to beleaguered Navarrese garrisons. In the main he achieved much, although he was too late to save some garrisons from the dauphin's forces. In early July Lancaster arrived before the walled town of Verneuil-sur-Avre. The inhabitants fled to the citadel, which was taken by storm after three days of assault and numerous casualties. The town was plundered. On 8 July Lancaster withdrew from Verneuil-sur-Avre, no doubt well aware of the presence of Jean's much larger army only a few hours' march away. Jean set off in pursuit and by nightfall was about 5km from Lancaster's army at l'Aigle. To the west of l'Aigle was an extensive forest which was unsuitable for a set-piece battle. Nevertheless, Jean sent heralds challenging Lancaster to battle. Lancaster replied that he had achieved

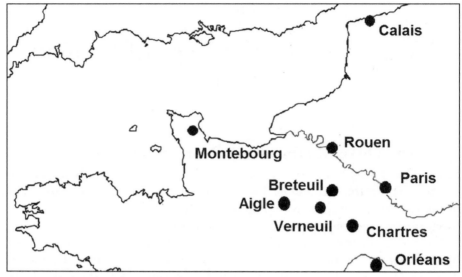

Normandy and Breteuil, 1356.

what he had set out to do and now had pressing business elsewhere, but Jean could have his battle if he blocked the way. Perhaps Lancaster hoped to draw Jean into the forest but if so the king was too wise to fall into that trap. Nevertheless, with his superior strength he could have pursued Lancaster but instead allowed him to leave unimpeded.

The Siege of Breteuil

As Lancaster returned to his headquarters at Montebourg in the Cotentin Peninsula, King Jean decided to take the fortress of Breteuil, 80km south of Rouen and the only remaining Navarrese stronghold in eastern Normandy. He laid siege around 12 July. This was an unimportant castle and the siege itself of no consequence for the events which were to follow the Black Prince's departure from Bordeaux. The interest is largely that once again we see Jean, much as at Aiguillon ten years before, becoming fixated on a siege as a point of honour to the detriment of the more important task of raising his army to confront the Black Prince.

While in the vicinity of Verneuil-sur-Avre the Duke of Lancaster had driven off a French force besieging the castle. Before leaving, he had ensured that Breteuil was well provisioned with food, and its Navarrese garrison proved resolute. The castle had been built by William the Conqueror and its square construction and high towers should, in theory, have rendered it vulnerable to mining. The besiegers filled the ditches around the castle and set about undermining the walls. When these efforts failed, Jean decided to attempt to take the fortress by assault. Work was set in hand to construct a large, wheeled tower to carry men to the walls. According to the chronicler Jean Froissart, this tower had three storeys, each capable of sheltering 200 men. The work of ditch filling and construction took a month, and it was August before an assault could be made. The defenders had had plenty of time to prepare for the attack. The assault failed and the tower was destroyed with burning arrows, resulting in heavy French casualties. As the siege dragged on fruitlessly, the Black Prince continued to move north. It eventually became clear even to Jean that the priority must be to counter the prince. On 20 August, with the Black Prince some 320km away and only 130km from Tours, Jean paid the garrison a large sum of money to surrender the castle. They were allowed to march away to rejoin the Navarrese forces in the Cotentin.

Generalship

The interest in this short phase of the war lies not so much in Jean's conduct of the siege of Breteuil but in his overall conduct of operations and disposition of his forces as the storm clouds gathered. In the early summer of 1356 Jean was certainly faced with a complex situation: much of Normandy was in the hands of men loyal to his enemy Charles of Navarre, the arrival of the Duke of Lancaster to support the Navarrese, the threat of an invasion by Edward III, and the prospect of a further *chevauchée* by the Black Prince in an as yet unknown direction. To add to his problems he faced difficulties in raising the funds necessary to sustain the war and the mobilisation of his army was progressing slowly.

Faced with this complex situation, he seems to have been plagued by uncertainty and indecision. The planned despatch of the Count of Poitiers to the Languedoc as a counter to the Black Prince was cancelled, he failed to pursue the Duke of Lancaster and thus perhaps eliminate one of the armies which threatened his realm, and finally he settled down to besiege and attempt to take by storm a minor castle of little consequence. In the event his lack of pursuit of Lancaster proved not to be a problem in the short term since, as we shall see later, Lancaster was unable to cross the Loire and join forces with the Black Prince before the Battle of Poitiers. However, in the longer term the failure to eliminate the Anglo-Navarrese army in Normandy left the English in effective occupation of Normandy after Jean's defeat at Poitiers.

Jean's hesitation was certainly due in part to problems in financing and raising his army. Also, the risk of leaving the north of France and Paris vulnerable to attack by Edward III must have weighed heavily on his mind. Nevertheless, decisive action early in the summer might well have resulted in an entirely different outcome for the French. Three centuries earlier King Harold had been faced with the twin threats of invasion by the Norwegian king, Harald Hardrada, in the north of England, and William, Duke of Normandy, in the south. Harold had marched rapidly to the north and defeated the Norwegians at Stamford Bridge and had then returned south with equal rapidity to face William at Hastings. Of course, he lost the Battle of Hastings but, nevertheless, his strategy of attempting to defeat the two armies separately had been sound. Jean, however, failed to take the initiative and allowed events to unfold until he had but one choice: to conclude the siege and march south to intercept the Black Prince, who had already wreaked considerable havoc as he advanced north.

Jean's preoccupation with Breteuil was another example of his inability to grasp the bigger picture and his propensity to allow his sense of pride and honour to guide his conduct of the war.

Chapter 8

The Poitiers Campaign
1356

The Battle of Poitiers was the only occasion when Jean II and the Black Prince faced each other in battle. The victory of the prince and his Anglo-Gascon army over the French king's numerically superior army gives us a direct contrast between the military competence and leadership of the two men.

The Black Prince's *Chevauchée*

When the Black Prince set out from Bergerac on 4 August 1356 no one could have known that the climax of his *chevauchée* towards the Loire would be battle between the prince and King Jean 5km south-east of Poitiers. The English strategy that year had been for three English armies to operate in France, led respectively by Edward III, who would disembark at Calais, the Black Prince coming from Aquitaine, and the Duke of Lancaster, who would land in Normandy. When the Black Prince moved north from Bergerac, Jean II was, as we have seen, engaged in the siege of Breteuil 150km north of the Loire. His 16-year-old son Jean, Count of Poitiers, was at Bourges 290km north-east of the prince.

The Black Prince's initial intention was to move towards the Count of Poitiers at Bourges, but at this moment he still expected to join forces with his father and Lancaster. Writing after the Battle of Poitiers, the prince stated that 'the sovereign cause for our going towards these parts was that we expected to have had news of our said lord and father, the king, as to his passage'. He also stated that he was intent upon joining up with Lancaster, 'of whom we had certain news that he would make haste to draw towards us'. If the rendezvous with the king had happened, then the prince would have been subordinate to his father and his chosen strategy. As it turned out, unforeseen events thwarted the king's expedition to France. Thus, although he would not have been aware of this for some time, the prince would be left only with the hope of joining forces with Lancaster and the responsibility for any set-piece encounter with the French would rest with him.

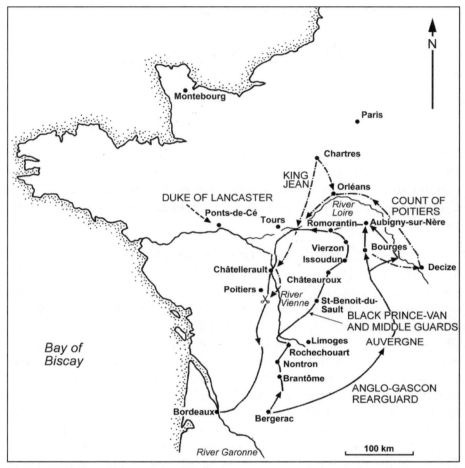

The Poitiers *Chevauchée*, August to October 1356.

Within the concept of the strategy of the *chevauchée* it is implicit that the Black Prince would seek battle with either the Count of Poitiers or Jean. Preparations for the operations of 1356 began shortly after the return from the 1355 *chevauchée*. As far as we can judge, casualties during the 1355 *chevauchée* were light, but nevertheless 600 additional archers were recruited in England and supplies of bows, arrows and bowstrings procured. No attempt was made to procure siege equipment and the preparations were indicative of an offensive and battle-seeking strategy.

The Black Prince, having left a substantial force at Bergerac to guard Aquitaine against the Count of Armagnac, set out on a generally northerly route towards the Loire. The rearguard under the command of Sir John

Chandos and Sir James Audley took a more easterly route through the Agenais, the Auvergne, the Limousin and Berry to converge with the main body of the army near Bourges.

The prince kept his aim firmly in view during his advance north from Bergerac: the objective of battle required the conservation of fighting strength. Men and weapons (arrows, bows and bowstrings) could not be replaced once the army had left friendly territory. There are numerous examples during the march north of his determination to maintain his aim and not waste men and materiel.

On 8 August the prince arrived in the vicinity of Brantôme. The town is a natural choke-point on the route north, standing on an island in an ox-bow bend of the river Dronne. It was fortified with ramparts overlooking the wide, natural moat formed by the river. To the west, immediately across the river, stands a Benedictine abbey, founded by Charlemagne, which was protected by fortifications on the river side, with natural protection behind from cliffs 60m high. To the east high ground again rises steeply more than 60m above the town. The road north passes through the town over bridges spanning the river to the south and north. There is a narrow strip of land between the town and the high ground to the east, which currently carries a minor road, which could afford a passage past the town. However, it would be well within bow-shot of the ramparts and not a sensible option.

The prince remained in the vicinity of Brantôme until 10 August. It is likely that the time spent here was due to consideration of the options for moving north. The choices were the possibility of an assault of the town to force a passage, reconnaissance for an alternative crossing, and negotiations to attempt to persuade the garrison to allow the prince's army to pass. In the absence of an unmolested passage through or close to the town, the option of taking the town by assault would probably have been feasible even without siege equipment. However, it would certainly have involved unwanted casualties. Action at this stage, with the nearest substantial French force 230km away with the Count of Poitiers at Bourges, would deplete resources early in the campaign without the prospect of provoking the French into battle. In the event the crossing of the Dronne was made at Quinsac, 13km to the north-east, and casualties associated with an assault were avoided.

The next choke-point, at Nontron, 15km north of Quinsac, was reached on 11 August. The approach to Nontron from the south involves a steep descent into the valley of the Bandiat, which runs across the line of approach just before reaching the town. Behind the river is an escarpment rising 60m above the valley floor. The town is on a steep rocky spur jutting out from the escarpment like an upturned boat before broadening out to the north. Nontron had come into hands sympathetic to the Anglo-Gascon cause in 1345, but it had been retaken by the French in the

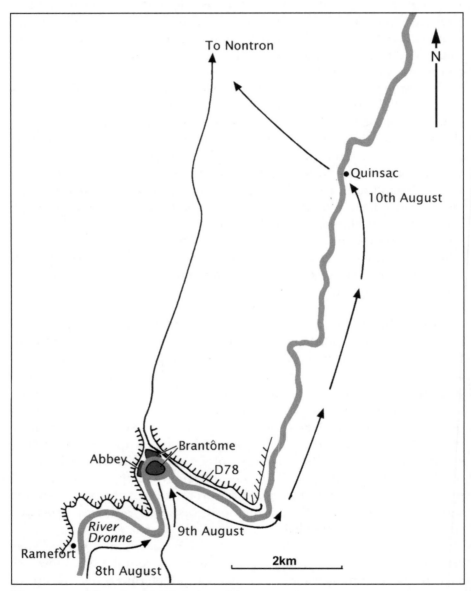

The passage of Brantôme, 8–10 August 1356.

autumn of 1352 and it would have been in French hands in August 1356. Thus, with the road north running through the town, Nontron would have presented a significant obstacle. However, in a letter dated 29 May 1357 one Ietier de Maignac forfeited 'all his goods, either in the manor of Nontron or elsewhere, since the said de Maignac is accused of having delivered the castle of Nontron into the hands of the enemies of the Viscount of Limoges'. It is probable that this letter relates to the surrender of the castle to allow the passage of the prince, and his army passed through the town unmolested. Once again, casualties were avoided.

On 12 August the prince's army had a march of 40km to Rochechouart, just short of the Vienne. The most direct route from here would have been to cross the river at either Chabanais or St-Junien. Instead the prince turned west for a 20km march to La Péruse. Two days later the army turned north-east and crossed the Vienne at the ancient ford at Manot. The route chosen added some 50km to the march, compared to taking the more direct route via either Chabanais or St-Junien. The reason for the chosen route was again consistent with avoidance of casualties. Both towns had had bridges over the river since at least the thirteenth century. The drawback with crossing the Vienne at either of these towns was that both bridges were in the vicinity of fortifications. Chabanais straddled the river, with the stone bridge linking the two parts leading directly into the gates of the castle on the north bank, which was surrounded by a ditch on the other sides. A crossing at Chabanais would have required the reduction of the castle to secure the crossing. This would probably have entailed an assault through the town and across the bridge, since fording the river, although quite shallow here in dry weather, would have been likely to be impractical in the wet summer of 1356. At St-Junien the medieval town stood a few hundred metres back from the river and the Pont Notre Dame, but those crossing the bridge would inevitably move within bow-shot range of the town's ramparts.

The Vienne had symbolic significance as the ancient frontier of Aquitaine. By and large, until crossing the river little offensive action had been taken. On crossing the river banners were unfurled – an indication that hostilities had been joined – and from now on the army embarked on the looting and burning characteristic of a *chevauchée*.

While the Black Prince had been preparing for his campaign, as we saw in the previous chapter, events had been unfolding further north with the Duke of Lancaster's campaign and Jean's siege of Breteuil. Of great significance for the prince's campaign, around the time that the Black Prince left Bergerac, an Aragonese galley fleet allied to the French arrived at

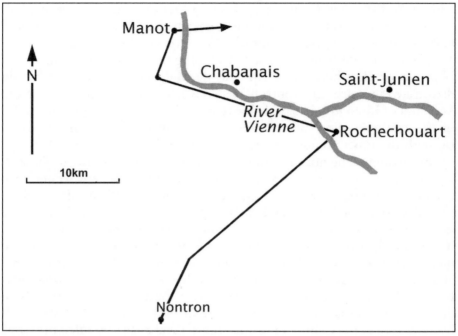

Crossing the Vienne, 14 August 1356.

the mouth of the Seine and on 10 August was seen off the coast of Kent. Ships intended for Edward III's expedition to France were ordered to take shelter in port. The expedition was put on hold and by 26 August troops designated to go to France with the king were redeployed for coastal defence. The threat posed by the Anglo-Gascon army should surely have been the priority for Jean. However, much as at Aiguillon ten years before, he became fixated on the siege of Breteuil as a point of honour to the detriment of the more important task of raising his army to confront the Black Prince. It was only on 20 August, with the Black Prince some 240km away, that Jean raised the siege to concentrate on the most immediate and serious threat: countering the army of the Black Prince. He moved towards Chartres, where an army was summoned to muster. The marshal, Jean de Clermont, was sent to organise the defence of Touraine, and two detachments, one under the leadership of Philippe de Chambly, otherwise known as Grismouton, and the other led by Jean de Boucicaut and Amaury de Craon, were sent south on reconnaissance missions as the king set about gathering his army. The Count of Poitiers had been ordered to redeploy from Bourges and by 20 August was at Decize, 80km south-east of

Bourges, with orders to hold the line of the Loire. Subsequently he withdrew to join his father's gathering army.

When Jean finally decided to raise the siege of Breteuil, the Black Prince was at St-Benoît-du-Sault, only 120km south of the important town of Tours on the river Loire. Three days later the Anglo-Gascon army arrived before Châteauroux. The defence was in the hands of André de Chauvigny. The town's defences were in a poor state of repair and the prince's troops were able to enter without difficulty. However, the castle, in the north-west corner of the town, with one wall close up to the river Indre, proved to be another matter. The prince's men, in an attempt to force an entry, filled an ox-cart with oil and dry wood with the aim of burning the draw-bridge and gate. The defenders showered the attackers with missiles, and the cart escaped from those man-handling it towards the gates and fell into the ditch. The attackers suffered some casualties, including one knight. The prince called off the assault and, in an attempt to achieve the surrender of the castle, sent four Gascon knights forward under a sign of truce. One of the Gascons, the Lord d'Albret, told André de Chauvigny: 'My lord, the prince sends greetings to you as his close relation, in whom he has great confidence, and asks you to open the fortress, for as you are his relation, you should respect his rights more than those of others.' De Chauvigny's reply was courteous but uncompromising: 'Gentlemen, I thank my lord the prince for his recognition of our relationship, but as for opening this place, in truth, I cannot do so, for my father holds it for the King of France to whom he has sworn an oath and my father has ordered that I neither open nor surrender this place.'

D'Albret told him that, if he failed to surrender, then 'certainly tomorrow you have an assault'. With this objective in mind, the strength of the castle was now assessed, with two knights protected by shield-bearers going forward to make a reconnaissance. They identified the weakest part of the defences, and marked it with oats for the benefit of the assailants. The prince now held a council to consider the options. The consensus was that the defenders were determined and valiant, that an attack would cost many men, and that success was not certain. In view of the overall aim to do battle with the French king and thus to conserve resources to that end, an attack was not deemed necessary; the assault was abandoned, and orders given for a departure the next day, 25 August.

On Sunday, 28 August the Black Prince with the advanced and middle-guards arrived at Vierzon, having sacked the town of Issoudun en route from Châteauroux. On the same day the rearguard was at Aubigny-sur-Nère, 40km north-east of the prince. Although the main bodies of the

French and Anglo-Gascon armies were far apart, with Jean II still at Chartres, 160km to the north, both armies were conducting reconnaissance. On 28 August the first contact was made. A French reconnaissance party under the command of Grismouton probing south of the Loire came across a detachment of the Anglo-Gascon rearguard reconnoitring towards the river. Although the Anglo-Gascon detachment was considerably less numerous than the French force, they had much the better of the encounter. Grismouton's men were routed, with many killed and eighteen knights and men-at-arms captured.

On the following day, Monday, 29 August, the prince moved 25km west from Vierzon along the river Cher to Villefranche-sur-Cher, in the vicinity of which there was further contact with the French. There was an ebb and flow in fortunes during the day, but with the day in the end going with the prince. The start of events was a clash between the Lord of Caumont for the prince and some of the French force, resulting in the capture of eight French knights and men-at-arms. From these prisoners the prince learnt that a French army was assembling and moving towards Orléans with the intention of doing battle with the Anglo-Gascon army. He was also able to confirm that Grismouton's party encountered the day before had been sent to gather intelligence. Similarly, it became apparent that the prisoners taken on the Monday were part of a second scouting party in the vicinity under the command of the Lords Craon and Boucicaut, possibly amounting to 300 men-at-arms. Later in the day Craon and Boucicaut ambushed and captured a small Anglo-Gascon foraging party, together with their booty, with ten men-at-arms under Sir John Willoughby and Ralph Basset. However, reinforcements quickly came to their relief, and some 150 of the French were captured and the English prisoners released. The remaining French fled with Craon and Boucicaut and, finding the drawbridge down and the gates open, took refuge in the castle at Romorantin, 8km north of Villefranche.

On the next day, Tuesday, 30 August, all three divisions of the prince's army converged on Romorantin. The town fell with little if any resistance. The following day the army attacked the castle where Craon and Boucicaut had holed up. The outer walls were scaled and the gates forced with little difficulty. The French withdrew further to the keep. The prince and his council decided that they would remain until they had taken the castle.

At first sight this departure from the policy to date of avoiding sieges seems strange. Why would the prince now take the risks associated with a siege of losing valuable resources and remaining static with the loss of initiative that could entail? After all, only a week earlier at Châteauroux he had rejected a siege precisely because he wished to conserve his resources for battle with the French main army. The answer seems to be that the situation had changed to the extent that he now knew King Jean was approaching with a view to do battle. If he remained at Romorantin and laid siege to the castle, this might provoke the French into an ill-timed attack. In this context, from a contemporary account, it seems that the prince thought the enemy army was about 50km away, much closer than was in fact the case.

The keep at Romorantin proved to be a tough nut to crack. On 31 August there were two notable casualties among the prince's forces, with Bernadet d'Albret and a knight in the company of the Captal de Buch both killed. The next day three successive assaults were made, but the keep still held. A change of tactics was required, and the emphasis was placed on undermining and setting fire to the keep. This was achieved over the next two days to the extent that by Saturday, 3 September the keep was burning so badly that the garrison had no hope of extinguishing the fire with their remaining stocks of water and wine. Their choice was between losing their lives to the fire and surrender. They opted for surrender. Now that Romorantin had been reduced, fresh intelligence came that King Jean was moving towards Tours. Clearly the French were not as close as had been thought, and there was now little point in remaining at Romorantin. The prince and his council now had a new target to make for, and, having rested their troops on the Sunday, they set out towards Tours on Monday, 5 September.

Manoeuvre

After the prince's departure from Romorantin, until the Battle of Poitiers two weeks later, both armies entered a phase of manoeuvre. For Jean, during the coming days it was a question of continuing to marshal his forces and of maintaining contact with the Anglo-Gascon army either to bring it to battle in a favourable position for the numerically superior French forces, or to trap it, cut it off from its route back to Gascony and force its surrender. However, there have been two distinctly different views concerning the prince's objective. The predominant view has been that the Black Prince was seeking to avoid battle and that he was attempting to disengage and return to Bordeaux with his booty. The historian H.J. Hewitt argued that 'The best way from Romorantin to Bordeaux lay in going west along the Cher and, at some suitable point, turning south.' Even a cursory glance at a map shows that this is nonsense. A quicker escape could have been achieved by either retracing the route taken in the previous month or cutting south-west to pick up the route from Poitiers to Bordeaux. In either case he could have kept well ahead of King Jean. Indeed, even if he had marched at only 20km a day, the average distance covered on march-days since leaving Bergerac, he would have reached Poitiers on 13 September, well ahead of King Jean, who arrived at what was to be the battlefield on Sunday, 18 September. If escape had been his aim, he could have moved much faster. The other view is more probable: that his objective was to join battle provided that this could be done in a favourable position, and that he manoeuvred his army accordingly, ensuring that he avoided becoming trapped in the process. This is entirely consistent with the prince's objectives for the *chevauchée* and demonstrates his determination to maintain the aim of his campaign. An understanding of this phase of the *chevauchée* after the departure from Romorantin until arrival in the vicinity of the battlefield twelve days later is instructive for gaining an insight into the prince's conduct of operations.

Before departing from Romorantin, the intelligence available to the prince from prisoners was that King Jean was gathering his army and 'had made up his mind for certain to fight with us, at whatever time we should be on the road towards Tours, he meeting us in the direction of Orléans'. The prisoners had also reported that the bridges across the Loire had been destroyed, although it is probable, in view of the need for the French to cross the river, that some of them at least were simply well guarded. This much we know from the prince's letter written to the City of London in October. We do not know what news he had at this stage of either Lancaster's progress or of the nature of the French forces at Tours, but it seems that a detachment from the prince's army may have made a reconnaissance towards the Loire at Amboise.

In any event, it was towards Tours that the prince advanced from Romorantin, arriving at Montlouis-sur-Loire on Wednesday, 7 September. He was now 10km to the east of Tours. The medieval city stood on the left bank of the Loire, which served to protect its northern side, and it was, therefore, vulnerable to attack from the south without the need to cross the river. This vulnerability had been recognised by Jean who, in March 1354, had issued a charter to the town to galvanise the townspeople in their work of improving the town walls and ditches. Provision was also made to improve the arrangements for local defence with seven companies of town militia raised. In addition, by the time the prince arrived, there was a large French force in the city with the Counts of Poitiers and Angers and Marshal Clermont. It is unlikely that the prince planned to assault Tours, but it is possible that he hoped to entice the French out for battle

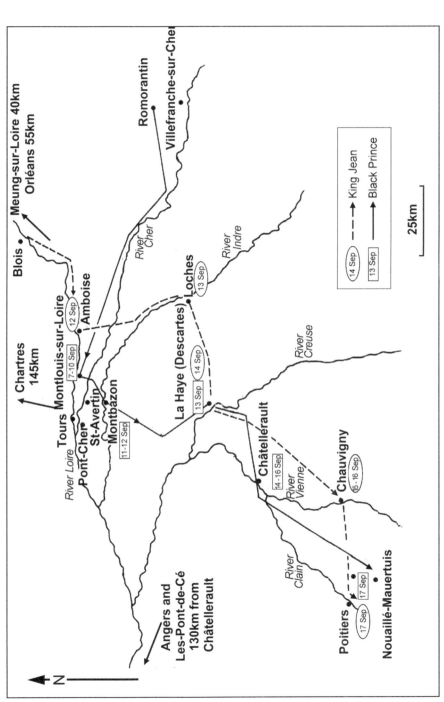

Romorantin to Poitiers.

before King Jean brought further troops to the scene. This may have been the motive for attacks which took place against the suburbs.

Meanwhile more contingents had been joining the French army at Chartres. As his army continued to grow, Jean moved towards the Loire, reaching Meung-sur-Loire on Thursday, 8 September, still 80km north-east of the prince. He continued south-west along the north bank of the Loire, reaching Blois and crossing the river there on Friday. He was now only 45km from the prince's position at Montlouis and on the same side of the river. With the Loire in front and the Cher behind him, the prince would have been mindful of the potential dangers of his position if he remained at Montlouis. Here the two rivers are only 6km apart and they gradually converge to meet 10km to the west of Tours. A further consideration was that the bridges across the Cher in the vicinity of Tours, at Pont-Cher and St-Avertin, had been cut, and small villages burnt down to avoid them being of use to the Anglo-Gascon army. Now that King Jean had crossed the Loire, the destruction of the bridges would have increased the risk of the prince being bottled up in the funnel between the Loire and the Cher.

No doubt other crossings to the east of Tours had been held by the prince's army to secure his rear, but in a day, or two at the most, the French could close the trap. As it was, on 11 September Jean moved 30km to Amboise, only 12km east along the Loire from Montlouis. He paused briefly to await other contingents crossing at Meung, Orléans, Blois, Tours and Saumur, but it was time for the prince to move if the trap were to be avoided. Of necessity this move must be to the south. Although this would take him closer to Bordeaux, this did not indicate a desire to disengage from the French. If he had wished to do that he would surely have moved at a greater speed than he did. Indeed, it seems that he was moving at a pace which might still allow for a rendezvous with the Duke of Lancaster, although it must now have been clear that there was no longer any prospect of bringing the two armies together near Tours. However, the prince clearly still had hopes of effecting a union with the duke's army, for in his letter to the City of London he wrote, 'and on departing from thence [Montlouis], we took the road so as to pass certain dangers by water, and with the intention of meeting with our most dear cousin, the Duke of Lancaster, of whom we had certain news that he would make haste to draw towards us'.

The Indre flows east to west only a few kilometres south of the Cher before joining the Loire. A short move beyond the Cher would simply replicate the risk of entrapment a little further south. Thus, the prince needed to move beyond the Indre. This he did on Sunday, 11 September, crossing both the Cher and the Indre and arriving at Montbazon.

The prince, through application of the principle of war of security to give himself freedom of action and limit his vulnerability to hostile threats, now had room to manoeuvre since the next serious obstacle, the river Creuse, was 30km to the south. He remained at Montbazon on the Monday. While there he received a visit from the Cardinal of Périgord, who came to try to persuade the prince to negotiate either a truce or peace. The cardinal told him that the dauphin was at Tours with 1,000 men-at-arms and that the king was drawing near and intended to join the battle on Wednesday, 14 September. Presumably this news was intended to persuade the Black Prince of the advantages of suing for peace. He was having none of it, and politely rebuffed the cardinal's approach as he explained in his letter to the City of London:

> Upon which parley we made answer to him, that peace we had no power to make, and that we would not intermeddle therewith, without the command and the wishes of the King, our most dear lord and father; nor yet as to a truce were we at that time of opinion that it would be the best thing for us to assent thereto, for there we were more fully certified that the King [of France] had prepared in every way to fight with us.

The final clause is a further indication that the prince did not wish to avoid the chance for battle, but in addition his approach reflected the terms of his indenture with his father which gave him some restricted powers to agree a truce:

> And if it shall happen that the prince is besieged or so beset with enemies that his person is in peril, and no rescue can come in time, then, to save himself and his men, he may help himself by making a truce or armistice, or in any other way that seems best to him.

Even if the prince had been inclined to negotiate a truce, at this stage he was neither 'so beset with enemies that his person was in peril' nor without hope of rescue in the shape of the Duke of Lancaster. A truce, which would have allowed the French to tighten the net further, to the disadvantage of the Anglo-Gascons, would certainly have been premature. The discussions with the cardinal having proved fruitless, the prince moved on again on Tuesday. He covered 40km, reaching the river Creuse and spending the night at La Haye, now called Descartes, on the east bank of the river.

Meanwhile, Jean had also been on the move and on the Tuesday night rested at Loches, a massive Plantagenet fortress built by Henry II, 30km north-east of the prince. At this point the French were not in a position to block the Anglo-Gascon army's route south, but it was while the prince was at La Haye that he received information of the position of the French and the news that Jean was trying to get ahead of him to cut him off. It would seem that Jean was afraid the Anglo-Gascons would escape to the south, and the attempt to overtake them made eminent good sense for the French. However, for the prince, the prospect that he might be trapped and held at bay as his provisions dwindled was not a happy one.

On Wednesday, 14 September the prince moved 25km to Châtellerault on the east bank of the river Vienne. On reaching the town the Anglo-Gascon army had moved on sufficiently, or so it must have seemed, to keep ahead of the French. However, the Black Prince still needed to be alive to the risks of becoming trapped while keeping in touch with the enemy so as to be able to bring them to battle. Also, if he still held out hopes of meeting the Duke of Lancaster, he needed to avoid moving too far too quickly. Thus, he remained at Châtellerault for two days. Meanwhile, the French had moved rapidly, passing through La Haye on Wednesday, and moving on to secure the bridge at Chauvigny on the river Vienne. Jean had overtaken the prince and was 30km south-east of him. Meanwhile Lancaster, as the French were approaching Chauvigny, had tried unsuccessfully to force a crossing of the Loire at Les-Ponts-de-Cé 120km distant. The prince could not have been aware of the news at this point, but all hope of joining up with Lancaster had now gone.

The prince then executed a bold stroke. Hearing on Friday evening that the French would be moving from Chauvigny to Poitiers the next day, he determined to attempt to intercept the French column on the march. The Anglo-Gascon army had more than 30km to cover if they were to catch the French. They could not move quickly enough if they tried to stay with the baggage train, and so instructions were given for it to cross the bridge to the west of the river Vienne that night to avoid impeding the combat elements the next morning as they hastened to find the French. This action was entirely consistent with Sun Tzu's principle that where speed is of the essence, it may be necessary to separate a flying column from the baggage train.

On the Saturday morning the prince set off, hearing fresh news that the main French army was on the move towards Poitiers, where there were other French troops. The prince moved quickly across country and, and having crossed the main road from Chauvigny to Poitiers, emerged from woods to find that the main body of the French army had already passed. However, 200 Anglo-Gascon men-at-arms fell on the rearguard. The French were unprepared for combat, since some at least were wearing ostrich-feathered caps rather than their bascinets, and were taken by surprise. In the ensuing engagement with 700 French knights and men-at-arms, the French were put to flight, with 240 killed or captured. In Jean Froissart's account there is the suggestion of a trap being sprung by the prince, with the French, upon seeing the prince's scouts, donning their helmets, unfurling banners and pursuing the Anglo-Gascons, only to find themselves drawn into contact with the main force. The prince admits to losses, but we do not know how many. Some of the prince's men pursued the routed French towards Chauvigny, but the majority of the army was held back in case of a French counter-attack. In the event this did not materialise, but the prince camped for the night near the scene of the engagement so that, in his own words, 'we might collect our men', which presumably included the baggage train and those who had pursued the French. An unfortunate consequence of this choice for an overnight bivouac was a shortage of water for the men and horses. The Saturday halt was probably in the vicinity of Savigny-Lévescault, 10km south-east of Poitiers. King Jean and the French were only a few kilometres away, somewhere between Poitiers and the eventual battlefield.

Let us now look at what contemporaries, or near-contemporaries, had to say of events in this phase of the *chevauchée*. There are some general comments in the chronicles to the effect that when the prince heard that Jean was approaching, he turned for home. One contemporary stated that the 'English took the road to go to Poitiers'. However, another is quite specific: 'the prince eager for battle ... led his army towards the camp of the usurper'. Chandos Herald, in relating the movement of the French and the prince's response, states that 'they [the French] departed from Chartres and rode without any hesitation straight towards Tours. Very noble was their array. The news then reached the prince, and good tidings did they seem to him; towards Poitiers he took his way.' This short passage is ambiguous. Was the prince's delight due to the approach of the French or because they were heading towards Tours and this gave him time to move away from them towards Poitiers? Other contemporary evidence includes a report from Sir Henry Peverel, and a letter written by Bartholomew de Burghersh, and three letters from the prince, one to the Prior of Winchester Cathedral, the second to the Bishop of Worcester, and the third to the City of London. The letters to the Prior of Winchester Cathedral deal with fact and not intentions, and Burghersh's letter is also very matter of fact, only briefly alluding to intentions when he talks of crossing the Loire to 'pass into France'. The prince's letter to the Bishop of Worcester is, however, explicit: 'we had news that the King of France with great strength very close to those marches [Bourges, Orléans and Tours] came to fight with us, and we approached so that battle was joined between us'. In his letter to the City of London the prince is also explicit over his intentions. As a general intent he states that 'it was our purpose to ride forth against the enemies in the parts of France', and he also links the intelligence that Jean was seeking battle with his decision to move towards him at Tours. Similarly, he explains the halt at Châtellerault because he was 'waiting to know for greater certainty of him'.

It would be interesting to know what Jean thought the prince was trying to achieve. One writer gives a tantalising taste of what might have been the king's view: 'when he [King Jean] knew for certain that they were so close to him, he thought that they would wait for him, and that the next day or the one after it would be necessary to fight them'. What are we to make of the last clause? Was Jean himself keen to fight, or did he simply see battle as inevitable? As we shall see later, on the eve of battle he and his advisers were in two minds as to whether or not the best course was to starve the prince into submission rather than take the risks of battle.

What the prince's movements during this phase of manoeuvre show us is his tactical appreciation of the situation and his skilful execution of the necessary movements to strike what Clifford Rogers rightly describes as 'the delicate balance between avoiding a trap and not avoiding a battle'. His itinerary from Romorantin was no more nor less than sound tactical movement to maximise the opportunities to join forces with the Duke of Lancaster, to keep the initiative, to stay close enough in touch with the French that King Jean would not be tempted to give up the chase, and yet avoid being trapped. The risk of entrapment was entirely linked to the position of the two armies in relation to major rivers. The prince's movement out of potential traps is exemplified by his departure from Montlouis and the passages of the Cher and the Indre before halting at Montbazon, and his crossing of the Creuse and the move to Châtellerault, followed by another halt. In each case he paused long enough to stay in touch and then moved on again to ensure the security of his army before the next trap could be sprung. All the while he kept the opportunity for battle alive. His bold move on Saturday, 17 September not only gave him a successful morale-boosting skirmish, but it also brought the two armies into close proximity. There was now the opportunity for battle without the prince facing the risk of entrapment with a major obstacle at his back.

The Prelude to Battle

The manoeuvre phase which had characterised operations since the prince and his army left Romorantin was now over and the armies were at last in close proximity. The most pressing need for the Anglo-Gascon army as the sun rose on Sunday, 18 September 1356 was to find water, and, if possible, other provisions for men and horses. The nearest water source was the river Miosson, only about 4km from the overnight bivouac. The Benedictine abbey of St Junien on the banks of the river in the village of Nouaillé-Maupertuis and the *commanderie* of the Knights Hospitaller at Beauvoir were close at hand and could be expected to provide at least some provisions for the army. Once the men and horses had been fed and watered as best they could, attention then turned to the best course of action. If the prince were intent on avoiding battle the obvious move, with the French somewhere to the north between the Anglo-Gascon army and Poitiers, was to continue south towards Bordeaux and safety at all speed. Instead, opting to take offensive action, he advanced towards the French and selected a position for battle:

> And on the morrow we took our road straight towards the King, and sent out our scouts who found him with his army; and he set himself in battle array at one league [6km] from Poitiers, in the fields; and we went as near to him as we could take up our post, we ourselves on foot and in battle array, and ready to fight with him.

So where was the battle fought? There are numerous primary sources which deal with the battle. However, they vary in detail, are often obscure, and are imprecise concerning the location. As a consequence it has proved impossible over the years to resolve the many differing accounts with certainty, and there have been significantly different interpretations. My conclusions, in common with those of others, inevitably involve a large measure of conjecture. A debate on the location of the battlefield and the deployment of the prince's army here would be something of a distraction from discussion of the conduct of the battle by the two commanders. My analysis of the location of the battlefield is at Appendix 1. In summary, my interpretation is that the battlefield was to the north-west of the village of Nouaillé-Maupertuis, with the Anglo-Gascon army arrayed along the axis of the road running north from the Gué de l'Homme. The sketch maps used below to illustrate the progress of the battle might seem to imply that it is possible to reduce a medieval battle to accurate plans of well-ordered blocks of men moving to some master-plan in disciplined parade-ground fashion. This is of course not the case, and such maps cannot accurately represent the chaos of battle. The sketch maps are nothing more than aids provided to guide the reader through the main events of the combat based on my interpretation of the battlefield.

The Anglo-Gascon army was probably about 6,000 strong: 2,000 archers, 3,000 men-at-arms and 1,000 sergeants (possibly foot soldiers or squires). It was divided into three divisions, probably with a more or less equal distribution of men-at-arms and sergeants between them. In addition, there were 400 men-at-arms in reserve around the prince's banner. Reports of the fighting imply that the archers were in two blocks deployed on the flanks. If, for the sake of argument, we divide the men-at-arms and sergeants equally, then we have 1,200 men fighting on foot in each division, with an additional 400 men in reserve with the prince. We also have 1,000 archers with each of the van and rearguards. Thus, if the men-at-arms were arrayed in four ranks, as the historian Clifford Rogers argues was typical of the period, each division would have a frontage of around 300m. Rogers proposes that at the Battle of Agincourt archers were probably deployed in seven ranks with a frontage of 1m per man. If we assume a similar formation at Poitiers, we would have a block of archers on each flank, each with a frontage of about 140m.

There is a key description of the battlefield in the chronicle of Galfridi le Baker:

> he [the prince] perceived that there was near-by on one side a hill, encircled with hedges and ditches on the outside, but with different land inside, on one side a pasture thick with thorn bushes, but, on the other side sown with vines, and the rest of it arable land. And in the arable part of it he thought a French column lay. Between us and the hill was a broad deep valley, and a marsh which was fed by a certain stream. At a fairly narrow ford the prince's column crossed the stream, with its wagons, and coming out of the valley across ditches and hedges occupied the hill, where amid the thickets they were easily hidden by the natural fortification of the place, which lay higher than the enemy. The field in which our first and second columns lay was separated from the open ground which the French occupied by a long hedge with a ditch on the far side, one end of which fell away into the marsh aforementioned. The Earl of Warwick, commander of the first column, held the slope going down to the marsh. In the upper part of the hedge, a good way from the slope, was a certain large gap or hiatus, which carters made in the autumn, distant a stone's throw

from which lay our third company, which the Earl of Salisbury commanded. The enemy, seeing the standard of the prince, previously
visible, but now starting to move and to be hidden from their eyes by
the slope of the hill, thought that he was trickling away ...

From this description it seems that the vanguard on the left, under
Warwick, and the prince's division were close together, but that they were
separated initially from the rearguard under Salisbury on the right. Based
on the assumptions above and Baker's description, the army could have
deployed over an overall frontage of around 1,200m with archers on the
flanks, centred on the prince on the spur near the Croix de la Garde.

A road runs north from the ford at the Gué de l'Homme, as it did then.
A little to the north, near Bernon, the modern road turns left but a length
of farm track continues north on what was probably the route of the
original track. This section of road is bordered on both sides by thick
hedges typical of the region. Their importance is evident in the contemporary descriptions of the battle. Such hedges are planted with two rows
of saplings 1m or more apart and undergrowth develops between the two
rows. They frequently grow to several metres in height and as they grow
the saplings become trees embedded within the hedge. They are formidable obstacles. They would have slowed the attackers and given the
defenders an initial advantage until the hedges had been breached.

A particular feature of the battlefield which also drew the attention of
the chroniclers was a gap in the hedge. With hedges along the sides of the
road, and, assuming that the prince's division, as indicated by Baker's
account, had occupied the higher ground initially, then the gap in the
hedge for the carters would be somewhere to the north of the Croix de la
Garde, with Salisbury's rearguard stepped back somewhat to put them a
'stone's throw' from the gap. Some interpretations of the battlefield imply
that the gap was to allow a road to pass, but since we are told that the gap
was opened in the autumn by carters this does not make sense. They must
have been opening a gap to allow access either to fields or to woodland.

We have no precise information on the French position. One analysis
suggests that on the night of Saturday, 17 September the French army was
positioned with its right flank near the right bank of the Miosson, 1.5km
north-west of les Bordes, and its left towards la Cardinerie and Beauvoir.
If this is correct, then the prince's deployment would have brought him
within sight of the French about 1,200m away, but one source records that
there was only a bow shot between the two armies and the French may
have moved forward close to a line south-east of les Bordes. From that

position the French would have a clear view of the location of the Anglo-Gascon rear and middle-guards, but with the road falling away towards the Gué de l'Homme, the position of the vanguard and the prince's reserve would be masked by the terrain. Chandos Herald tells us that: 'as I have heard, the one camped before the other, and pitched their tents so near that, by Saint Peter, they watered their horses at the same river'. It is not clear whether this is supposed to refer to the positions on Saturday night, after the engagement between the prince and the rearguard of the French, or the positions taken up on Sunday. However, on the assumption that the prince's army was short of water on the Saturday, it seems more likely that he means when the armies were deployed. That both should use the water of the Miosson is very likely, given the meandering course of the river.

Accounts of the battle give varying numbers for the strengths of the forces deployed. However, the figure of 6,000 men is widely accepted as the probable strength of the Black Prince's army. The figures for the French vary widely from 11,000, cited in letters by Bartholomew de Burghersh and Henry Peverel, to Froissart's 60,000. There are numerous other figures in between, but an assumption that at the start of the battle the French outnumbered the prince's men by around two-and-a-half to one is probably not far off the mark.

Having moved his army into position along the road north from the Gué de l'Homme, the prince and his advisers would no doubt consider the possible turn of events. Sunday was likely to be free of fighting under the provisions of the doctrine of the Truce of God, which tried to prevent combat on holy days, although the prince could not count on this and would need to be on his guard. Meanwhile the French army continued to grow as fresh contingents arrived, adding perhaps an additional 1,000 men-at-arms during the day. If battle did not come on Sunday, then on the Monday morning it would not be possible to prevaricate. If the French attacked then so be it. The prince would be able to adopt the preferred English tactic of the period of fighting a defensive action with his archers and dismounted men-at-arms. Although the size of the French host led some in the prince's army to mutter about the number of troops left behind at Bergerac to defend Aquitaine, many of his captains had been at Crécy and they would be confident that, given the right circumstances and God's blessing, they could prevail against the numerically superior French army. Recent successes during encounters with French reconnaissance parties, the siege at Romorantin and Saturday's engagement with the French rearguard would have added to their confidence.

However, if the French did not engage early on the Monday, the situation could rapidly deteriorate. The prince's men were short of supplies, and the longer they stayed put, the greater the risk of them being starved into submission. As things stood, they had an escape route over the fords of the Miosson, but the distance from the northernmost French positions round the east of the woods to the Gué de l'Homme was no more than 5km. A substantial French force could easily be in a blocking position within a couple of hours of first light. Although both Sun Tzu and Vegetius argue for allowing the enemy an escape route, albeit in the latter case to allow the enemy to be pursued and destroyed, it is something of a mystery why the French did not cut the way south, particularly since the option of holding the Anglo-Gascons in position and starving them into surrender was under consideration on the Sunday. If the French did not show signs of engaging soon after first light on Monday, then the prince would have to consider withdrawal. This should not be seen as a sign of wishing to avoid battle. It would be a prudent measure to avoid being trapped as the advantage moved towards the enemy as their army grew and the provisioning situation for the prince's men became more acute. A move south and the chance to feed and water men and horses would possibly present another opportunity for battle.

In any event, on Sunday morning the prince's army had watered and fed as well as circumstances allowed and had moved into position facing the French. Meanwhile Talleyrand, the Cardinal of Périgord, still had hopes for peace. He approached the king and suggested that in view of the might of his army in comparison with the handful in the prince's army, it would bring him more honour to secure a peaceful outcome than to risk the lives of many when it was not necessary. With Jean's agreement, he rode out towards the Anglo-Gascon army with two fellow cardinals, the Bishop of Urgel, a fellow papal delegate, and the Archbishop of Rouen, an ambassador for the French. The English did not trust Talleyrand to be impartial, since both he and the Pope were French. Thus, initially the prince rebuffed his approach, suspecting that the cardinal was buying time for the French to supplement their forces, and telling Talleyrand to get on with it since this was a time for fighting and not sermons. However, having heard the cardinal out and held discussions with his council, he agreed to negotiations. These were conducted in the ground between the two armies by representatives of the king and the prince, under the chairmanship of Talleyrand. For the prince the negotiators included the Earls of Warwick and Suffolk, Bartholomew de Burghersh, John Chandos and James Audley. The result of the negotiations was the offer of terms by the prince. The details of the terms vary from one source to another but included some at least of the following provisions: the surrender to Jean of all the properties that had been captured from the French in the last three years, a large cash indemnity, the release of all prisoners, the hand in marriage of one of the king's daughters, and the promise not to take up arms against Jean for seven years. The sting in the tail was that the terms would be subject to King Edward's agreement. The prince promised to secure this quickly but, given the speed of communications and the imminence of battle, his sincerity in entering these negotiations must be questionable. Furthermore, the prince's indenture with King Edward empowered the prince to make a truce or armistice *in extremis*, and it seems very likely that he was simply buying time while he prepared for events on the Monday. During the negotiations King Jean asked for the surrender of the prince and 100 knights as a sign of good faith. Also, according to Chandos Herald, there was a proposal from Geoffroi de Charny for the battle to be settled by combat between 100 knights from each side. Warwick's reported reply is interesting, in that it implies that perhaps the French were seeking to select a field for the battle which would offer them better circumstances. If so, this would clearly not be in the interest of the English and the Gascons, outnumbered as they were, and Warwick replied:

> Sire, what will you gain by this encounter? You know well that you have more men-at-arms and steel clad, by four times than we are, and we are on your territory; here is the field and the place, let each side do its best. Nowhere else will I be, nor agree to any other conditions. May God defend the right, as it shall seem best to him.

It seems that Jean may have been inclined to accept the terms on offer, and some of his advisers were of the opinion that he should do so. However, many of his entourage were opposed to such a step, and in the argument Marshal d'Audrehem implied that Marshal Clermont was lacking in courage, to which he retorted: 'You will not be brave enough today to put the muzzle of your horse to the backside of mine!' The Bishop of Châlons reminded the king of the damage done throughout his realm by King Edward, the Duke of Lancaster and the prince. He also reminded him of his inaction to date to exact revenge on the English, and expressed incredulity that Jean, bearing in mind his strong position, should be negotiating with the prince when he could have little confidence in his good faith. He was strongly supported by Marshal d'Audrehem, Geoffroi de Charny and Earl Douglas, a Scot in Jean's service with 200 men-at-arms, who argued that given the relative strength of the armies, the fact that the

French were on their home soil, and the difficulty the Anglo-Gascon army was in with provisions, 'by common reason it could not come to passe [*sic*] that the Englishmen should at that time prevaile [*sic*]'. The position of the prince's army with regard to provisions, and the possibility of holding the Anglo-Gascons in position and forcing their surrender, would no doubt have figured in the king's deliberations with his advisers. Having taken counsel, Jean refused all terms and demanded the surrender of the prince and his army, trusting in his mercy. The appeal to his sense of honour and duty outweighed the more pragmatic advice of those who sought to neutralise the prince's army without the uncertain risks of battle.

When the prince heard that his terms had been rejected by the king, he is said to have announced that he would willingly put himself in God's hands, and that he only had one life, and he would prefer to risk death than live in shame. There was an offer from the king of a formal truce until the Monday morning, provided that the prince undertook not to depart under cover of night. The prince was not going to be caught like this and replied to the effect that he had not come to these parts with the assent of King Jean, and would stay or go at his own pleasure. Talleyrand was mistrusted by the prince and his advisers, but he was not held in much greater regard in some quarters in the French camp. As Chandos Herald put it, 'and on both sides it was said "This cardinal has betrayed us".'

It could be argued that these negotiations revealed the reluctance of the prince to fight, and Chandos Herald adds some weight to this with his comment that 'and willingly, as I think, [the prince] would have been spared the action, could he have avoided it'. However, none of the other principal sources make similar reference, and we should see the negotiations within the religious context of the times. Strange as it may seem to us today, God's support for his cause would have been very much in the prince's thoughts. To reject the cardinal's overtures without negotiation, particularly on a Sunday, a day of the Truce of God, would have been tempting providence.

It is likely that both the king and the prince saw the prospects of a peaceful issue as remote, and both would be considering the coming battle. For the prince, whose army had been together for six weeks on this campaign, the allocation of captains and their companies to divisions was in accord with the organisation to date. Warwick would command the van with Oxford, with numerous Gascon lords including the Captal de Buch, the prince commanded the centre with John Chandos and James Audley, and the rearguard lay with Suffolk, Salisbury and Sir Maurice Berkeley. On the French side, King Jean assigned the vanguard, comprising (according to Chandos Herald) men-at-arms, infantry and crossbowmen to the two marshals, Audrehem and Clermont, and the Duke of Athens, Constable of France. The vanguard also included a number of men-at-arms from Lorraine, modern Switzerland and Savoy, under the leadership of the Counts of Saarbruck, Nassau and Nidau. The dauphin, the Duke of Normandy, commanded the second division with the Duke of Bourbon. The king's brother, Philippe, Duke of Orléans, took command of the third division. A fourth division was constituted under the command of the king, with his three sons Louis, Jean and Philippe.

King Jean also had to decide on his tactics. He knew, of course, of the standard tactic for the English to fight on foot. He would also have known how effective the archers could be. The experience of Crécy ten years before, when the archers had exacted a terrible toll and the mounted French men-at-arms had been defeated by the dismounted English, would have been much in the minds of the king and his advisers. Jean sent forward four knights to reconnoitre the prince's position, who advised him that:

> Sire, they are in a very strong position, and we can see and imagine that they are prepared for battle, very well and very cleverly arrayed. They have taken the length of a road well-fortified with hedges and bushes, and have lined this hedge, from one end to the other, with their archers such that one cannot enter, nor ride in the road, save being among them if one wants to take this road or fight them. This hedge has only one way in and out, where only four men-at-arms could ride abreast, and the same goes for the road. At the end of this hedge, where one can neither go nor ride, are their men-at-arms, all on foot, and they have put in front of them archers in the manner of a harrow. It is very well organized it seems to us, for whoever wants or is able to come up to them by feat of arms, will not be able to do so save among the archers who will not be easy to defeat.

When he had heard the reports from the reconnaissance party, Jean asked for advice on how best to fight. Eustace de Ribemont advised that he should select 300 men-at-arms to make a mounted attack, 'to split and open and disrupt the English archers, and then our divisions, which are large, powerful, and well equipped with good men-at-arms, to follow quickly on foot, for there are too many vines for the horses'. This advice was supported by William Douglas, since this was the practice of the Scots. The king readily agreed, and orders were given to facilitate fighting on foot by shortening lances and removing spurs.

Battle

With the prospect of peace gone, the prince addressed his army, and no doubt held a council to finalise plans for the Monday morning. Sunrise on 19 September would have been at 5.40am, with the two armies facing each other and arrayed for battle. Shortly thereafter the cardinal arrived in the English camp to try once again to secure a peaceful outcome. It was clear to all that his efforts were in vain, and even the cardinal in the end had to concur that there was now no option but battle. At some point the prince sent Sir Eustace de Daubriggecourt and another knight, probably the Gascon Petiton de Curton, to reconnoitre the French position. The unfortunate Sir Eustace, having become involved in combat with Louis de Recombes, was overwhelmed by Louis' companions and made prisoner.

The armies faced each other for almost two hours after sunrise. However, the longer the prince waited, the worse his position would become as the French army grew in strength and the Anglo-Gascon shortage of supplies became more acute. The prince stated that:

> the battalions on the one side and the other remained all night, each one in its place, and until the morrow [Monday], about half prime [7.30am]; and as to some troops that were between the said main armies, neither would give any advantage in commencing the attack upon the other. And for default of victuals, as well as for other reasons, it was agreed that we should take our way, flanking them, in such a manner that if they wished for battle or to draw towards us, in a place that was not very much to our disadvantage, we should be the first; and so forthwith it was done.

Chandos Herald describes the prince as outlining the plan for disengagement thus:

> At first you [Warwick] will cross the pass and protect our carriages; I shall ride after you with all my knights, so that if you meet with any mischance, you may be reinforced by us; and the Earl of Salisbury shall also ride after me, bringing up our rearguard; and let each be on his guard, in case they fall upon us. Each may dismount and engage as quickly as he possibly can.

The instruction to 'protect our carriages' can be interpreted as the baggage train moving across the Miosson that morning, but it could mean that some at least of the baggage train was already positioned south of the river. Certainly it would have been prudent, in view of the possibility of needing to disengage, to leave non-essential vehicles south of the Miosson on the Sunday to minimise the risk of congestion at the crossing, retaining north of the river only those carts carrying necessary provisions and stocks of arrows.

French awareness of the movement of the Anglo-Gascon army precipitated the start of the battle, with Baker telling us that the French saw 'the standard of the prince, previously visible, starting to move and to be hidden from their eyes by the slope of the hill'. This is consistent with the prince moving off to the south between the road and the wood, where he would become partially hidden from French view by the reverse slope of the spur, with Warwick already having moved off out of sight of the French because he was further down the slope. It is likely that by the time the French realised what was afoot, both the van and middle-guards of the Anglo-Gascon army had started to move from their positions. On a modern parade ground well-drilled troops can move off simultaneously in large numbers but this is unlikely to have been possible with troops in the fourteenth century. No matter how well disciplined they were, they would have tended to move off much as a queue of cars when traffic lights change to green, with movement extending progressively down the line. Thus, it is probable that the vanguard would be well under way before the prince's middle division moved off, and that Salisbury would still be stationary by the time Warwick was crossing the Miosson.

The 300 French cavalry assigned to the destruction of the prince's archers had been divided into two squadrons, each commanded by one of the two marshals. Marshal d'Audrehem concluded that the English were seeking to disengage, and considered that there was no time to lose if they were to be prevented from escaping. Marshal Clermont and William Douglas took a different view, and cautioned against haste. However, Audrehem set off and Clermont, apparently goaded into action by a mixture of insults and pride, followed. It may be that the speed of the response was the undoing of the attack. Clearly there would have been some confusion, and the Constable, the Duke of Athens, would have taken a few minutes at least to get the dismounted troops of the French vanguard moving. In addition, the distances from the French vanguard to the two wings of the Anglo-Gascon army would be significantly different. If the cavalry were somewhere in the vicinity of les Bordes, they would have had about 500m to cover to reach Salisbury's rearguard and possibly as much as 1,000m to the left flank of Warwick's vanguard. Thus, Audrehem's cavalry on the right of the French would quickly outstrip the infantry, who of necessity would be some way behind the mounted troops when

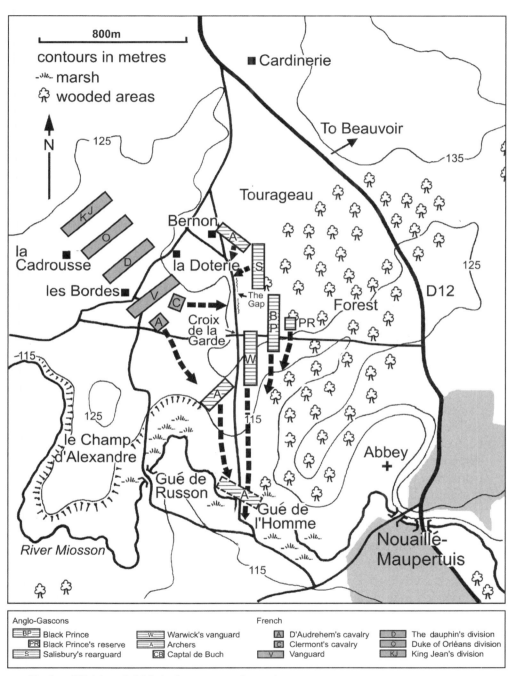

Battle of Poitiers: initial deployments and opening moves.

contact was made, and would probably be in contact with Warwick after about seven minutes. On the left, Clermont's cavalry would probably take about three minutes to come into contact with Salisbury and could expect the infantry to be closer on their heels, assuming that the Constable took the initiative to advance promptly when he saw the cavalry move.

A coordinated attack at a more measured pace may well have caught the prince's army at its most vulnerable, with infantry coming into contact quickly after the cavalry on both wings. However, the die was cast and the mounted troops of Marshal d'Audrehem and Marshal Clermont fell upon the vanguard and the rearguard respectively. It seems that Warwick had at this point already crossed the Miosson with a part of his force, but there was an initial clash between some of Warwick's mounted men-at-arms and Audrehem's cavalry. This initial encounter led to some hesitation on Audrehem's part, but he renewed the attack heading south-east down the spur of land converging with the road and the Gué de l'Homme. It appears that by now elements of the French vanguard on foot were coming into contact since Audrehem's men turned their armoured horses face-on to protect them from the English archers, who had been positioned in the marshy ground close to the river, most probably as a prudent measure to cover the initial stages of the withdrawal. Oxford, recognising what was happening and that the shooting of the archers was proving less effective than it might be, left the prince's company and took the archers forward to allow them to strike the horses in their unprotected flanks. It is probable that the archers were not deployed where the current marsh is most visible. If they had been, it is difficult to see how their shooting could have been effective with the very steep ground to their north. Furthermore, the slope would have been difficult for cavalry to descend and a head-on confrontation between archers and cavalry would have been most improbable. It is more likely that the archers were close to the Gué de l'Homme and were then moved to the left along the edge of the marshy ground to engage the cavalry in the flank. The result of this movement and the shooting from the flank was chaos as some horses fell, taking their riders with them, and others turned and ran into those coming behind. The men on foot were now exposed to the shooting from the archers. Those of Warwick's men-at-arms who had already crossed the Miosson, realising what was happening, had now recrossed the river and joined the fray.

Meanwhile, on the English right flank Clermont led a determined attack with the aim of exploiting the gap in the hedge to fall on the vanguard. This implies that the prince's division was separate from the van, as would be expected if they were now both moving, and Clermont, with the aim of cutting off the withdrawal, intended to move across the prince's front, which he could do safely if the archers were on the flanks with Warwick's and Salisbury's divisions. Salisbury anticipated the problem and countered Clermont by moving forward with his men-at-arms and positioning his archers so that they were protected by the hedge and were able to shoot at the French mounted men-at-arms. Since Clermont, goaded into action, had set off promptly and had a shorter distance to cover than Audrehem, the first action was between his men and those of Salisbury, as reflected in Salisbury's words reported by Chandos Herald: 'Advance, Sirs, in God's name! Since it hath pleased Saint George that we who were the rear, should now be the front, let us take care to do honourably.' We know little of the part played by the French dismounted men-at-arms, infantry and crossbowmen in this initial phase of the battle, other than that the Constable, the Duke of Athens, lost his life. Among the mounted elements of the vanguard, Clermont was killed and Audrehem captured. William Douglas fled the field, possibly in fear of his treatment if, as a Scot, despite in theory being subject to a truce between England and Scotland, he should fall into English hands. In a disastrous start to the battle, the king had lost three of his key commanders. Also among the dead was Robert de Duras, Cardinal Talleyrand's nephew, and a further member of the cardinal's family, the Châtelaine d'Emposte, had been captured. According to Froissart, the prince was enraged that members of the cardinal's entourage had joined the fight. He gave orders for Duras' body to be carried to the cardinal with the prince's compliments. He also ordered that d'Emposte should be decapitated, but was dissuaded by Sir John Chandos from carrying through this act. Also the defeat of the French vanguard meant that fortunes changed for Eustace Daubriggecourt, who was freed from his captors.

There had been no general pursuit of the remnants of the French vanguard. As successful as this opening encounter had been for the prince, the battle was far from over. The Anglo-Gascon vanguard closed up with the prince's division, probably on the spur near the Croix de la Garde, and waited for the next phase. The dauphin's division now advanced to join battle. Baker tells us that this was a harder and longer fight than that with the vanguard, lasting two hours, and at some time early in this phase the Anglo-Gascon rearguard must also have closed up. At some stage the French penetrated the gap in the hedge, but the shooting of the archers was so intense that they were driven back beyond it again. The dauphin's banner-bearer, Tristan de Maignelières, was captured, and the division fell back, albeit in good order. The Earl of Suffolk seems to have played a

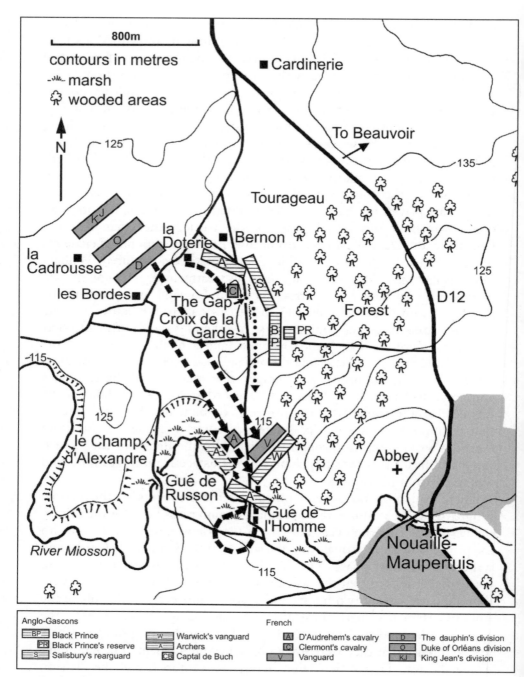

Battle of Poitiers: attack of the vanguard.

key part in this phase, moving among the men to encourage them and to restrain the less experienced from foolhardy pursuit of the retiring French. The Duke of Bourbon was among the French dead, and among the English casualties was Sir Maurice Berkeley, who, wounded and isolated, was taken prisoner.

The prince's men were exhausted and many were wounded, but they kept their composure and did not pursue the French. They now awaited the next onslaught, and in the meantime moved wounded men away from the immediate area of combat, laying them under hedges and bushes. Men with broken or damaged weapons replaced them with those of the fallen, and archers went forward to recover arrows, including pulling them from the dead and wounded. Much would depend now on the 400 chosen men who had been kept in reserve with the prince's standard. No doubt his close advisers Sir John Chandos, Sir James Audley and Sir Bartholomew Burghersh were with him. Of these it is noteworthy that Chandos remained close by the prince throughout, and that Audley single-mindedly pursued the combat without thought of personal gain. Neither of them joined in the later pursuit of prisoners to secure ransoms. Also among the men close to the prince were Sir Walter Woodland, carrying the standard, William Shank and William de Harpenden in attendance on the standard, Sir Nigel Loring, John de la Haye, Sir William Trussell, Sir Alan Cheyne and Sir Baldwin Botetourt, all of whom received annuities from him in recognition of their service at the battle.

The next division into action should have been that of the Duke of Orléans, but instead it, or at least a great part of it, left the field of battle and withdrew towards Chauvigny. With the duke went the king's sons (except for the youngest, Philippe, who remained with his father to the last), perhaps on the king's instructions to preserve the lives of the princes. What remained of the Duke of Orléans' division seems to have made a somewhat half-hearted attack which was driven off. To many in the English camp it must have seemed that, after three phases of combat, the day was theirs, since the common practice was for a medieval army to comprise three divisions. However, the remaining French troops, including the survivors of the crossbowmen, now rallied to the king's fourth division. The final act was about to begin.

King Jean had held his division to the rear, which gave the English some breathing space as he advanced, but nevertheless the exhausted English and Gascon troops, having successfully withstood three successive attacks, watched with fear and consternation as the king's division, described as arrayed in a broad and dense body, approached. They had every reason to

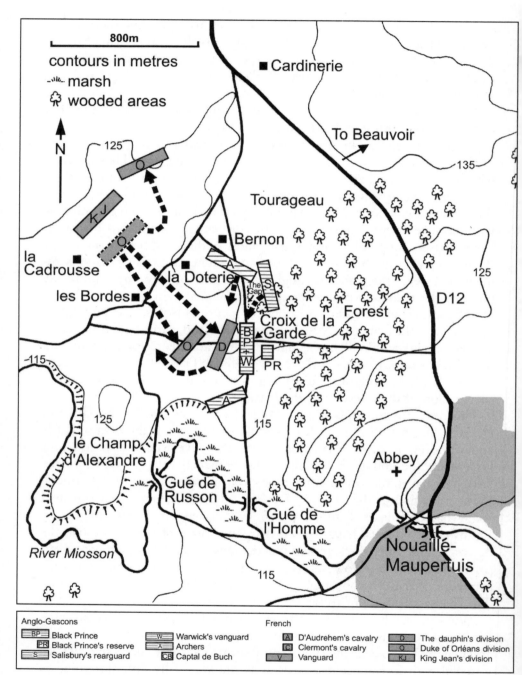

800m

contours in metres

-ᴗᴵᴵᵘ- marsh

🌳 wooded areas

N

125

O

KJ

O

■ Cardinerie

To Beauvoir

135

Tourageau

■ Bernon

la
Cadrousse ■

les Bordes ■

■ la Doterie

A

S
The
Gap

Croix de la
Garde

B
P
+
W

D12

125

Forest

O   D

PR

-115-

125

A

115

le Champ
d'Alexandre

Gué de
Russon

Abbey
+

River Miosson

Gué de
l'Homme

Nouaillé-
Maupertuis

115

🌳 🌳

🌳 🌳

Anglo-Gascons			French			
BP	Black Prince	W	Warwick's vanguard	A	D'Audrehem's cavalry	D	The dauphin's division
PR	Black Prince's reserve	A	Archers	C	Clermont's cavalry	O	Duke of Orléans division
S	Salisbury's rearguard	CB	Captal de Buch	V	Vanguard	KJ	King Jean's division

Battle of Poitiers: attacks of the Dauphin's and the Duke of Orléans' divisions.

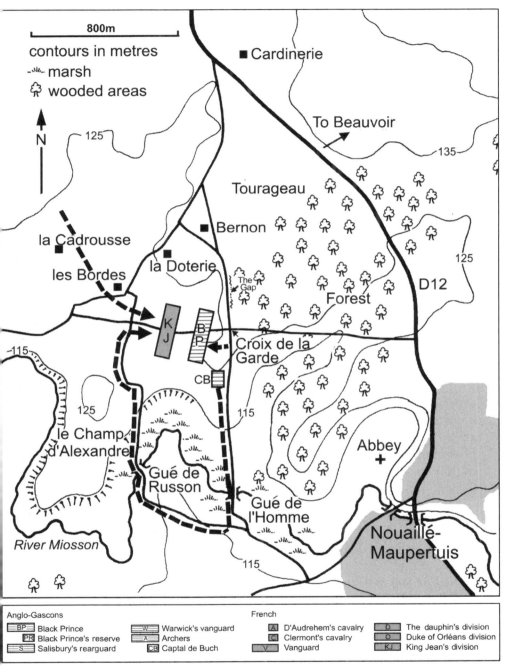

Battle of Poitiers: the final phase.

be concerned since this fourth battle brought fresh men-at-arms as well as those who had rallied from the earlier fighting. In addition, with the *Oriflamme* banner flying above the French, the traditional signal that no prisoners would be taken, they would have been clear of the fate that awaited them if they lost the day. According to Baker, one of the prince's men close to the prince cried out: 'Ah, we are beaten!' The prince, however, was having none of this and rebuked him: 'You're a liar and a fool! How can you say we're beaten while I am still alive?' No doubt there is some licence in this account, but it is indicative of the challenge facing the prince. His army had fought courageously, but was faced with having victory snatched away. The prince's response was to seize the initiative, and he took two decisive steps. First, he despatched the Captal de Buch with 60 men-at-arms and 100 archers, all mounted, to move round behind the French. Secondly, possibly in part to stiffen the resolve of his men as they saw the Captal apparently leaving the field, he called 'Advance, advance banners!', and moved down the slope of the spur towards King Jean's advancing men. Froissart states that for this advance the prince and his men remounted. This is not reported by other writers and is improbable, given that the fighting that followed was clearly intense and hand-to-hand. The battle was now renewed. This phase started with an exchange of shooting between French crossbowmen and the English archers. The archers were proving less effective than hitherto as the French advanced with their shields across their chests and their heads turned away from the shooting, but in any case the archers had soon exhausted their already depleted supplies of arrows and joined the hand-to-hand fighting with anything that came to hand. It is possible that Warwick had earlier left the field in pursuit of fleeing French troops, but if so, he returned in the nick of time to add his forces to those of the prince. However, it seems that the decisive stroke was delivered by the Captal de Buch who:

> made a wide sweep, retreating down the slope of the hill [the spur near Croix de la Garde] which he and the prince had recently left and, circling the battlefield, reached a point just below the original position of the usurper [King Jean]. From there he rode up to the battlefield by the path just taken by the French and suddenly burst out of hiding, signalling his presence to our men with the noble banner of St George.

The Captal de Buch's appearance behind the French, with his archers shooting into the less well protected sides and rear of the men-at-arms, led to many now fleeing the field. Tradition has it that the final combat took place inside a loop of the Miosson on the Champ d'Alexandre. If so, it may be that the flanking attack by the Captal crossed the river to the south over the Gué de l'Homme, recrossed at the ford further to the west at the Gué de Russon, followed the track north and then turned to come onto the hill. Alternatively, if the final combat, as seems more probable, was taking place further north, on the ground to the west of Croix de la Garde, he may have taken his men across the Gué de Russon, along the track north and then along the re-entrant between les Bordes and la Cadrousse to shield him from the view of the French.

King Jean remained fighting to the last, with his youngest son Philippe at his side shouting warnings: 'Father, look out to your right! Look out to your left!' Among those to fall was Geoffroi de Charny, seen by many of his contemporaries, English and French alike, as the epitome of chivalry, bearing the *Oriflamme*. There was an unseemly scramble to receive the surrender of the king, with many claiming to have taken him, with cries of 'Surrender, surrender, or you are dead!' The king, recognising his position as hopeless, wished to surrender to the prince: 'To whom should I surrender, to whom? Where is my cousin the Prince of Wales? It is to him that I wish to speak.' Froissart records that Denis de Morbek, a knight from Artois who had been exiled from France following a murder committed in his youth and now in the service of Edward III, intervened: 'Sire, he is not here, but surrender to me and I will lead you to him.' Subsequently Bernard de Troyes claimed that it was he who had taken the king prisoner, but in due course King Jean gave testimony that he had surrendered to de Morbek. To all intents and purposes the battle was now won, but the fighting continued as the English pursued the fleeing French, many of whom lost their lives outside the gates of Poitiers which remained closed to them.

It had been a hard-fought battle, and the result had been uncertain throughout much of the day. One chronicler tells us that in the past one could almost always judge the outcome of a battle from the release of the sixth arrow, while at Poitiers when each archer had fired 100 arrows the result remained uncertain. As calm settled over the battlefield the scale of the French losses would become apparent. The prince's account named twenty nobles killed and reported another 2,426 men-at-arms killed, with forty-two senior nobles and a further 1,933 men-at-arms taken prisoner. Attention was rarely given to the losses of those of lower social status, but the letter entitled 'News of the Prince Overseas' from Sir Henry Peverel to the Prior of Winchester refers to 500 common folk captured and 3,300 slain. Many of the senior personages killed and captured are listed with the sources. French sources tend to give lower figures, with one account stating that 800 were killed and 700 captured. Indicative of the ambivalent role of the Church in the medieval period is the capture of the Archbishop of Sens and the death of the Bishop of Châlons fighting with the French. It was not uncommon for there to be a large discrepancy in casualty numbers between the victors and the defeated, with many killed in the rout that often concluded a medieval battle. Nevertheless, reports of English casualties – forty to sixty killed, including four men-at-arms – seem improbably low. However, we have no other means to judge them.

After the battle the prince's army rallied and set about gathering in and tending the wounded. The prince lodged on the battlefield that night. Among the wounded was Sir James Audley, the prince's close associate, who was brought in seemingly near death. The prince is said to have been entertaining the king to dinner when Audley was brought in and he left his guest to tend personally to Audley, raising his morale with the news of the capture of the king. It is said also that the prince waited on the king, and during dinner asked him: 'Fair cousin, if you had taken me today, as by the grace of God I have taken you, what would you have done with me?' The king did not answer, and the prince did not press the point.

Geoffrey Hamelym, a groom in the prince's chamber, was despatched with the tunic and bascinet of King Jean as evidence of his capture, and a messenger was sent with letters. The news was known in England by 10 October, when King Edward gave orders for the proclamation of the victory.

Once again a smaller English army had prevailed over a much larger French force. No doubt the skilful combined arms approach of the English with the mix of archers and dismounted men-at-arms had much to do with it. No doubt also the continuity of service with so many men in the Anglo-Gascon army being old comrades in arms, and also, most unusually, notwithstanding the interlude between the 1355 and 1356 *chevauchées*, having been together for a year, contributed to the discipline that the Anglo-Gascons displayed in the battle. Crécy had started with an ill-disciplined French charge against a disciplined English army, and much the same had happened here with a precipitate charge by the marshals. Perhaps the reported sighting by the French army of an armed and mounted knight flying to and fro in the sky and fighting against them would be seen by some as a reason for the defeat, but many more in France would see it as a result of the cowardice and treachery of much of the nobility of France.

Generalship

Jean and the Black Prince were faced with very different situations in the summer of 1356. The prince had perhaps the most straightforward task, although fraught with risk and danger, as commander of an army with clear objectives: to follow his father's directives, to carry the war to the French with the strategy of the *chevauchée*, to seek battle if the right conditions were present, and if possible to join forces with Edward III and the Duke of Lancaster.

The challenge facing Jean was much more complex. As king, he bore the overall responsibility for defence of his realm as well as command in the field. On the strategic front he faced potential invasions from England and a further raid launched from the English stronghold of Aquitaine. To add to the complex situation, he also had to deal with internal problems. First and foremost there was the rebellion in Normandy as a consequence of his quarrel with the King of Navarre. Furthermore, he had to be prepared to support the somewhat recalcitrant Estates of the Languedoc in the south which, after the Black Prince's incursion of the previous year, had reserved tax revenue in 1356 for defence of their region.

King Jean

At the start of the summer of 1356 the nature of the English threat began to become clearer to King Jean. By mid-June the Duke of Lancaster's expeditionary force was operating in Normandy and the Black Prince's army was reassembling in Aquitaine. It was unclear to the French at this point what the prince would do: would there be a repeat of the Languedoc *chevauchée* of the previous autumn or would the Anglo-Gascons strike north or east? The French were probably also uncertain at this point whether or not Edward III planned to invade in the north, although that would have been a reasonable assumption in view of events in 1355.

The armies of Lancaster and King Jean had come into contact near l'Aigle on 8 July. Lancaster, having failed to tempt Jean into battle in a position favourable to the Anglo-Navarrese army, withdrew to his headquarters in the Cotentin. Jean had seen off one threat, at least for the time being. He was now presented with a choice: wait to see how events unfolded or take the initiative. Taking the initiative implied offensive action to counter the Black Prince. This would leave the king with the risk of Edward III landing in his rear while he was preoccupied with the prince. However, if he could engage and destroy the Black Prince's army before Edward's arrival, and certainly before the armies had had the chance to join forces, this would have greatly increased his chances of overall success. In addition, if he could engage the prince before he set off on campaign, he could minimise the damage to his realm and prevent a further invasion of the Languedoc.

In the event he allowed himself to be drawn into renewing the inconsequential siege of the Navarrese castle of Breteuil. He had sent the Count of Poitiers to Bourges, but this was essentially a precautionary and defensive measure which still left the initiative to his enemies. By late July the situation was becoming clearer. Around 22 July the Black Prince had left La Réole and set off on the short march of around 50km to Bergerac. The target for the prince was now more likely to be the north or east rather than the Languedoc. Shortly thereafter Jean learned that orders had been given on 20 July for an English army to assemble at Southampton for an expedition to France in mid-August. The prince then left Bergerac on 4 August and moved north. Jean would have been aware of this shortly thereafter. Perhaps this was the moment to raise the siege and strike against the prince before Edward III could arrive and deploy his army? In assessing Jean's actions we do not know whether or not the deployment of the Aragonese galleys in the channel in early August was planned to attempt either to deter or to disrupt Edward III's crossing. Perhaps it was simply customary raiding of English shipping and south coast towns which had the fortuitous effect of the cancellation of the king's expedition. However, if the deployment of the Aragonese fleet had been a strategic move, then now would have been the moment to move south to counter the Black Prince. However, Jean remained obsessed with the siege of Breteuil, and it was only on 20 August, when the Black Prince and his army had penetrated well into French territory, that he acted, when he now really had no choice. Certainly until Edward III's threatened invasion had been countered then Jean's hesitance to leave his capital and northern France exposed while he moved south to deal with the prince is perhaps understandable. Nevertheless, this cannot justify his personal obsession with Breteuil. His delay and lack of a strategic plan with a clear aim was a significant deficiency in his preparations for the summer of 1356. He had missed the chance to take offensive action while he could still take the initiative.

Once he had decided to muster his army and move against the Black Prince, however, we see an entirely different commander. Up to the point when the two armies met on the field of battle, Jean pursued an aggressive and well-executed campaign. The Count of Poitiers was recalled to concentrate the French forces for the anticipated engagement of the prince's army. It could be argued that the count could have been deployed to cut off the prince's line of march back to Bordeaux, but that would have risked his defeat by a numerically superior force. Reconnaissance units were sent out to gather intelligence of the prince's movements. The Loire, particularly in view of the heavy rains that had fallen that summer, was a natural line of defence. Jean had clearly recognised the risk to Tours, standing to the south of the river, and had reinforced the town. He had also ordered bridges to be broken, with some being retained but defended to allow the passage of his army. He also appears to have recognised the danger of the Duke of Lancaster's army moving south to join the prince. The bridge over the Loire at Les Ponts de Cé further west was well guarded to prevent Lancaster crossing the river. He had taken appropriate measures to ensure the security of his army and provide the best possible conditions for his planned offensive action. Once he had crossed the Loire, he pursued his objective with determination and moved at considerable speed. When the prince left Montlouis on 11 September, Jean was still north of the Loire but within five days he had overhauled the Anglo-Gascon army. Perhaps the only criticism that can be levelled against the king in this phase is that through neglect of security, his rearguard was ill-prepared when intercepted by the prince.

When the two armies deployed on the battlefield on Sunday, 18 September 1356 the advantages seemed to lie with the French. Jean's army was considerably superior numerically (and the balance of forces was continuing to grow in his favour as more men arrived), the Anglo-Gascons were encumbered by a baggage train which inevitably impeded their potential speed of march if they sought to escape, and the prince's men were short of supplies. The prince had adopted a strong defensive position, but if he were forced to withdraw, he would have to cross the Miosson. There were potential crossing points at the two fords at the Gué de Russon and the Gué de l'Homme and two bridges in the village of Nouaillé-Maupertuis south-east of the battlefield. That Jean did not close at least some of the crossings of the river to restrict the chance of the prince disengaging successfully and channelling the retreating Anglo-Gascon army towards a chosen choke-point was a tactical error. It seems particularly strange that the king did not choose to encircle the prince's army on the Sunday when two options were still under consideration: to starve the Anglo-Gascons into submission or to join them in battle.

On the Sunday there was, as we have seen, discussion between the king and his advisers on the best course of action. If the king's objective was to neutralise the prince's army, then there would have been a great deal of merit in following Vegetius' advice to adopt famine to subdue the Anglo-Gascon army. Vegetius' judgement that fortune can have too great an influence on battle should perhaps have weighed more heavily in the argument, particularly in view of the fact that the prince was recognised as holding a very strong defensive position. In the event Jean was swayed by the opinion of many of his advisers that it was inconceivable that the depredations of the prince's army over the last year should go unpunished. Once more Jean's sense of honour appears to have played a significant role in his decision-making at the expense of military judgement. The king's third son Jean, Count of Poitiers and from 1360 Duke of Berry, drew lessons from Poitiers. In 1415, at the age of 75, he argued that a battle lost was a disaster but a king lost was a catastrophe. His advice that his nephew King Charles VI should not lead the French army at Agincourt prevailed.

Although the decision to fight had been taken, the French did not make the first move and instead of taking the initiative waited for the prince to start to leave his positions. This, however, perhaps had some merit since the Anglo-Gascons would be more vulnerable as they disengaged and moved off. However, to exploit this situation a well-coordinated response was needed. In the event the start of the French action was ill-disciplined and uncoordinated, a strong indication that the prince's withdrawal had been neither anticipated nor planned for. Eustace de Ribemont's advice that the dismounted men-at-arms should follow quickly on foot had been overtaken by events with disastrous consequences. A better coordinated initial attack with the dismounted elements of the vanguard following closely behind the marshals would probably have resulted in a better start, instead of the destruction of the cavalry squadrons and the loss of the constable and both marshals. Similarly, if the other divisions had moved more swiftly to the attack, denying the prince's army any respite, the French could well have won the day through force of numbers. Certainly a cardinal principle of war – 'concentration of force' – had been ignored. Sun Tzu's axioms concerning the dangers of attacking uphill and pursuit of an army simulating flight had also been ignored by Jean, but perhaps the greatest weakness in Jean's conduct of the battle was a complete lack of command and control.

The Black Prince

The prince's preparations for the summer of 1356 started early in the year. Orders were issued in February for 1,000 bows, 2,000 sheaves of arrows and 400 gross of bowstrings, and in March Edward III authorised the levy of 600 archers as reinforcements. We do not have precise figures for losses during operations in the Languedoc the previous year, but they seem to have been low. These reinforcements arrived in Bordeaux on 19 June along with the bows, bowstrings and arrows as well as additional horses and victuals. The additional archers ensured that the army was better pre-pared for battle and offensive action with the prospect of battle with the French. The additional supplies and horses show a clear appreciation of the importance of ensuring the sustainability of the army. Bows, arrows and bowstrings could not be replaced once the army had moved into French territory. As in 1355, the preparations of the prince and his advisers were methodical and thorough.

Once on the march the prince kept his primary objective clearly in mind: battle with the French, either the Count of Poitiers near Bourges or Jean. His avoidance of the risk of casualties and the expenditure of arrows in bypassing Brantôme, his apparently negotiated passage of Nontron, the crossing of the Vienne at the ford of Manot rather than attempting to take by force the bridges at Chabanais or St-Junien, and the decision not to attempt to take by force the castle at Châteauroux all demonstrate his determination to maintain the aim. The siege and capture of Romorantin was at first sight a departure from this policy. However, if, as seems prob-able, the objective was to tempt Jean to come to the town's rescue, then it shows the prince's ability to adapt his plans while remaining consistent with maintenance of the aim.

Once it had become clear to the prince that a crossing of the Loire would not be possible, then his movements as he withdrew to the south were prudent measures to ensure the security of his army, but at the same time he kept open his options for offensive action and for cooperation with Lancaster until it became clear that the duke's army could not meet him. Once at Châtellerault he could have sought to avoid the French as they gathered in the vicinity of Poitiers. Instead he opted for a bold stroke, taking offensive action with a surprise attack on the French rear-guard. One aspect of the phase of the operation after leaving the Loire which gave the prince problems was maintaining sustainability of victuals. The presence of large numbers of French troops in the vicinity would have restricted opportunities for sending out foraging parties, and also the French themselves would have been competing for supplies. This defici-ency was a critical factor in the prince's decision to withdraw on the morning of Monday, 19 September.

In preparing for the anticipated battle the prince followed the well proven tactics developed by Edward III. He adopted a strong defensive position on higher ground than the French, and arrayed his men-at-arms on foot with the intention of enticing Jean to attack his position. It seems, in contrast to the divided views among Jean's advisers, that there was no dissent among the Anglo-Gascon leadership. In part this may have been because the choice between battle and surrender was stark. The decision to withdraw would also have been inevitable once the French stayed put on the Monday morning. Disengaging from the enemy in close contact is a dangerous and challenging manoeuvre. Vegetius advises that 'the enemy must also be prevented from noticing your retreat and attacking at once'. With the two armies in sight of each other, the prince could not achieve this in totality. However, using the lie of the land as cover, the vanguard and his reserve division were able to start moving off without immediate detection, thus gaining some precious time – time which was, perhaps, instrumental in triggering the precipitous attack of the French cavalry.

There was a strong contrast between the ill-coordinated French attack and the disciplined response of the Anglo-Gascon army once it needed to regroup and hold its ground. It is evident that there was effective command and control, with appreciation of the lack of effectiveness of the archers engaging Marshal d'Audrehem's cavalry and their redeployment by the Earl of Oxford. Similarly, at the crucial moment of the battle, when the fourth of the French divisions advanced on the exhausted Anglo-Gascon army, the Black Prince was still capable of appreciating the situation, taking critical decisions and exercising effective command and strong leadership. It is unlikely that the deployment of the Captal de Buch with mounted men-at-arms and archers was pre-planned, yet it was well judged to deal the decisive blow of the battle and demonstrated the prince's ability to adapt to the situation in the heat of battle. This small force of 160 men had a disproportionate effect: an example of economy of effort. Importantly, the prince was shrewd enough a commander to recognise that the morale of his exhausted men was fragile and that the movement of the Captal de Buch and his men could be misconstrued and lead to the army being routed. By seizing the initiative and calling on his men to advance towards the enemy, he would have taken the minds of the less resolute off the fact that the battle hung in the balance. Since the prince's senior commanders had been with him for more than a year, and many had served with him before, the strong sense of team spirit and the morale founded on success over many months and the resulting self-confidence must have played a strong part in the unity of command.

* * *

The critical difference between King Jean and the Black Prince was their exercise of command and control. Jean lost control from the outset, while the prince was able to maintain effective control throughout the fighting.

Chapter 9

The Battle of Nájera
1367

Background

As we saw in Chapter 1, the Black Prince was not overly enthusiastic about the prospect of leading an army into Spain to help restore Pedro the Cruel to the throne of Castile. He distrusted and disliked Pedro and was rightly wary of the allegiance of Charles, King of Navarre. The Kingdom of Navarre was largely in northern Spain, with Pamplona its capital, but included part of modern France north of the Pyrenees. The route to Castile from Aquitaine necessitated safe passage through Navarre by way of the Pyrenees. Similarly, secure lines of communication back to Aquitaine required at least the neutrality of Charles of Navarre. The prince's mistrust of both Pedro and Charles was well placed, but he recognised the political importance to his Principality of Aquitaine and to England of Castile being a friendly neighbour rather than being allied to France. Whatever his personal reservations, he was also obedient to the wishes of his father. Thus in February 1367 he set out on the campaign which was to result in his last great victory but was to prove disastrous for both his health and the future of Aquitaine.

The army that the prince gathered for his expedition to Castile was drawn from a variety of sources. There were English and Welsh troops already stationed in Aquitaine, reinforcements brought from England by the prince's younger brother John of Gaunt, men serving under Gascon barons, and bands of English, Breton and Gascon *routiers* (some of whom had only recently fought for Henry of Trastamara, Pedro's half-brother who had taken his throne), Hainaulters led by Eustace Daubriggecourt, who had fought with the Anglo-Gascons at Poitiers, Castilians loyal to Pedro, a mixed band of exiled Spaniards, and Aragonese with the Count of Orsana and the exiled King James of Majorca. Among the Gascon barons were men such as Jean, Count of Armagnac, who had been enemies in the past but, since the Treaty of Brétigny, now owed allegiance to the Black Prince as Prince of Aquitaine.

As is so often the case when trying to assess the strength of medieval armies, it is difficult to determine the size of the respective forces. Chroniclers give widely varying figures. Of the chronicles the two most comprehensive and contemporary accounts are, for the Castilian side, by Pedro López de Ayala, standard bearer for the Spanish Order of the Sash, and, for the Anglo-Gascon side, by Chandos Herald. Both of these men were present at the battle but unfortunately their figures do not tally. Chandos Herald tells us that there were 30,000 men in the prince's army, while Ayala gives us a figure of 7,000. The former figure would have been a very large army for the period, and 7,000, not dissimilar in size to the army of around 6,000 men that the prince took on campaign in 1355 and 1356, seems more plausible. This army, which with non-combatants was perhaps 10,000 strong, gathered at Dax in the foothills of the Pyrenees in January 1367.

Henry was poorly placed to confront this formidable army, which the French king Charles V described as containing 'the flower of the chivalry of the world'. He had paid off much of the army which had put him on the throne the year before, although he had retained Bertrand du Guesclin and some 1,000 men and the Englishman Hugh Calveley with 400 men-at-arms and some archers. On the positive side, in the autumn of 1376 the Breton Olivier de Mauny had brought a company of Bretons to support Henry. Numerically, if Ayala is to be believed, Henry had perhaps 4,500 men-at-arms and cavalry and an unspecified number of infantry. Thus, the armies may well have been similar in size and it is possible that the Black Prince had a slight numerical superiority. On the quantitative side, the Anglo-Gascons had an advantage. Over recent years armour had developed more rapidly in northern Europe and the men-at-arms with the prince were in general better protected than their adversaries, with the exception of those of French and Breton origin. In addition, the lightly armed Castilian cavalry were well suited to the type of combat prevalent in Spain but were ill equipped to face heavy northern European cavalry, let alone English archers with the formidable longbow. Few in the Castilian army, other again than the French and Bretons in Henry's service, had experience of facing the English longbow. This was a factor which was to prove important for the outcome of the battle. Henry also faced a further problem: the Aragonese in his service were likely to rebel if Pedro returned to Castile. Henry also faced problems with the loyalty of those ostensibly in his camp. He could certainly not count on Hugh Calveley once the Black Prince mobilised his army. Even the loyalty of his own household troops became doubtful when his ability to pay them was exhausted.

The obvious course of action for Henry was to prevent the Black Prince from crossing the Pyrenean passes, which could be held by a relatively small number of men, and thus thwart the invasion before it had started. Thus, in late December 1376 Henry met Charles, King of Navarre, at the town of Santa Cruz de Campezo on the border between Navarre and Castile. The ever duplicitous Charles, fearful of the consequences if the prince failed to restore Pedro to the throne, sold his soul to Henry for the cession of the frontier town of Logroño and a small sum of cash. With this deal secured, and keen to reduce the expense of maintaining his army, Henry felt confident enough to dispense with the service of many of his Bretons and also of the company of Hugh Calveley. This proved to be a fatal error: with immediate effect Calveley could now be counted on by the Black Prince. The latter, less than pleased by Charles's duplicity, instructed Hugh to invade Navarre to remind the king of his commitments in the Treaty of Libourne, which he had signed only a few months previously. Advancing rapidly from Castile, Hugh Calveley took a number of towns and was within 30km of the Navarrese capital of Pamplona when Charles saw the error of his ways. He sent an emissary to the prince at Dax disavowing his agreement with Henry and promising to keep the Pyrenean passes open for the prince's army. The stage was now set for the start of the campaign.

The Campaign

With the pass across the Pyrenees secure, the Black Prince's army started to move across the mountains into Spain. The route taken was from St-Jean-Pied-du-Port across the Col de Bentarté at an altitude of 1,300m, descending through the pass of Roncevalles, scene of the legendary last stand of Charlemagne's rearguard and the death of Roland in 787, into the plains of Navarre beyond. This was a risky undertaking in the depths of winter, which probably explains why the army crossed in three divisions on successive days rather than as a single unit. On Monday, 14 February 1367 the vanguard under the command of John of Gaunt and Sir John Chandos set out. The centre with the Black Prince, Pedro and Charles of Navarre followed the next day, and the rearguard under James of Majorca and Jean d'Armagnac followed on the Wednesday. The crossing of the first two divisions was carried out in atrocious conditions of snow and ice, with men and horses suffering greatly. The rearguard appears to have had milder weather, but nevertheless the march would have been arduous. The army assembled at the Navarrese capital of Pamplona, and was able to take advantage of plenteous supplies in relatively friendly territory.

Charles of Navarre had been as good as his word in that he had accompanied the Black Prince across the Pyrenees and had contributed 300 men-at-arms. However, as usual he had hedged his bets. He had no wish to be involved in the fighting to come and had cooked up a plot to be ambushed by the Breton Olivier de Mauny and held until the war was concluded. Needless to say no one was fooled by this stratagem and Charles was treated with derision across Europe.

When news of Charles's return to the Anglo-Gascon fold and the arrival of the Black Prince in Navarre reached Henry, he hastily set up his headquarters at Santo Domingo de la Calzada, about 40km from the frontier with Navarre. Bertrand du Guesclin and a number of French *routier* captains were summoned to join the Castilian army, but they brought with them probably only some 1,000 men-at-arms, others being left behind to defend Aragon. A number of Aragonese followed. Faced with a powerful and experienced enemy army, Henry initially wisely elected to conduct a campaign of harassment of foraging and scouting parties. The objective was to force the withdrawal of the Black Prince for want of supplies.

The Nájera Campaign.

Henry was an experienced soldier and he probably concluded himself that this was the best strategy. However, he had also been advised by Charles V of France, conscious of the disastrous defeats suffered by his grandfather at Crécy and his father at Poitiers, to avoid pitched battle with the Black Prince. Du Guesclin also urged him to do likewise.

The Black Prince's objective, as it had been for Henry the year before, was the town of Burgos, capital of the ancient County of Castile. To reach the town he needed to cross the river Ebro. The Ebro is a substantial river and at its height in the spring as melting snow runs in from the mountains. Chandos Herald described the river as being swift and fierce in 1367, and fording the river would have been at best problematic. The most logical route to reach his objective would have been to cross the Ebro by the bridge at the frontier town of Logroño, which was in the hands of men loyal to Pedro, and take the pilgrim road towards Santiago de Compostela through Santo Domingo de la Calzada. A scouting party sent out under the command of Sir Thomas Felton joined forces with Sir Hugh Calveley near Logroño, which tends to support the idea that the Black Prince did indeed initially intend to follow this route.

However, instead he elected to take a more northerly route through Basque territory and the Castilian town of Vitoria-Gasteiz, with the intention of crossing the Ebro at Miranda de Ebro and then moving on to Burgos. This route took him through mountainous countryside which was sparsely populated and poorly cultivated, with the result that fodder was difficult to find. On the higher ground the army was also exposed to more adverse winter weather. It is impossible to say with certainty why the Black Prince opted for this route. It has been suggested that he may have chosen this route because after Charles of Navarre's latest trick he was uncertain of the security of supply though Navarre and wished to take a route closer to the coast that would facilitate communication with Aquitaine. However, even with this northern route the Black Prince's army was still more than 50km from the nearest port, and supply overland from the coast would have required the diversion of substantial numbers of men to protect baggage trains crossing difficult terrain. In addition, the strength of the army should have meant that taking supplies, by force if necessary, in western Navarre would not have been too great a challenge. It may be that he took this route because he hoped to outflank Henry and take him by surprise. However, the Black Prince was an experienced soldier accompanied by many competent advisers. They would surely have appreciated that it was unlikely that the army could pass undetected through Basque and then Castilian territory. With Henry's headquarters at Santo

Domingo de la Calzada, the Castilian army had a shorter route than the prince, some 50km, to reach Vitoria-Gasteiz. If the Black Prince had been hoping to achieve strategic surprise he was to be sorely disappointed. An alternative hypothesis, favoured by the historians L.J. Andrew Villalon and Donald J. Kagay in their comprehensive study of the Nájera campaign, is that the Navarrese guides, on whom the Anglo-Gascon army would have needed to place much reliance, were instructed by the King of Navarre to follow a route that took the Black Prince out of Navarrese territory as quickly as possible. If this is correct, then it would have had the advantage for Charles of avoiding the passage of the Anglo-Gascons through the more prosperous agricultural region of his kingdom. Whatever the reason for the route chosen, the plan was an uncharacteristic blunder on the part of the Black Prince. The result was great difficulty sustaining his army since, in view of the terrain and the season of the year, supplies proved difficult to find on the march. It was only after 65km of the march to Vitoria-Gasteiz that plentiful supplies were found at Salvatierra, which surrendered after minor resistance.

The army rested for several days at Salvatierra and finally reached Vitoria in early March. As the army approached Vitoria, 25km beyond Salvatierra, news reached the Black Prince from Sir Thomas Felton, who had gone on ahead with a scouting party, that there had been a skirmish with Henry's army, which was also converging on Vitoria. If the plan had been to outflank and surprise Henry it had failed. Nevertheless, hopeful of battle, the Black Prince drew up his army in battle order outside Vitoria. Henry was not to be tempted, and opted for harassment of foraging parties with light cavalry.

The Prince then suffered two set-backs as a result of the harassing tactics of Henry and du Guesclin. Henry sent out two mounted companies under the command of his brother Don Tello and the French Marshal d'Audrehem, who after his capture at Poitiers had been released on parole against payment of his ransom. Don Tello was the first to strike, falling upon Sir Hugh Calveley's men who were about to join the Black Prince's army. They were caught by surprise in camp and many were killed in their beds. The baggage train was also badly damaged. Don Tello rode on and fell upon the vanguard of the main army. However, by now John of Gaunt had been wakened by the noise of the attack on Calveley's men and was rallying his division in battle order. The Black Prince and Sir John Chandos had also been alerted and the centre division was coming to John of Gaunt's aid. This was too much for Don Tello and his men and they were driven off. Meanwhile at Ariñez, 6km south-east of Vitoria, Marshal d'Audrehem attacked the company of Sir Thomas Felton, comprising around 400 men-at-arms and archers. They were considerably outnumbered and, despite forming up on high ground where they could not be reached by horsemen, they were eventually overwhelmed. They were all killed or captured, with Sir Thomas among the prisoners. A kinsman of Sir Thomas, Sir William Felton, was among the dead. These two surprise attacks demonstrated a surprising and uncharacteristic lack of attention to security on the part of the prince.

These set-backs were followed by bad weather. In addition, the army was faced with great difficulty in finding supplies, and the longer the army remained stationary, the worse the situation would become. There were two options: to try to press on to Burgos via Mirande de Ebro or to move south to cross the river at Logroño in friendly territory. To attempt to continue towards Burgos across the mountain passes and force a passage of the Ebro at Miranda de Ebro in bad weather in the presence of the enemy and with a serious shortage of supplies would have been foolhardy in the extreme. After remaining near Vitoria for around two weeks the Black Prince decided to withdraw around 22 March and take the road through Logroño. He was no doubt encouraged by reports received earlier from Sir Hugh Calveley and Sir Thomas Felton that this route provided better opportunities to find fodder and provisions.

Villalon and Kagay consider three possible routes back through Navarre, two across the hills and a third retracing the army's outward route from Pamplona. Contemporary accounts are not precise and ambiguous, and arguments can be made for all the routes. Whichever route was adopted, the march was undertaken in harsh conditions. On arriving in southern Navarre the army paused for several days in the vicinity of Viana before turning south-west to reach the frontier at Logroño on 1 April. Meanwhile Henry had moved south via Miranda de Ebro and Haro to block the Black Prince's onward path to Burgos by securing the bridge over the Najerilla at Nájera, a little over 20km to the west of the prince's army.

At Logroño the prince replied to a challenge received from Henry a month before in which, having expressed surprise that the prince should invade his realm, he had asked the prince to indicate the route that he would take in order that they could meet in battle. This was the last thing the prince would have wanted to do at a time when perhaps he still hoped to surprise Henry by taking the northern route via Vitoria. In his belated reply the prince demanded that Henry renounce the crown which he had usurped and in return offered to mediate between him and Pedro. He addressed the letter to the Count of Trastamara. This had the no doubt desired effect of enraging Henry, who replied in insulting terms, addressing the prince as 'Edward Prince of Wales, who call yourself eldest son of the King of England and Prince of Aquitaine'. He continued by accusing the prince of being much attached to vainglory. He proposed that the two sides appoint representatives to select a field of battle. The prince saw this as delaying tactics, and no doubt he wanted to choose the time and place of battle himself.

The following day, 2 April, the Black Prince advanced 10km west to Navarette. Henry's army was 12km further to the west, to the east of Nájera. Behind Henry's army was the river Najerilla. A bridge crossed the river into the town. To the west of the town the ground rises steeply but to the east, where Henry's army was positioned, the ground is flat. Thus, the army had the river Najerilla, the town and high ground behind them and open terrain in front.

Henry had decided to abandon the tactics of harassment and hit and run which had stood him in good stead to date and instead to fight a pitched battle. We cannot be sure of his motives. It is possible that he feared that without a decisive victory his already waning support would disintegrate totally. He may also, much as Jean was at Poitiers, have been driven by a sense of honour that required him to fight; if so, the provocative letter from the Black Prince may well have goaded him to do so.

The Battle of Nájera

If Henry had positioned his men behind the Najerilla they would have been constrained by the town, which is only some 200m wide before the ground rises steeply some 150m above the plain to the east. However, he would have had a strong defensive position which would have proved a significant challenge to the Black Prince. If his objective were simply to stop the Anglo-Gascon army in its tracks and force its withdrawal due to lack of supplies, such a position would have been ideal. However, having chosen to fight, he perhaps feared that the Black Prince would not attempt battle with near numerical parity in the face of such a strong position. He may also have reasoned that his light cavalry would have been of little use in such circumstances. Whatever his reasons, he chose to deploy his army with the river at his back. The exact location of the Franco-Castilian army cannot be determined with certainty. It was, however, certainly astride the road from Logroño orientated to the east to face the anticipated line of approach of the Black Prince. About 3km to the east of Nájera is the minor river Valde. There is no mention of this river in contemporary accounts, and perhaps it was of such little significance that it would neither have been a major obstacle nor offered much protection. Certainly when I saw it at the end of a hot summer it was little more than a trickle running in a narrow gulley. About 10km to the north-east of Nájera, just to the north of the road from Navarette, is a hill rising around 250m above the surrounding plain. This feature was to be exploited by the Black Prince during his approach to Henry's army.

During the night of 2 April 1367 the Castilian army was camped to the east of the river Najerilla with a plentiful supply of water available from the river. At first light the army moved out of camp towards Navarette, probably some kilometres east of Nájera but less than half the distance between the town and Navarette, 14km away. They had an easy march across the open plain. Henry and du Guesclin positioned the most experienced and capable troops in the centre. This multi-national division of Castilians, Aragonese and Franco-Breton mercenaries was drawn up on foot slightly in front of the rest of the army. These men were under the command of du Guesclin with Marshal d'Audrehem and a further French noble, the Bègue de Villaines. The left flank of this division, also dismounted, comprised the elite Castilian knights of the Order of the Sash commanded by Henry's brother Sancho.

On the two flanks of this dismounted body of men were two divisions of Castilian and Aragonese cavalry. These were predominantly light horsemen, although a significant number seem to have been heavily armoured in the north European fashion. In contrast to the familiar armoured knights of the heavy cavalry, the light horsemen carried a light shield, a sword and javelins which could be used either as projectiles or for stabbing at close quarters. In comparison to the men and horses of the heavy north European cavalry, they were poorly protected, wearing at best light chain mail rather than plate armour. Their purpose was not close combat but harassment to try to disrupt formations, followed by a charge when an opportunity arose. They were effective troops in combat against similar lightly armed troops in the kind of skirmishing common in the Iberian Peninsula. As was seen near Vitoria they could also be effective against heavily armoured knights in the right circumstances. However, they were not well equipped to combat heavily armoured dismounted men-at-arms or English archers. The division of cavalry on the left flank was commanded by Henry's younger brother Don Tello, who was not noted for his reliability, despite his success near Vitoria earlier in the campaign. The division on the right, probably more numerous than that on the left, was commanded by the Aragonese nobleman Don Alfonso, Count of Denia.

Henry took command of a further division of mounted men stationed behind du Guesclin's division. The deployment was completed by a large number of infantry, predominantly local levies, who seem to have played little part in the battle to come. There also seem to have been a number of infantrymen equipped with slings, javelins and crossbows. These may have been either positioned on Henry's right or deployed as a skirmish line in front of the mounted cavalry.

While Henry's army broke camp and deployed for battle, the Black Prince's army moved out from Navarette where they had camped for the night. The prince had a surprise in store for Henry and du Guesclin. The obvious route to take was along the pilgrim road which skirted to the south of the higher ground north-east of Nájera. Instead, he marched north-west from Navarette, moving behind the high ground and appearing from an unexpected direction. Henry and du Guesclin now faced the not inconsiderable challenge of manoeuvring their army to face north-east rather than east to avoid being taken in the flank.

As the Anglo-Gascon army approached, the men dismounted and their horses were led away. The vanguard, under the command of the prince's brother John of Gaunt and Sir John Chandos, occupied the centre of the battle formation. Behind him was the main body of the army commanded by the Black Prince. Facing Don Tello on the left of the Castilian army

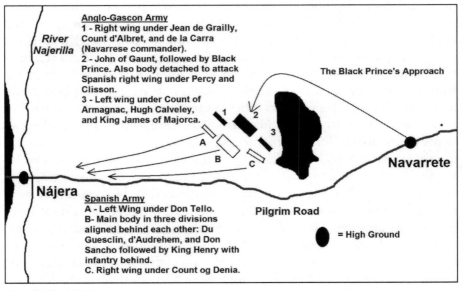

The Battle of Nájera.

was the Anglo-Gascon right wing commanded by the Captal de Buch, the Lord d'Albret and Martin Enriquez de la Carra with his Navarrese troops. The left wing of the prince's army was under the command of the Count of Armagnac, Sir Hugh Calveley and James IV, King of Majorca.

There was a significant difference between this battle and the famous earlier English victories at Crécy in 1346, Poitiers in 1356 and later at Agincourt in 1415. On these occasions the English were badly outnumbered and fought defensive battles once attacked by the French. It is true that at Agincourt the English archers advanced towards the French and shot at the French cavalry to provoke an attack, but the dismounted men-at-arms stood their ground and waited for the French to charge. In addition, this expedition was not a *chevauchée* like the campaigns either of Edward III in 1346 or the Black Prince in 1355 and 1356 where battle was an objective if the right circumstances could be found. In Spain in 1376 the objective was first and foremost to restore Pedro to the throne of Castile. This would almost certainly require battle. At Nájera the situation was different from the other famous English battles in another aspect: the Black Prince's army was not significantly outnumbered; indeed, it may even have had a small numerical advantage. Furthermore, the army was critically short of supplies and matters had to be brought to a head. Chandos Herald's account of a speech by the Black Prince before the battle demonstrates this point graphically: 'Today, Sirs, has no other termination, as you well know, but in famine, for want of food we are well nigh taken. And see here and there our enemies, who have food enough, bread and wine and fish, salt and fresh, from the river and the sea; but those we must now obtain by the dint of sword and spear.' The Black Prince could not wait for Henry to attack.

It is not clear who made the first move. According to Chandos Herald, John of Gaunt launched the first attack against the Castilian centre division with the words: 'Banner, advance, advance! Let us take God to our rescue, and each do his honour.' However, Pedro López de Ayala tells a different story. He recounts that as the armies faced each other, a Castilian contingent broke ranks and went over to Pedro. According to Ayala, Henry, to prevent further defections, started the battle, sending forward light cavalry to attack the Anglo-Gascon left. As the Castilian centre was engaged by John of Gaunt, Henry seems to have wheeled right to attack the Anglo-Gascon left, possibly in part to rally and encourage his men after the initial attack by the Count of Denia's cavalry had been repulsed. He launched a series of unsuccessful cavalry attacks with the combined divisions of the centre and the right under Denia against the English left.

It was in the centre that the most ferocious fighting developed as John of Gaunt's vanguard clashed with du Guesclin and his strong division. It seems that both divisions advanced on each other, possibly on the part of du Guesclin's division in an attempt to neutralise the effectiveness of the English archers, who could not shoot when the two armies were engaged in hand-to-hand combat. With du Guesclin's division offering stout resistance, the Black Prince entered the fray with the main body of his army. Some of the Black Prince's men pushed directly forward to support Gaunt, while others under Lord Percy and Olivier de Clisson moved to their left, extending the English line in the centre and outflanking du Guesclin's men to their right. In contrast to Jean at Poitiers, where he had launched attacks with successive divisions as the preceding division was driven back, here the Prince exercised effective concentration of force.

The critical action, however, occurred on the flanks of the Castilian army. On the left Don Tello waited passively as the Captal de Buch's division advanced on foot. By remaining stationary, they would have been dangerously exposed to shooting by the English archers. But Don Tello not only failed to attack, he also decided to flee the field of battle. Bereft of its leader, the left flank of the Castilian army disintegrated and turned in flight. Some of the Captal's men pursued the fleeing troops to prevent them rallying, while the remainder wheeled left to take the men of the Order of the Sash on the left of du Guesclin's division in the flank. With attacks on both of his flanks, du Guesclin's situation was becoming critical.

On the Castilian right the cavalry under the Count of Denia, now reinforced with Henry's men, fought hard, even charging uphill to the Anglo-Gascon position, attempting to outflank the Count of Armagnac and Sir Hugh Calveley's men and attack the Black Prince's baggage train. During this fighting on the Castilian right a skirmish line of infantry using slings and javelins joined in an unequal contest with English archers. The cavalry fared no better against the shooting of the archers, and after successive attacks on the Anglo-Gascon left had failed, they finally broke and ran from the field. With the divisions on both of the Castilian flanks in flight, it was clear to Henry that the battle was lost. He could expect no mercy if he fell into the hands of Pedro and took flight. It seems that the infantry to the rear took no part in the battle. Henry had failed to concentrate his force and take advantage of all of the men at his disposal. The English archers and the men-at-arms of the Black Prince's army now closed in on du Guesclin's division. These men held out as long as they could and few had the chance to flee. The two principal chroniclers, Ayala and Chandos Herald, are broadly in agreement that up to 500 men-at-arms were killed. Those captured included the principal commanders du Gues-clin, Marshal d'Audrehem, the Bègue de Villaines, Henry's brother Sancho and the Aragonese commander the Count of Denia, who had joined the fight in the centre rather than flee when the right flank broke.

As was so often the case in medieval battles, it was during the rout that many of the casualties occurred. The situation for those fleeing the field at Nájera was particularly unfavourable. In front of them was the river Najerilla, crossed by a single bridge leading into the town. According to Chandos Herald, 7,700 men were slaughtered as they struggled to cross the river. With the steep escarpment rising behind the town, those who did manage to cross the bridge now had no choice but to try to flee along the two roads running north and south. In the inevitable congestion as men were bottled up, more prisoners were taken and a further 1,000 men were reported by Chandos Herald as being killed. The victory was over-whelming.

The Aftermath

The immediate aftermath of the battle was marked by disputes between the Black Prince and Pedro over the treatment of prisoners and the inability, or unwillingness, of the restored King of Castile to pay his debts for the army. The prince, in contrast to Pedro, showed a strong sense of honour towards his prisoners. The Black Prince considered that Marshal d'Audrehem, who had not fully discharged his ransom after his capture at the Battle of Poitiers, was in breach of his associated oath not to take up arms against the prince until he had paid his ransom. He had thus acted dishonour-ably in fighting in the battle. The prince appointed an impromptu court of chivalry to try the case. The court, comprising twelve knights – four English, four Gascon and four Breton – decided in the marshal's favour on the technicality that he had not taken up arms against the prince but against Pedro. The prince accepted their judgment.

In due course, the Black Prince had no option but to withdraw with Pedro's debts unpaid and in late August he crossed the Pyrenees once again to receive a hero's welcome back in Aquitaine. On the personal side, the Black Prince contracted a disease in Spain which was to lead to steadily deteriorating health until his death in 1376. Henry escaped to France and in less than two years returned to Castile with French support. In mid-March 1369 Henry surprised and routed Pedro's army near Montiel. Pedro took refuge in the castle above the town but was lured out of his sanctuary by du Guesclin's promise to help him escape. A hand-to-hand fight between Pedro and Henry followed as the king found that his erstwhile saviours had betrayed him. But Henry was helped by his followers and Pedro was killed. The throne returned to Henry, who was to reign for a further ten years.

The irony of this great victory was that it sowed the seeds for the resumption of the Hundred Years War. The result was the loss of the English gains secured through the Battle of Poitiers and the Treaty of Brétigny. The reason for this was in essence the failure of Pedro to pay for the cost of the campaign. The Black Prince was faced with paying these costs himself, and to do so raised new taxes across the Principality of Aquitaine. These taxes were very unpopular, not least among powerful barons including the Lord d'Albret and the Count of Armagnac. Albret and Armagnac appealed to the French king, Charles V. He summoned the prince to appear in Paris to answer complaints over taxation. This interference in territories ceded by the French at the Treaty of Brétigny was too much for the Black Prince. The French came to the aid of the rebellious Gascons and by 1369 the war was again in full flood.

Generalship

The Black Prince's victory at Nájera secured his reputation as one of the great commanders of the Hundred Years War. That the victory ultimately served as a catalyst for the renewal of the war with France and the reversal of English fortunes and the loss of the gains made during the first phases of the war cannot be laid at his door. This had much more to do with the perfidy of Pedro and his failure to pay the costs of the war as he had agreed.

The test of any campaign is the outcome and the achievement of the aim. The aim in this case was not to conduct a *chevauchée* but to restore Pedro to his throne. In this respect the campaign must be judged a success. However, although the battle was won, this owed much to Henry's strategic error in choosing to fight a set-piece battle, against the advice of those who had more experience of fighting English armies. If Henry had chosen to continue to harass and disrupt the Anglo-Gascon army and its foraging parties, the Black Prince would in all likelihood have found his army in a very precarious position due to a shortage of supplies for horses and men, and it is quite probable that he would have been forced to withdraw.

The timing of the campaign was unusual. Crossing the Pyrenees in winter and then campaigning in northern Spain in adverse weather was far from ideal. This raises the question why did the Black Prince set out at this time of year when he must surely have appreciated the supply problems that this would create? The answer is probably one of necessity rather than choice. Once the army had begun to muster in July 1366, it needed to be paid and also provisioned. The longer he delayed, the more the costs of the expedition would rise. Furthermore, it is possible that he wanted to move out of his principality as quickly as possible to remove the demands on his own population. Additionally, it may have been the case that, having intervened with Hugh de Calveley's men to force Charles of Navarre to reverse his decision of December 1376 to close the Pyrenean passes to the Anglo-Gascon army, he feared further treachery if he did not act promptly to cross the mountains. The army was beset with problems in finding sufficient food throughout the campaign. The victory at Nájera secured much-needed supplies at a time when the army was on the verge of starvation. If Henry had not given battle and lost, the Black Prince could have been faced with either the collapse of his army's morale and its subsequent disintegration or an ignominious withdrawal, having failed in his aim.

A further imponderable is the decision to take the northern route through Vitoria-Gasteiz rather than the direct, well-known pilgrim route towards Burgos. As discussed above, there are several possible reasons why the prince chose this route. Whatever the reason for it, the result was that, by marching through inhospitable terrain with a low population density and little cultivated land, the problems of supply were exacerbated. Furthermore, the prince remained in the vicinity of Vitoria for several weeks despite his army suffering at the hands of the Castilian light cavalry and it being apparent that Henry would not be tempted down from his dominant positions controlling the route to Miranda de Ebro to join the prince in battle. The longer the army remained *in situ*, the further afield the foraging parties needed to roam, increasing their vulnerability to attack. Perhaps this decision to remain near Vitoria reflected either a continuing hope to bring Henry to battle or uncharacteristic indecision on the part of the prince. The overall result of his decisions over timing, route and immobility near Vitoria was that, in contrast to his *chevauchées* of 1355 and 1356, the Black Prince experienced great difficulties in maintaining the sustainability of his army.

Nevertheless, in due course the prince had sufficient flexibility of mind to change his strategy and return to the more direct route along the pilgrim road through Logroño. Once Henry had decided to give battle, the Black Prince's generalship cannot be faulted. He achieved surprise by moving to the north of the high ground to advance unseen until late in the approach to the Castilian army. Despite this approach route, he was able to bring his men into contact with the enemy in good order and concentrate his force to best effect. Although we do not know the precise disposition of the English archers, it is clear that their tactical employment in concert with the men-at-arms had a devastating effect, particularly against the Castilian light cavalry. The character of this battle was different from both the Battle of Crécy and the Battle of Poitiers where the prince had fought previously. On those occasions the English had been significantly outnumbered and had fought defensive battles with the archers shooting at the advancing French. At Nájera the Anglo-Gascon army took the offensive. The prince demonstrated sufficient tactical flexibility to adapt his use of archers to the offensive role. On the debit side, the set-backs near Vitoria when he was taken by surprise by the raids of Don Tello and Marshal d'Audrehem reflect a surprising lack of sense of security for such an experienced commander.

It is probably a reflection of the Black Prince's reputation and leadership that he was able to maintain the morale of his army throughout the campaign, despite the privations of shortages of supplies and adverse weather, to achieve one of the greatest victories of the Middle Ages.

Conclusions

Chapter 3 discussed briefly the principles of war of the Chinese theorist Sun Tzu, the Roman general Vegetius and the modern British armed forces. Common to all these principles is the importance of logistics and the ability to sustain an army. The Black Prince's conduct of the 1355 and 1356 *chevauchées* was generally exemplary in this respect, despite the shortage of supplies being a factor in the prince's decision to attempt to disengage when the anticipated French attack did not materialise on the morning of the Battle of Poitiers. In Spain in 1367, however, the Black Prince's reliance on local provisions in sparsely populated and poorly cultivated countryside in winter nearly resulted in disaster. The corollary of sustaining one's own army is the recognition and exploitation of weaknesses in the enemy situation. At Poitiers Jean had the opportunity to hold the prince in position and prevent his withdrawal, forcing either surrender or a negotiated settlement, but his sense of duty and pride were such that he could not countenance such an approach. In view of the destruction wrought by the Black Prince for almost a year, he took the risk of battle. He ignored Vegetius' stricture that famine is preferable to battle, where fortune can have too great an influence, and which, he believed, should only be fought under great necessity or when the occasion is advantageous. However, sustainability in the English case, with their reliance on archers, also included an effective system for manufacture and resupply of arrows, bows and bowstrings. This system was proven between the 1355 and 1356 *chevauchées* of the Black Prince. The English also had the capacity to provide reinforcements, another element of sustainability, for the prince during the spring of 1356, despite the simultaneous demands for Edward III and the Duke of Lancaster.

Surprise is also a common and long-established principle of war. This was notable in strategic terms in 1355 in the Black Prince's crossing of the Garonne and the Ariège, where he completely wrong-footed the Count of Armagnac. At Nájera in 1367 he exploited the terrain to achieve tactical surprise. In the prelude to Poitiers he achieved surprise by intercepting the French rearguard on the march, exemplifying Sun Tzu's principle that where speed is of the essence, it may be necessary to separate a flying column from the baggage train.

The importance of knowledge of the country in which the army is operating is essential for any commander. Operating internally, Jean II and his advisers would have had such information readily to hand during all of his operations. The Black Prince's advisers, particularly the Gascons, had some knowledge of the lands of Gascony beyond the extant and often fluid borders of Aquitaine, but in addition the prince made extensive use of scouts and guides during his 1355 *chevauchée*. His difficulties in the early part of his 1367 campaign in Spain may have owed something to a lack of knowledge of northern Spain among his senior staff and to duplicity on the part of guides provided by Charles of Navarre.

There are a number of Sun Tzu's axioms which came into play in the Battle of Poitiers concerning the dangers of attacking uphill, pursuit of an army simulating flight, and falling for bait offered by an enemy. Jean ignored the dangers of attacking uphill. The prince was probably genuinely attempting to disengage from the French, but the outcome was similar to a simulated flight to the extent that Jean allowed an uncoordinated attack on the withdrawing Anglo-Gascon army.

Selection and maintenance of the aim is the master principle of war for the British armed forces. A single, clearly defined, commonly understood and unambiguous aim is the key to successful military operations. The historian H.J. Hewitt, when considering the Black Prince's *chevauchée* of 1355, wrote: 'that this campaign lacked a strategic plan is largely true, but it is also a truism of all warfare in the fourteenth century'. This is difficult to square with the planning of campaigns by Edward III and his chosen use of the *chevauchée* to achieve his objectives. As Mollie M. Madden points out, the indenture of the Black Prince given to him by Edward III before his expedition to France in 1355–56 laid out his strategic objectives in general terms and a letter from the king addressed to the prince before he set out was explicit: 'for the reformation of the situation and control of our Duchy of Aquitaine and other lands and places in our Kingdom of France, and for the recovery of our lands and rights, which have been wrongly occupied by our rebellious subjects'. Similarly, the king himself set out clearly his strategic objectives during the Crécy campaign of 1346 in a letter to King Philippe VI.

King Jean and his advisers, on the other hand, lacked a strategic vision of how to counter simultaneous threats. He was also indecisive in terms of tactics and even on the eve of battle with the Black Prince near Poitiers in

1356 was still uncertain whether to attempt to destroy the Anglo-Gascon army or force its surrender through famine.

The Black Prince's 1367 Nájera campaign was different in nature to a *chevauchée*, where battle was a goal but not the only measure of success. In 1367 the goal was not plunder and destruction but defeat of the Castilians to restore the throne to Pedro. Throughout his operations the Black Prince did not allow himself to be diverted from his aims. However, although selection and maintenance of the aim is a primordial principle of war, it proved to be a weakness on the part of Jean who stuck stubbornly to his tactical aims to take Aiguillon in 1346 and Breteuil in 1356. He should have recognised that these sieges were of relatively little importance compared with the greater aim of at best defeating and at least neutralising large enemy armies which presented a much greater threat than the small garrisons of a minor castle and small, albeit strategically important, town.

Maintenance of morale is a timeless principle of war. Dissatisfied or demoralised soldiers cannot be expected to fight well. Many, or indeed perhaps all, in the army led by the Black Prince in 1355–56 would have been driven in part by the goal of personal enrichment through booty and ransoms, but nevertheless it is clear that he was an inspirational leader. Over the year that his army had been together a strong sense of cohesion had clearly been established, in part due to the success of the 1355 *chevauchée*. This was critical to the army holding together at the moment of crisis during the Battle of Poitiers when to many it seemed that they were about to be overwhelmed by King Jean's final attack on the exhausted Anglo-Gascons. He was conscious of the fragility of his men's morale at this moment and personally rallied his men to lead them into an attack on Jean's division as he sent the Captal de Buch on his flanking manoeuvre to take the French army in the rear. Poor logistic support leading to a shortage of food and water for men and horses can be expected to have an adverse impact on morale, and it is perhaps a strong indication of the Black Prince's leadership that the morale of his army held together sufficiently well in adverse conditions to secure victory in the battle at Nájera. Jean also seems to have been capable of inspiring his men, but during his greatest test at Poitiers his army disintegrated. Perhaps this had much to do with detachments continuing to arrive on the eve of battle and with his army not having had the chance to develop a cohesive sense of purpose through serving together.

Both Jean and the Black Prince recognised the importance of offensive action to gain advantage, sustain momentum and seize the initiative. This was the essence of the *chevauchée*, with the Black Prince's deep penetration of enemy territory forcing the French to react to his manoeuvring rather than take the initiative. He also took offensive action in the interception of the French rearguard before Poitiers and in his attack on the Castilian army at Nájera. Jean also successfully exploited offensive action in his pursuit and successful interception of the Anglo-Gascon army before Poitiers.

Security was important to medieval armies, particularly when operating in enemy territory. The *chevauchée* was vulnerable to harrying of scouting and foraging parties and if, as in the case of the Crécy campaign, the French were in close pursuit, this could present a serious risk. In Spain in 1367 the Black Prince's foraging parties were vulnerable to Spanish light cavalry. Uncharacteristically, poor security in Spain was evident in the surprise attacks by Don Tello and Marshal d'Audrehem when the army was near Vitoria.

Concentration of force to maximise combat effectiveness was equally important to medieval combat as today. The ill-coordinated French attack on the Anglo-Gascon army at Poitiers meant that King Jean II was unable to concentrate his force and exploit to the full his considerable numerical superiority. In contrast, the Black Prince brought all his forces into play at Nájera, while the infantry in Henry's army were not brought into action.

The principle of economy of effort, judiciously exploiting manpower, materiel and time in relation to achieving objectives, was in the medieval period perhaps more applicable at the strategic level. However, it can be seen at the operational level in the Black Prince's operations of 1355–56. This was exemplified in 1355 with his detachment of the rearguard away from the line of march of the bulk of the army to sack the important town of Limoux. In 1356 we see a similar application of this principle with the rearguard advancing to the east of the main line of advance of the army before rejoining the middle-guard and vanguard on the approach to the Loire.

Flexibility in military operations is the ability to change readily to meet new circumstances. The Black Prince was able to adapt to a considerable change of circumstances when it became clear in September 1356 that the planned rendezvous with armies led by Edward III and the Duke of Lancaster would not be possible. At the Battle of Poitiers he also had the flexibility, and presence of mind, to recognise the precarious position of his army as it faced the attack of Jean's fourth division. His decision to send the Captal de Buch on a flanking manoeuvre with mounted men-at-arms and archers proved decisive. In the Spanish campaign, although he could be criticised for taking some time to reach his decision, he was sufficiently flexible to change his plan when it became apparent that he could not achieve his aim by remaining near Vitoria. Perhaps in the circumstances he had little choice, but at the tactical level he was also flexible in adopting an offensive approach at Nájera, in contrast to the defensive posture which was the preferred concept of operations for English armies of the period and which had brought success at Crécy and Poitiers.

The importance of cooperation is reflected in the British principles of war. This embraces teamwork and a sharing of dangers, burdens, risks and opportunities in war. When the Black Prince embarked on his expedition of 1355–56, he was given an experienced team of subordinate commanders, many of whom had served with him on the Crécy campaign of 1346. It is clear that these men, and the Gascon barons who joined his army, recognised the need for cooperation. In contrast, disputes between the advisers to King Jean II, in particular between his two marshals Clermont and Audrehem, not only on the eve of the Battle of Poitiers but also as battle was joined, demonstrated a serious lack of understanding of the need for cooperation.

What conclusions can be drawn on the relative merits of the Black Prince and King Jean II? Jean's military career, and indeed his reign, was marked indelibly by his disastrous defeat at Poitiers. His two major sieges were also marked by failure. In contrast, the Black Prince had one of the most successful military careers of the period. The victory at Poitiers was due in large part to his tactical sense, personal leadership, coolness and presence of mind under great pressure, the maintenance of effective command and control in the confusion of battle, and the ability to respond flexibly to changing circumstances. It has been argued that he owed much to the quality of the senior commanders with him. This may be true, but it says much for his qualities as a leader and commander that he was able to maintain the cohesion of these men without apparent dissent. In contrast, Jean's senior commanders were unable to suppress their personal differences. The Black Prince's campaign in Spain came close to failure, and a more astute commander than Henry may well have been able to defeat the prince without recourse to battle. However, once again the cohesion of his army, despite the privations it had suffered and the set-backs near Vitoria, won the day. In the end, results speak for themselves.

Sun Tzu drew attention to what he considered five dangerous faults in a general: recklessness which leads to destruction; cowardice which leads to capture; a hasty temper which can be provoked by insults; delicacy of honour sensitive to shame; and over-solicitude for his men. Jean II can certainly not be accused of either cowardice or over-solicitude for his men. However, his character was marked by a hasty temper and a sense of honour that overrode other considerations. In view of the significant numerical superiority of his army at Poitiers, it would be stretching a point to argue that his attack was reckless. Nevertheless, his decision to attack was certainly influenced by those of his advisers who argued that to do otherwise would be an affront to his honour as king after all the destruction wrought by the Black Prince during the preceding year. At Aiguillon and Breteuil he continued to maintain the sieges for too long due to his sense of honour and pride prevailing over more important strategic considerations. However, despite his failings in the field, Jean did recognise the need for military reform and with his ordonnances of 1351 and proposals for a permanent army in 1363 paved the way for subsequent reforms which contributed to the final expulsion of the English from France almost 100 years later.

The Black Prince was also a man of considerable personal courage and was honourable within the standards of his time, as shown by his attitude towards what he saw as the excesses of Pedro the Cruel, and his acceptance of the judgment of the court of chivalry after the Battle of Nájera which ruled against him and in favour of Marshal d'Audrehem. He could be hasty of temper, as at Poitiers when he ordered the decapitation of the Châtelaine d'Emposte after his capture. However, he was open to persuasion and accepted Sir John Chandos' argument that to do so would be dishonourable. He was a bold commander, ready to take risks, but could not be described as reckless. The rewards granted to many after Poitiers, even to some of humble birth, demonstrate that he recognised the contribution of others, but this was not over-solicitude for his men. He clearly expected loyalty and courage from those who served in his armies but gave the appropriate recognition. Overall, he was a pragmatic commander.

The Location of the Poitiers Battlefield

The chronicler Jean Froissart tells us that the battle took place 'somewhat close to Poitiers in the fields of Biauvoir [*sic*] and Maupertuis', and 'in the fields of Maupetruis [*sic*] two leagues from Poitiers'. Biauvoir is unambiguous: it is the small settlement of Beauvoir, 8km south-east of Poitiers, close to Froissart's 'two leagues'. Maupertuis has been the subject of debate over the years, hinging on whether this was a place or a description. It has been suggested that Maupertuis was the current farm of la Cardinerie, 1.5km to the west of Beauvoir, based on a concession which passed land named Maupertuis to a Richard Delyé, known as Cardin, in 1495. However, this is not conclusive and Maupertuis may have been a description of a place rather than a proper noun. It has been asserted that Maupertuis means 'bad road', and that this description was applied to the minor road running from north to south to the west of the woods at Nouaillé. Unfortunately it is not quite as clear-cut as that, with *pertuis* having a variety of meanings in Ancient and Middle French, including a hole, hollow, den, hiding place or passage. Thus, although the description Maupertuis can conveniently be applied to the road, it could equally well be applied elsewhere.

In the nineteenth century there were reported to be a number of local names – *le champ de la bataille, la masse* (mound) *aux Anglais* and *l'abreuvoir* (watering place) *aux Anglais* – in the vicinity of la Cardinerie and the settlement of les Bordes to the south. Unfortunately these names are on neither modern maps nor cadastral plans going back to Napoleonic times and they do not help to locate the battlefield. It has also been claimed that archaeological finds were made in the area in the eighteenth and nineteenth centuries, including jewellery said to belong to King Jean found near la Cardinerie. There were also said to be signs of defence works still visible in the nineteenth century. Even if all this information were correct it would give us little useful help, since the places mentioned are dispersed across a wide area.

The chronicle *Eulogium Historiarum* gives us a brief description of the English position as being near a dense wood with pasture lands and glades

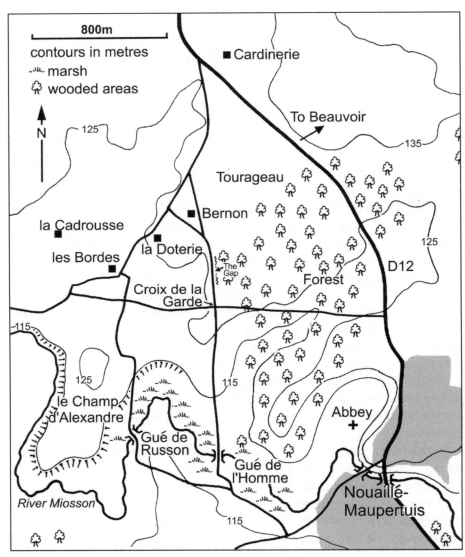

The Poitiers Battlefield.

with a ditch, surmounted by a high thorn hedge. This hedge was described as having one gap, wide enough for only four men-at-arms to pass at a time. This is too general to be of any great help, other than the proximity to a dense wood, possibly that to the west of the abbey of Nouaillé.

According to Jean Froissart's account, on the Sunday King Jean sent forward four knights to reconnoitre the prince's position, with Eustace de

Ribemont credited with making the report to the king. On his return he was asked by the king: 'And how do they lie?' This is said to have been Ribemont's description of the English position:

Sire, they are in a very strong position, and we can see and imagine that they are prepared for battle, very well and very cleverly arrayed. They have taken the length of a road well fortified with hedges and bushes, and have lined this hedge, from one end to the other, with their archers such that one cannot enter, nor ride in the road, save being among them if one wants to take this road or fight them. This hedge has only one way in and out, where only four men-at-arms could ride abreast, and the same goes for the road. At the end of this hedge, where one can neither go nor ride, are their men-at-arms, all on foot, and they have put in front of them archers in the manner of a harrow. It is very well organized it seems to us, for whoever wants or is able to come up to them by feat of arms, will not be able to do so save among the archers who will not be easy to defeat.

Although this places emphasis on a road and hedges, it does not give us enough information on its own to determine the location of the Anglo-Gascon deployment. The chronicler Galfridi le Baker gives the most detailed description:

he [the prince] perceived that there was near-by on one side a hill, encircled with hedges and ditches on the outside, but with different land inside, on one side a pasture thick with thorn bushes, but on the other side sown with vines, and the rest of it arable land. And in the arable part of it he thought a French column lay. Between us and the hill was a broad deep valley, and a marsh which was fed by a certain stream. At a fairly narrow ford the prince's column crossed the stream, with its wagons, and coming out of the valley across ditches and hedges occupied the hill, where amid the thickets they were easily hidden by the natural fortification of the place, which lay higher than the enemy. The field in which our first and second columns lay was separated from the open ground which the French occupied by a long hedge with a ditch on the far side, one end of which fell away into the marsh aforementioned. The earl of Warwick, commander of the first column, held the slope going down to the marsh. In the upper part of the hedge, a good way from the slope, was a certain large gap or hiatus, which carters made in the autumn, distant a stone's throw from which lay our third company, which the Earl of Salisbury commanded. The enemy, seeing the standard of the prince, previously visible, but now starting to move and to be hidden from their eyes by the slope of the hill, thought that he was trickling away ...

Although Baker talks of 'a broad deep valley' and 'a hill', these terms can give a distorted impression of the terrain. There are valleys and hills, but this is not hilly countryside and land features are of a modest nature. The maximum change of elevation across the whole battlefield area is no more than 35m.

The most distinctive features in the description given by Baker are the 'fairly narrow ford' and the 'marsh'. The 'fairly narrow ford' could be either the Gué de l'Homme, on the road north to the west of the forest, or the Gué de Russon, crossed by the track towards les Bordes. From the Gué de Russon to the east, following the bend in the river, is an area of very marshy land, with a steep bank rising to the north. It is tempting to assume that this was the extent of the marsh at the time of the battle, but even after a prolonged spell of dry weather the ground further round towards the Gué de l'Homme is wet under foot. Indeed, seeing the Miosson today, particularly after a period of dry weather, gives a very misleading picture. It is only about 5m wide, slow running, and meanders gently on its way. However, heavy rain can dramatically change the character of the river, and as recently as 1982 the modern road bridge was carried away by flood water. It is likely that in the wet conditions experienced in the summer of 1356 the marsh extended out as much as 150m from the river in places, mainly on the northern side, and from west of the Gué de Russon to well to the east of the Gué de l'Homme.

The historian A.H. Burne sets out an alternative view of the location of the marsh and suggests that there was a minor watercourse and marshy area in the re-entrant near the settlements of la Cadrousse and Bernon. There is now no trace of a watercourse here, but the nature of the vegetation certainly indicates that it could be marshy in wet periods. He concludes that the army was deployed behind a hedge, orientated along a track running across the north-west edge of the area called Tourageau, with its left flank anchored on the marsh, and the right flank protected by trenches and wagons. It is difficult to see how this squares with other elements of Baker's description, including the 'broad deep valley' and the hill occupied by the prince's column which 'lay higher than the enemy', or indeed a ford in the vicinity unless the now absent watercourse was once much more significant. Also, Burne's location of the prince's army places the gap in the hedge described in Baker on the axis of the current

D12 road to Nouaillé. This does not fit with the statement that the gap was opened by carters in the autumn, which implies that the gap was opened in a hedge alongside a road to allow access into either the forest for wood gathering or cultivated land at harvest time. The case for the marsh and the deployment of the armies being where Burne suggested is not convincing.

Although the *Eulogium Historiarum* mentions dense woods, Baker does not refer to the woods at Nouaillé. This may have been because their extent and nature have changed since the fourteenth century and that at the time this was an area of thickets of bushes and young trees and not the mature woodland we see more than 600 years later. The absence of comment on the woods might tend to support the case for the view being from the Gué de Russon, but equally there are substantial woodlands to the west and south of the Champ d'Alexandre which we might have expected Baker to mention if this were the location and we cannot draw conclusions from this absence of evidence. It is possible to visualise the description given by Baker from both fords. From the vicinity of the Gué de Russon he would have seen the hill with Champ d'Alexandre about 1km distant, and if this is the view that the prince saw, then we could envisage the army deployed near the Champ d'Alexandre, facing north-east across the throat of the large loop in the Miosson. The weakness with this position is that there are steep banks around the spur, which would make it a dangerous position if the army were pushed back by a French attack or the prince sought to withdraw as he did. Although today the slopes are obscured by trees, the line of the road south from les Bordes which traverses the contours is evidence of the difficult nature of the slope. A better position can be found looking back to the north from south of the river somewhere near the Gué de l'Homme. From here the prince would have looked across the valley of the Miosson and seen rising ground, stretching away for about 1.5km to the north and a hill, more properly a spur coming out from the higher ground to the north-east, near Croix de la Garde. If this were his view, then the deployment could have been along the axis of the road to the west of the woods at Nouaillé, possibly Jean Froissart's 'length of a road well fortified with hedges and bushes'. It would be easier to disengage from such a deployment than from the Champ d'Alexandre, and there would not be the same risk of being driven back to steep slopes. There is also more space for manoeuvre here. The last sentence of Baker's description relating to the opening moves of the battle – 'The enemy, seeing the standard of the prince, previously visible, but now starting to move and to be hidden from their eyes by the slope of the hill' – is also consistent with the prince's viewpoint being near the Gué de l'Homme since the ground to the east of the road falls away and would have obscured part of the view of the French of the Anglo-Gascon army. On balance I believe this to be the more probable location for the prince's army.

Notes

Chapter 1: Edward of Woodstock, 'The Black Prince'

There are several excellent biographies of the Black Prince: Richard Barber's *Edward Prince of Wales and Aquitaine*, Michael Jones's *The Black Prince* and two volumes by David Green, *The Black Prince* and *Edward The Black Prince, Power in Medieval Europe*. Volumes 1, 2 and 3 of Jonathan Sumption's history of the Hundred Years War, *Trial by Battle*, *Trial by Fire* and *Divided Houses*, also give useful coverage of the career of the Black Prince during the war. The chronicle by Chandos Herald, *The Life and Feats of the Black Prince*, gives a flattering account of the life of the Black Prince. Volumes 2, 3 and 4 of *The Black Prince's Register* give a wealth of information on the administration of the prince's demesnes. For a re-appraisal of casualties at Limoges, see *The Black Prince* by Michael Jones.

Chapter 2: King Jean II, 'The Good'

The main sources for the short biography of King Jean II are two biographies in French: *Jean II, 1350–1364, Fils de Philippe VI* by Georges Bordonove and *Jean le Bon* by Jean Deviosse. I have also drawn on Volumes 1 and 2 of Jonathan Sumption's series of books on the Hundred Years War, *Trial by Battle* and *Trial by Fire*.

Chapter 3: The Principles of War

Sun Tzu's *The Art of War* and *Vegetius: Epitome of Military Science* are recommended for those who wish to understand these treatises in more depth. Mollie M. Madden's *The Black Prince and the Grand Chevauchée of 1355* and Clifford J. Rogers' *War Cruel and Sharp, English Strategy Under Edward III, 1327–1360* are valuable sources for a detailed explanation of the strategy, operational conduct and sustainability of an Edwardian *chevauchée*.

Chapter 5: The Siege of Aiguillon, 1346

Alis, R-L., *Histoire de la Ville d'Aiguillon et de ses Environs depuis l'Epoque Gallo-Romain jusqu'à nos Jours*, gives a valuable account of the siege of Aiguillon. Jonathan Sumption, in *Trial by Battle*, gives an excellent account of the siege. Kenneth Fowler's *The King's Lieutenant, Henry of Grosmont, First Duke of Lancaster 1310–1361*, gives a good account of Lancaster's campaign in Aquitaine in 1345–46, including Bergerac, La Réole and Aiguillon. See Chaudru de Crazannes, 'Notice sur le Castrum d'Aiguillon' in the *Revue Archéologique*, for a description of the town and fortifications of Aiguillon.

Chapter 6: The Black Prince's *Chevauchée* in the Languedoc, 1355

There are a number of printed primary sources which deal with the 1355 *chevauchée*: Galfridi Le Baker de Swynebroke's *Chronicon*, Jean LeBel's *Chronique*, Jean Froissart's *Oeuvres* and the *Chroniques*, and Robertus de Avesbury's *De Gestis Mirabilibus Regis Edwardi Tertii*. Baker's *Chronicon* gives the itinerary for the *chevauchée*, and the letters of the Black Prince and his advisers can be found in Avesbury. Among secondary sources my *In the Steps of the Black Prince, The Road to Poitiers 1355–56* and Mollie Madden's *The Black Prince and the Grande Chevauchée of 1355* deal with the itinerary in detail and Madden's book is particularly valuable concerning the sustainability of the expedition. Other secondary sources dealing with the *chevauchée* are: Hewitt's *The Black Prince's Expedition*, Burne's *The Crécy War*, Sumption's *Trial by Fire* and Barber's *Edward, Prince of Wales and Aquitaine, a Biography of the Black Prince*. See Craig Lambert, 'Taking the War to Scotland and France, The Supply and Transportation of English Armies by Sea', for an examination of the logistics of moving the Black Prince's army to Bordeaux and Yuval Noah Harari's 'Strategy and Supply in Fourteenth-Century Western European Campaigns' for an analysis of the size of non-combatant elements for fourteenth-century armies. The description of the Landes comes from *The Pilgrim's Guide, a 12th Century Guide for the Pilgrim to St James of Compostella*, and that for the defences of the *cité* of Carcassonne from *The Historical Monuments of France*. See my *In the Steps of the Black Prince* for a discussion of the crossing places of the Garonne and Ariège.

Chapter 7: Normandy and the Siege of Breteuil, 1356

Contemporary sources covering this period of the war include *La Chronique des Premiers Valois*, *Récits d'un Bourgeois de Valenciennes*, Jean Froissart's *Chroniques* and volume 1 of *Grandes Chroniques de France*. Jonathan Sumption's *Trial by Fire* gives the most comprehensive secondary account.

Chapter 8: The Poitiers Campaign, 1356

There are many contemporary, or near-contemporary, sources which describe the Poitiers campaign. The *Eulogium Historiarum* gives the itinerary of the Black Prince's *chevauchée*. Other primary sources in printed form include Riley's *Memorials of London and London Life, in the XIIIth, XIVth, and XVth Centuries*, Galfridi Le Baker de Swynebroke's *Chronicon*, Jean LeBel's *Chronique*, Jean Froissart's *Oeuvres* and *Chroniques*, the *Anonimalle Chronicle 1333–1381*, the *Chronique des Quatre Premiers Valois (1327–1393)*, the 'Cronica' of Matteo Villani, *Knighton's Chronicle 1337–1396*, *Scalacronica, 1272–1363*, and *The Life and Feats of Arms of Edward the Black Prince by Chandos Herald*. Secondary sources include Crozet's 'Siège de Romorantin par le Prince de Galles 1356', Denifle's *La Désolation des Monastères, Eglises, et Hôpitaux en France Pendant la Guerre de Cent Ans*, Tourneur-Aumont's *La Bataille de Poitiers (1356) et la Construction de la France*, Burne's 'The Battle of Poitiers', Rogers' *War Cruel and Sharp, English Strategy Under Edward III, 1327–1360*, Hewitt's *The Black Prince's Expedition*, and Sumption's *Trial by Fire*. Rogers' 'The Battle of Agincourt' discusses the effectiveness of archers against cavalry and the speed of a cavalry charge from a standing start.

Chapter 9: The Battle of Nájera, 1367

The principal primary sources for the Battle of Nájera are those of Chandos Herald's *The Life and Feats of the Black Prince* and Pedro López de Ayala's *Crónica de Pedro I*. Both Chandos Herald and Ayala were present at the battle. Froissart, writing after the events, also describes the battle extensively. A number of secondary sources deal with the campaign and the battle at some length. Among these are Jonathan Sumption's *Divided Houses* and the biographies of the Black Prince by Richard Barber, *Edward Prince of Wales and Aquitaine, A Biography of the Black Prince*, and Michael Jones, *The Black Prince*. The most comprehensive secondary account of the campaign, the battle and the surrounding circumstances is *To Win and Lose a Medieval Battle, Nájera (April 3, 1367), a Pyrrhic Victory for the Black Prince*, by L.J. Andrew Villalon and Donald J. Kagay. This volume also contains translations of documents and chronicles relating to the battle.

Bibliography

Alis, R-L., *Histoire de la Ville d'Aiguillon et de ses Environs depuis l'Epoque Gallo-Romain jusqu'à nos Jours* (Agen and Ste-Radegonde, 1895).

Anonimalle Chronicle 1333–1381, ed. V.H. Galbraith (Manchester, 1927).

Avesbury, Robertus de, *De Gestis Mirabilibus Regis Edwardi Tertii*, ed. E.M. Thompson (London, 1889).

Barber, Richard, *Edward Prince of Wales and Aquitaine, A Biography of the Black Prince* (pb edition, Woodbridge, 2000).

Bel, Jean Le, *Chronique*, ed. J. Viard and E. Déprez (Paris, 1904–5).

Bordonove, Georges, *Jean II, 1350–1364, Fils de Philippe VI* (pb edition, Paris, 2010).

Burne, A.H., 'The Battle of Poitiers', *English Historical Review*, 53(209):21–52 (London, 1938).

Chronique des Quatre Premiers Valois (1327–1393), ed. Siméon Luce (Paris, 1861).

'Cronica', Matteo Villani, *Cronisti del Trecento*, ed. Roberto Palmarocchi (Milan, 1935).

Crozet, R., 'Siège de Romorantin par le Prince de Galles 1356', *Revue Historique*, 51(153): 187–92 (Paris, 1926).

Delachenal, R., *Histoire de Charles V*, vols 1 and 2 (Paris, 1909).

Denifle, Henri, *La Désolation des Monastères, Eglises, et Hôpitaux en France Pendant la Guerre de Cent Ans* (Paris 1899).

Deviosse, Jean, *Jean le Bon* (Paris, 1985).

Eulogium Historiarum, vol. 3, ed. F.S. Haydon (London 1863).

Fowler, Kenneth, *The King's Lieutenant, Henry of Grosmont, First Duke of Lancaster 1310–1361* (London, 1969).

Froissart, Jean, *Chroniques*, vol. 5, ed. Siméon Luce (Paris, 1874).

Froissart, Jean, *Oeuvres de Froissart, Chroniques*, vols 4, 5, 17, and 18, ed. Kervyn de Lettenhove (Brussels, 1867–77).

Galfridi Le Baker de Swynebroke, *Chronicon*, ed. E.M. Thompson (Oxford 1889).

Grandes Chroniques de France, Chronique des règnes de Jean II et de Charles V, ed. R. Delachenal, vol. 1 (Paris, 1910).

Green, David, *The Black Prince* (Stroud, 2001).

Green, David, *The Battle of Poitiers, 1356* (Botley, 2004).

Green, David, *Edward the Black Prince, Power in Medieval Europe* (Harlow, 2007).

Harari, Yuval Noah, 'Strategy and Supply in Fourteenth-Century Western European Campaigns', *Journal of Military History*, 64 (April 2000).

Hewitt, H.J., *The Black Prince's Expedition* (Manchester, 1958; repr. Barnsley, 2004).

Hoskins, Peter, *In the Steps of the Black Prince, The Road to Poitiers 1355–1356* (Woodbridge, 2011; pb edition, 2013).

Hunnewell, James F., *The Historical Monuments of France* (Boston and New York, 1898).

Jones, Michael, *The Black Prince* (London, 2017).

Knighton's Chronicle 1337–1396, ed. and tr. G.H. Martin (Oxford, 1995).

Lambert, Craig, 'Taking the War to Scotland and France, The Supply and Transportation of English Armies by Sea', PhD Thesis (University of Hull, March 2009).

Liddell Hart, Basil, *Thoughts on War* (London, 1944).

The Life and Feats of Arms of Edward the Black Prince by Chandos Herald, tr. Francisque-Michel (London and Paris, 1883).

Madden, Mollie M., *The Black Prince and the Grand Chevauchée of 1355* (Woodbridge, 2018).

Memorials of London and London Life, in the XIIIth, XIVth, and XVth Centuries, ed. H.T. Riley (London, 1868).

Notes from the 'Journal of John Henxteworth', tr. Edmund Rollo Laird Clowes (Duchy of Cornwall Archives).

The Pilgrim's Guide, a 12th Century Guide for the Pilgrim to St James of Compostella, tr. J. Hogarth (Confraternity of St James, London 1992).

Récits d'un bourgeois de Valenciennes (XIVᵉsiècle), ed. Kervyn de Lettenhove (Louvain, 1877).

Register of Edward The Black Prince Preserved in the Public Record Office, Parts II, III and IV (London, 1931–33).

Rogers, Clifford J., 'The Battle of Agincourt', in Andrew L.J. Villalon and Donald J. Kagay (eds), *The Hundred Years War (Part II)* (Leiden, 2008), pp. 37–132.

Rogers, Clifford J., *War Cruel and Sharp, English Strategy Under Edward III, 1327–1360* (Woodbridge, 2000).

Sabarthès, A., *Notes Historiques sur la Ville de Limoux* (Limoux, 1933).

Scalacronica, 1272–1363, ed. and tr. Andy King (Woodbridge, 2005).

Sumption, Jonathan, *Trial by Battle, The Hundred Years War I* (London, 1990).

Sumption, Jonathan, *Trial by Fire, The Hundred Years War II* (London, 1999).

Sumption, Jonathan, *Divided Houses, The Hundred Years War III* (London, 2009).

Sun Tzu, *The Art of War* (Amazon, 2014).

Tourneur-Aumont, J.M., *La Bataille de Poitiers (1356) et la Construction de la France* (Paris, Tours, and Poitiers, 1943).

Vegetius: Epitome of Military Science, tr. N.P. Milner (Liverpool University Press, 1993, 1996, 2001).

Villalon, L.J. Andrew and Kagay, Donald J., *To Win and Lose a Medieval Battle, Nájera (April 3, 1367), a Pyrrhic Victory for the Black Prince* (Leiden and Boston, 2017).

Index

Mentions of the Black Prince and King Jean are numerous and not included in the index.

Agen, 70
Agenais, the, 21, 111
Agincourt, Battle of, 58, 64, 90, 126, 161
Aigues-Mortes, 96
Aiguillon, 31–2, 49, 67, 69–77, 106, 114, 169, 172
Aimeri, Viscount of Narbonne, 94
Albi, 21
Albret, Lord of, 19–20, 115, 117, 161, 164
Alençon, Countess of, 35
Amboise, 118, 120
Amiens, 38
Amiens, Treaty of, 27
Angers, Castle, 5
Angers, Count of, 118
Angoulême, 31, 33, 69
Angoulême, Edward of, 14, 23
Anjou, Duke of, 48–9
Aquitaine, 14, 16, 18, 20–1, 37–8, 42, 58, 61–2, 69, 71, 74, 81–2, 113, 145, 151, 155, 163–4, 168
Ariège, river, 86–91, 103–4, 167, 180
Ariñez, 156
Arleux, 42
Armagnac, 85
Armagnac, Count of, 110, 151, 153, 161–2, 164
Arouille, 85
Artois, 41
Artois, John of, 41
Artois, Robert of, 7, 29
Arundel, Earl of, 8
Astarac, 86
Athens, Duke of, 71, 132, 134, 137
Auberoche, 31, 69
Auberoche, Battle of, 69, 73

Aubigny-sur-Nère, 115
Auch, Archbishop of, 86
Aude, river, 91, 94–5, 97
Audley, Sir James, 9, 12, 81, 101, 111, 129, 131, 139, 144
Audrehem, Marshal d', 17, 41, 130, 132, 134, 136–7, 150, 156–7, 159, 163, 166, 170–2
Auray, Battle of, 60–1
Auvergne, the, 111
Aveyron, the, 21
Avignon, 8, 15, 30, 36, 48, 95–6
Ayala, Lopez de, 152, 161–2

Badefol, Seguin de, 14
Bajamont, 77
Baker, Galfridi le, 88–92, 100, 126–7, 134, 137, 142, 175–7, 180–1
Bandiat, River, 111
Basset, Ralph, 116
Bassoues, 86
Baugé, Battle of, 61
Bazas, 21, 84
Béarn, 14, 75
Beaucaire, 96
Beaufort, Roger de, 22
Beauvais, 67
Beauvais, Bishop of, 71
Beauvoir, 125, 127, 173
Bel, Jean le, 11, 86, 96
Benedict XII, Pope, 29
Bergerac, 9, 31, 44, 69, 76, 109–11, 113, 118, 128, 146
Berkeley, Sir Maurice, 131, 139
Berkhamsted, 8
Bernon, 127, 176
Berry, 111

Berry, Duke of, *see* Poitiers, Count of
Béziers, 95
Blanchetaque, 88
Blois, 44, 120
Blois, Charles de, 29, 61
Blois, Margaret of, 33
Bohemia, King of, 27
Bonne de Luxembourg, Queen of France, 27, 32
Bordeaux, 9–12, 16–17, 21–4, 31, 38, 44–5, 72, 74, 81–2, 84–6, 97, 106, 117–18, 120, 125, 146, 148
Bordeaux, Richard of, 17
Bordeaux, Truce of, 44–5
Botetourt, Sir Baldwin, 139
Boucicaut, Jean de, 38, 106, 114
Boulogne, 39, 47
Boulogne, Cardinal of, 36
Boulogne, Jeanne de, 48
Bourbon, Duke of, 31, 48, 71, 132, 139
Bourbon, Jacques de, 86
Bourbon, Marguerite de, 19
Bourges, 43, 109, 111, 114, 124, 146, 149
Bourgogne, Jeanne de, 25
Brantôme, 111, 149
Breteuil, 43, 67, 106–9, 113, 115, 146, 169, 172
Brétigny, 47
Brétigny, Treaty of, 13–14, 18–20, 47–8, 61, 151, 164
Brignais, Battle of, 14
Brignolles, Battle of, 48
Briquebec, Robert Bertrand, 30
Brittany, 11, 14, 29, 37–8, 60, 80, 105
Brocas, Sir Bernard, 13
Burghersh, Sir Bartholomew de, 8, 13, 81, 123, 128–9, 139
Burgos, 155, 157, 165
Burgundy, 46, 48
Burgundy, Duke of, 30

Calais, 7–8, 11, 13, 22–3, 32, 46–8, 60, 67, 81, 87, 109
Calais, Truce of, 7
Calveley, Sir Hugh, 15–16, 60, 152–3, 155–7, 161–2, 165

Cambridge, Earl of, 20, 22
Canterbury, 14, 24
Capbreton, 15–16, 37
Capestang, 95–6, 104
Captal de Buch. *See* Grailly, Jean de
Carbonne, 58–9, 103
Carcassonne, 91–4, 97
Cardwell, Edward, 59
Carillo, Gomez, 17
Carra, Martin Enriquez de la, 161
Castelmoron, 70
Castets-en-Dorthe, 84
Castile, 16–17, 151–3
Castillon, Battle of, 58, 63
Caumont, Lord of, 72–4, 116
Cerda, Charles of La, Charles of Spain, 32–3, 35–6
Chabanais, 113, 149
Châlons, Bishop of, 59, 130, 144
Chambly, Philippe de, 114, 116
Champtoceaux, 29
Chandos Herald, 20, 123, 128, 130–3, 137, 152, 155, 161–3
Chandos, Sir John, 5, 14, 21, 60–1, 81, 101, 111, 123, 128–31, 137, 139, 153, 156, 160, 172
Charles IV, Holy Roman Emperor, 35–40
Charles IV, King of France, 26
Charles V, King of France, 11, 14, 19–21, 24, 28 , 31, 37, 39–40, 42, 44–5, 61–2, 103, 105, 121, 132, 137, 152, 155, 164
Charles of Spain. *See* Cerda, Charles of La
Charles the Bad, King of Navarre, 16, 19, 27, 33, 35–43, 45, 47–8, 61, 105, 107, 145, 151, 153–6, 165, 168
Charny, Geoffroi de, 7, 130, 143
Chartres, 43–4, 46, 114, 116, 120, 123
Châteauroux, 115–16, 149
Châtellerault, 122, 124, 149
Châtillon-sur-Indre, 31, 70, 71
Chauvigny, 122–3, 139
Chauvigny, André de, 115
Cher, river, 116–17, 120–1, 124
Cherbourg, 36–7
Cheshire, 6, 8, 12–13, 81
Chester, 8, 13
Cheyne, Sir Alan, 139

Clairac, 73
Clarence, Duke of, 61
Clausewitz, Carl von, 91
Clement VI, Pope, 13, 29–30
Clermont, Marshal, 86, 114, 118, 130, 132, 134, 136–7, 171
Clisson, Amaury de, 29
Clisson, Olivier de, 20, 29–30, 162
Cobham, Sir Reginald, 80, 85
Cocherel, Battle of, 19, 61
Cognac, 22
Conches, 43
Constanza, Queen of Castile, 23
Coq, Robert le, Bishop of Laon, 40
Craon, Armaury de, 114, 116
Crécy, 6, 13, 57, 62–3, 67, 76, 80, 88, 101
Crécy, Battle of, 31–2, 34, 74, 80, 87, 128, 144, 155, 161, 166, 168, 170–1
Creuse, river, 121, 124
Crèvecoeur, 42
Curton, Petiton de, 133
Cuxac-d'Aude, 95

Damazan, 72–3, 77
Daubriggecourt, Sir Eustace de, 133, 137, 151
Dauphin. *See* Charles V, King of France
Dax, 17, 152–3
Decize, 114
Denia, Count of, 159, 161–3
Derby. *See* Lancaster, Duke of
Descartes. *See* La Haye
Dordogne, River, 11
Douai, 42
Doublet, Colin, 41
Douglas, Earl, 130, 132, 134, 137
Dover, 47, 49
Dronne, River, 111
Duras, Robert, 137
Durfort, Gaillard de, 75

Ebro, river, 155
Edward III, King of England, 5, 7, 9–11, 13, 15–16, 19–20, 23, 26–32, 34–8, 41–3, 45–9, 55, 61–4, 67, 69, 74–6, 79–81, 87, 90, 93, 98, 101, 103, 107–9,
114, 130, 143–6, 148–9, 161, 167–8, 170
Emposte, Châtelaine d', 137, 172
Esplechin, Truce of, 29
Eu, Raoul de Brienne, Count of, Constable of France, 28, 32, 34, 42
Evreux, 35, 41

Fastolf, Sir John, 63
Felton, Sir Thomas, 156–7
Felton, Sir William, 157
Ferrers, Sir Thomas de, 8
Flanders, 6, 28–9, 59, 67, 75, 80
Flanders, Count of, 47
Foix, Count of, 88, 98
Fricamps, Friquet de, 41
Froissart, Jean, 10–11, 22, 88, 92, 107, 123, 137, 142–3, 173, 177

Garonne, river, 31, 69–77, 82, 84, 86–91, 98, 102–4, 167, 180
Gascony, 9, 12, 15–16, 37, 69, 74, 80–2, 84, 91, 98, 100–1, 103–4, 117
Gaston Phoebus. *See* Foix, Count of
Gaunt, John of, 22–3, 151, 153, 156, 160–2
Gimont, 100, 103
Grailly, Jean de, Captal de Buch, 80, 101, 117, 131, 142, 150, 161–2, 169–70
Granada, 15
Grismouton. *See* Chambly, Philippe de
Grosmont, Henry of. *See* Lancaster, Duke of
Gué de Maulny, 25
Guesclin, Bertrand du, 19, 61, 152, 154–6, 159–60, 162–3
Guines, 32

Hainault, Count of, 28
Hainault, County of, 76
Hamelym, Geoffrey, 10, 144
Harcourt, Godfrey of, 30, 42
Harcourt, John of, 41
Harcourt, Louis of, 36
Harfleur, 75
Haro, 157
Harpenden, William de, 139

Hastings, Sir Hugh, 75
Haye, John de la, 139
Helmuth von Moltke the Elder, 58
Henry II, King of England, 46, 56, 122
Henry V, King of England, 58, 61, 63, 90
Henry of Trastamara. *See* Trastamara,
    Henry of, King of Castile
Hertford, 45, 46
Hesdin, 38
Holland, Joan, 6, 13, 23
Holland, Sir Thomas, 13
Humbert II, Ruler of the Viennois, 30
Huntingdon, Earl of, 61

Indre, river, 120, 124
Innocent VI, Pope, 35–6, 48
Isabella, Queen of England, 45–6
Issoudun, 115

James, King of Majorca, 151, 153, 161
Jean I, King of France, 25
Jean, Count of Armagnac, 9, 14, 19, 21,
    38–9, 80, 82, 86, 88, 90, 95–6, 98,
    100–1
Jean, Count of Poitiers, 42
Joan, Countess of Auvergne, Queen of
    France, 26, 32
John, Duke of Lorraine, 6

Kennington, 8, 23
Knolles, Sir Robert, 60–1

l'Aigle, 35, 43, 105, 145
la Cadrousse, 143, 176
la Cardinerie, 127, 173
La Haye, 121–2
La Péruse, 113
La Réole, 69–72, 74, 76–7, 146
Lacroix-Falgarde, 88–90
Lancaster, Duke of (formerly Earl of
    Derby and Earl of Lancaster), 8, 11,
    36–8, 42–6, 69–72, 74, 76–7, 81, 88,
    105–7, 109, 113, 118, 120–2, 124, 130,
    145, 147, 149, 167, 170
Landes, 84–5
Langley, Edmund of, Earl of Cambridge,
    20

Langon, 82
Languedoc, 9, 38–40, 62, 80–2, 86, 95,
    102–3, 107, 145–6, 148
Le Fossat d'Aiguillon, 72
Le Mans, 25, 60
les Bordes, 127, 134, 143, 173, 176
Les-Ponts-de-Cé, 122, 147
Libourne, 11, 16, 44
Libourne, Treaty of, 16–17, 153
Lilies, Treaty of the, 48
Limoges, 6, 21–2
Limoges, Bishop of, 22
Limoges, Viscount of, 113
Limousin, the, 111
Limoux, 87, 170
Lionel, Duke of Clarence, 19
Lisle, Sir John de, 80–1
Loches, 122
Logroño, 153, 155, 157–8, 165
Loire, river, 42, 44, 107, 109–10, 115–16,
    118, 120, 122, 124, 147, 149, 170
Lombez, 86
London, 6, 8–9, 11, 20, 23, 37, 44, 46–7,
    49, 81, 91, 97
London, Treaties of, 13, 45–7
Lopez, Sanchez, 44
Loring, Sir Nigel, 139
Lorris, Robert of, Grand Chamberlain,
    36
Lot, river, 31, 71–4, 77
Louis X, King of France, 25
Louis, Duke of Anjou, 41
Lunac-d'Aiguillon, 71, 73, 75
Lynne, William, Dean of Chichester, 11

Maignac, Ietier de, 113
Malestroit, Truce of, 29–30
Manot, 113, 149
Mantes, Treaty of, 36
Mareuil, Lord of, 27
Marquefave, 98
Mauny, Olivier de, 152, 154
Mauny, Walter, 29, 31, 72, 76
Mediterranean, 91
Menil, Hugh, 72
Meung-sur-Loire, 120
Mézin, 101

Millau, 102
Minsterworth, Sir John, 60
Miosson, river, 125, 127–9, 133–4, 136, 143, 147, 176–7
Miranda de Ebro, 155, 157, 165
Mirande, 86, 157
Moissac, 70
Montbazon, 121, 124
Montebourg, 106
Montfort, Jean de, 29, 61
Montfort, Jeanne de, 29
Montiel, 163
Montlouis-sur-Loire, 118, 120, 124, 147
Montpellier, 95–6
Montreuil, 47
Morbek, Denis de, 143
Mortimer, Roger, Earl of March, 5

Nájera, 157–60
Nájera, Battle of, 17, 19, 60–1, 67, 156, 158–67, 169–72
Najerilla, River, 157–9, 163
Nantes, 29
Narbonne, 9, 31, 93–6, 98
Nassau, Count of, 132
Navarette, 158–60
Navarre, 16, 33, 151, 153–4, 157
Navarre, Philippe of, 42–3, 48, 105
Nidau, Count of, 132
Noé, 98
Nogaro, 85, 86
Nontron, 111, 149
Normandy, 28, 37–8, 40–1, 74–5, 81, 105, 107, 145
Normandy, Duke of, 69, 71
Northampton, Earl of, 29
Norwich, Bishop of, 59
Nouaillé-Maupertuis, 125, 147

Orléans, 116, 118, 120, 124
Orléans, Duke of, 48, 132, 139
Orsana, Count of, 151
Oxford, Earl of, 80, 101, 131, 136, 150

Pamplona, 16, 151, 153, 157
Parde, Martin, 9

Paris, 19–20, 24, 29–30, 32, 34–5, 39, 41, 45–6, 49, 108, 164
Patay, Battle of, 63
Pavia, Aimery de, 7
Pedro, King of Castile, 5, 15–18, 23, 151–3, 155, 157, 161–4, 169, 172
Pembroke, Earl of, 20–2, 61
Percy, Lord, 162
Périgord, 75
Périgord, Cardinal of, 45, 121, 129, 131, 137
Périgueux, 31, 69
Perrers, Alice, 23
Peverel, Sir Henry, 123, 128, 143
Philip the Bold, Duke of Burgundy, 71
Philippa, Queen of England, 5, 49
Philippe III, King of France, 3, 25–6
Philippe IV, King of France, 25–6, 33
Philippe V, King of France, 25
Philippe VI, King of France, 7, 25, 27, 29–32, 34, 74–6, 80, 94, 101, 168
Philippe, Count of Evreux, 26
Philippe, Duke of Orléans, 41
Philippe of Rouvres, Duke of Burgundy, 48
Phoebus, Gaston. *See* Foix, Count of
Picardy, 37, 39–40, 76, 81
Pinsaguel, 90
Pizan, Christine de, 79
Plymouth, 11, 44, 81
Poissy, 67, 88
Poitiers, 10, 118, 122–3, 125, 143, 149, 173
Poitiers, Battle of, 9, 12, 44, 48–9, 59, 62, 64, 67, 105, 107, 109, 117, 126, 133–44, 155, 161, 163–4, 166–72
Poitiers, Count of, 21–2, 48, 69, 101, 109–10, 114, 118, 146, 148–9
Poix, 67
Pont-Audemer, 43
Pont-Cher, 120
Ponthieu, County of, 47
Pontvallain, 60
Port-Ste-Marie, 70, 73

Quercy, the, 21, 71
Quinsac, 111

Rabastens, Raymond de, 21
Recombes, Louis de, 133
Reims, 19, 25, 35, 46
Ribemont, Eustace de, 132, 148, 175
Richard I, King of England, 56
Richard II, King of England, 23–4, 84
Richard of Bordeaux. *See* Richard II, King
   of England
Roche, Hugh de la, 22
Rochechouart, 113
Rodez, 21
Romorantin, 116–18, 124–5, 128, 149
Roncevalles, 153
Rouen, 29, 37, 41–2, 106
Rouen, Archbishop of, 129
Rouergue, the, 14, 21

Saarbruck, Count of, 132
St-Avertin, 120
St-Benoît-du-Sault, 115
St Denis, 28, 49
St-Jean-d'Angely, 34
St-Jean-Pied-du-Port, 153
St-Junien, 113, 149
St-Lô, 30
St-Lys, 80, 88
St-Macaire, 71, 82, 84
St-Omer, 39
St-Sauveur, 60
St-Thibéry, 95
Salisbury, Earl of, 13, 80, 85, 101, 127,
   131, 133–4, 136–7
San Vitale, Cardinal of, 45
Sancho, Henry of Trastamara's brother,
   159, 163
Santa Cruz de Campezo, 153
Santiago de Compostela, 155
Santo Domingo de la Calzada, 154–6
Saumur, 120
Save, river, 100
Savigny-Lévescault, 123
Scheldt, river, 28
Sens, Archbishop of, 59, 144
Shank, William, 139
Slim, Field Marshal Sir William, 62
Sluys, 29
Somerton, 45–6

Stafford, Lord Ralph, 31, 72
Stretelee, John, Constable of Bordeaux,
   11
Suffolk, Earl of, 10, 21, 80, 85, 101, 129,
   131, 137
Sun Tzu, 55–8, 122, 129, 148, 167–8, 171

Talbot, Sir John, 58, 63
Talleyrand. *See* Périgord, Cardinal of
Tancarville, Count of, 14
Taverny, 28
Tello, Don, 156, 159–60, 162, 166, 170
Thun-l'Evêque, 28
Tonneins, 72–3, 75, 77, 87
Toulouse, 71, 73, 75, 86–90, 97–9, 102–3
Touraine, 114
Tournai, 29
Tours, 107, 115, 117–18, 120–4, 147
Trastamara, Henry of, King of Castile, 15,
   18, 23, 60, 151–2, 154–7, 160–3, 165,
   171
Troyes, Bernard de, 143
Trussell, Sir William, 139

Umfraville, Sir Gilbert, 61
Urban V, Pope, 48
Urgel, Bishop of, 129

Vaas, 60
Valde, river, 158
Valence-sur-Baïse, 100
Valenciennes, 76
Valognes, Treaty of, 37–9
Valois, Charles de, 25–6
Valois, Joan of, 35
Valois, Philippe de, Count of Maine,
   25–6
Vannes, 29–30
Vegetius, 56, 58, 90, 129, 147, 150, 167
Verneuil-sur-Avre, 43, 105–6
Vessencourt, 67
Vienne, river, 21, 113, 122, 149
Viennois, the, 31
Vierzon, 115–16
Villaines, Bègue de, 159, 163
Villefranche-sur-Cher, 116
Villemur, John de, 22

Vincennes, Château de, 27
Vitoria-Gasteiz, 155–7, 159, 165, 171

Wallingford, 8
Warwick, Earl of, 10, 21, 80, 85, 101,
    126–7, 129–31, 133–4, 136–7, 142
Westminster, 24
William I, King of England, 106
Willoughby, Sir John, 116

Winchelsea, 8
Winchester, Bishop of, 97, 102
Winchester Cathedral, Prior of, 123, 143
Wingfield, Sir John, 88, 91, 102
Woodland, Sir Walter, 139
Woodstock, 5
Worcester, Bishop of, 123

York, 91